REVOLUTION IN AMERICAN DRAMA

Edmond M. Gagey

REVOLUTION
IN
AMERICAN
DRAMA

Essay Index Reprint Series

BOOKS FOR LIBRARIES PRESS
FREEPORT, NEW YORK

Library of Congress Cataloging in Publication Data

Gagey, Edmond McAdoo, 1901-
   Revolution in American drama.
   (Essay index reprint series)
   1. American drama--20th century--History and
criticism. 2. Theater--U. S.--History. I. Title.
PS351.G3 1971   812'.5'09   75-167343
ISBN 0-8369-2498-3

PRINTED IN THE UNITED STATES OF AMERICA
BY
NEW WORLD BOOK MANUFACTURING CO., INC.
HALLANDALE, FLORIDA 33009

To
SUSAN

PREFACE

O<small>F THE</small> numerous books on contemporary American drama few have attempted a panoramic survey of the field that would trace a little of the sweep of history and yet give an abundance of detail. Whatever its permanence, American drama of the past thirty years has proved its worth and significance in our literature. It has done far more than reflect passing fads and frivolities, which are themselves of considerable interest; it has portrayed the manners, voiced the creeds, and unveiled the psyche of a brilliant and erratic age. All this I have tried to record, allowing the playwrights to speak through their plays and critical dicta. I have sought to report objectively on this engrossing spectacle, and I have no personal axe to grind. While I have intended to offer a factual summary rather than a critical appraisal, I yet have not hesitated to give necessary evaluation to the material through selection, emphasis, attitude, and direct comment.

Among the more difficult problems have been those of selection and classification. Of the thousands of productions that have made their bid for favor on Broadway it has been impossible to consider every one. I have tried to include all significant plays, however, and yet to remain catholic in my approach, allowing space to the purely commercial theatre as well as to artistic and serious drama. The problem of classification has been solved by organizing the material under broad and general headings with special comment about plays that might equally well appear in different categories.

In all cases I have relied upon study of the plays themselves rather than on books about them. Since my main concern has been with professional drama, I have dwelt only briefly and occasionally with the amateur or provincial theatre, interesting and valuable as their work has sometimes been.

Needless to say, I am indebted. to the generous help and cooperation of numerous libraries and their staffs in Massachusetts and New York, especially the Harvard Theatre Collection, the Brander Matthews Museum at Columbia University, and the Theatre Section of the New York Public Library. For permission to quote specific passages I am grateful to the following: to Barrett H. Clark for a quotation from his book *Eugene O'Neill;* to Samuel French for a speech from Catherine Chisholm Cushing's *Pollyanna;* to Random House for several passages from S. N. Behrman's *Rain from Heaven* and Eugene O'Neill's *Anna Christie, Marco Millions,* and *Strange Interlude;* to Anderson House for quotations from Maxwell Anderson's *Winterset* and *Key Largo;* to *Theatre Arts* for a passage from the first number of this publication; to Moss Hart and George S. Kaufman for several brief quotations from *Once in a Lifetime;* and to the Irving Berlin Music Corporation for two lines from Irving Berlin's *Annie Get Your Gun.* Most of all am I indebted to the unfailing help and encouragement of my wife, Susan Maria Gagey, and to the critical and analytical assistance of Dr. William Bridgwater, editor of Columbia University Press.

E. M. G.

Bradford, Massachusetts
March 1, 1947

CONTENTS

Chapter 1

THE GREAT WHITE WAY
1912-1917

*I*N THE years before our entry into the First
World War, smugly indifferent to artistic and social forces
threatening its own complacency, Broadway went on its merry
way, attempting to live up to its appellation of the Great
White Way and dispensing entertainment to an eager public.
Klaw and Erlanger and the Shuberts were in their respective
heavens, and all was right with the world. Despite occasional
grumblings at the two-dollar top for orchestra seats, the theatrical patron of the period usually felt that he was getting his
money's worth. At the sedately ornate Empire Theatre, for
example, he might view the latest offering of Charles Frohman, the "Napoleon of the Drama," with at least one of the
galaxy of Frohman stars—perhaps Maude Adams, John Drew,
Ethel Barrymore, Billie Burke, or Otis Skinner. If the eager
customer happened to be interested in novelty of staging, he
might attend a production by David Belasco, famed as a
wizard of lighting, who was known to rehearse a play inter-
minably before the first tryout, occasionally keeping his actors
twenty hours at a single rehearsal, who thought nothing of
training an actress two years before her initial appearance,
and who transferred to the theatre with the most painstaking
accuracy the squeak of a pneumatic elevator, the setting of a
Childs Restaurant, or the wallpaper of a bedroom in a cheap
theatrical boardinghouse. Belasco, too, would provide a star;
it might be, among others, David Warfield or Mrs. Leslie
Carter or Frances Starr. In a lighter mood the enterprising

playgoer might purchase a ticket for the most recent George M. Cohan show—revue or farce—with the irrepressible George in the triple role of writer-director-star; or he might select one of Charles Dillingham's spectacles at the Hippodrome with such features as a parade of suffragettes, a gambol of cats on the rooftops of New York, daring high diving by Annette Kellermann, or an ice ballet with Charlotte, the Berlin skater. Whatever performance was finally chosen, the Broadway seeker after amusement would know there was little chance of his being disturbed unduly by contemporary problems or driven to painful thought. He would count on being moved to laughter or tears, with the strongest possible emotional stimulation. Whatever the production, he would be very sure of beholding a star. If he brought along a maiden aunt or adolescent daughter, he would have little fear that lines or situations would bring a blush to their tender cheeks or sully their female innocence. It was, on the whole, a pleasant world of escape and make-believe that was presented on the stage, a conventional and Freudless universe, not much more adult than the movies of a later age, and just about as sentimental. As romantic and escapist drama, the plays were not without merit; as manufactured products in the "show business," they brought fortunes to the successful producers and playwrights.

Who were the begetters of these engaging dramatic fictions? Many American producers, notably Charles Frohman, preferred European importations to native plays. While there was much talk of the Great American Play soon to be written, the Broadway dramatist, forced by the prevailing system to keep his eye on the box office if he wished to have his play presented at all, was more a clever craftsman than an artist. Unlike George Bernard Shaw, he was powerless to demand respect for the letter of his script, and by the time the directors, actors, and the play doctors had finished their amputations and revisions, his opus was often scarcely recognizable. Sometimes, one must admit, it was improved. Few would be so rash, however, as to rank the playwrights of 1912–1917 with those of the twenties. Augustus Thomas was still writing melodramas, and Eugene Walter attempting to equal his own *The Easiest Way* (1909). Charles Klein, who went down in 1915 on the "Lusitania," David Belasco, and Edward Sheldon were on the wane, despite occasional successes. Female dramatists were fattening their bank accounts on drippy sentimentalities—Jean Webster's *Daddy Long-Legs* (1914) for instance, or Catherine Chisholm Cushing's *Pollyanna* (1916). Rachel Crothers was already well-established as a dramatist of manners, social problems, and feminine psychology. She would be heard of later, as well as a ten-dollar-a-week law clerk, Elmer Reizenstein (later Elmer Rice), who startled Broadway by writing a novelty hit, *On Trial,* in his early twenties. Other playwrights showed promise, but there was no one to compare with Shaw, Barrie, or Galsworthy, whose work was currently appearing in New York.

While the Gay White Way had not as yet become the dramatic center of the world, it was at least supreme in the United States, and the astute Broadway producer flourished. Compared with that of later days, his lot was not such an unhappy one. The Authors' League was founded in 1911, but the Dramatists' Guild of this organization, with its keen eye for contracts, was not organized efficiently until 1926. Actors' Equity was still in the offing, and the director, if he chose, could be czar and curmudgeon to his players. The theatrical unions were neither as powerful nor as exacting as they eventually became. The "road" was slowly going into a decline, but it was still alive. According to William A. Brady, it used to account for seventy-five percent of a producer's profits. Brady was in a position to know, for he had lived for years on the returns from *Way Down East*—"Brady's Bread and Butter," as it was called by envious managers. Occasionally added income could be garnered from the stock companies. The movies, it is true, were beginning to offer competition, first in the small towns, then in New York itself, where such films as D. W.

Griffith's *Birth of a Nation* (1915) and *Intolerance* (1916)
drew immense crowds at a high admission price. Gasps of
horror were heard on Broadway, in 1915, when a legitimate
playhouse, the Knickerbocker Theatre, was acquired exclusively for Triangle films. The Strand, first of the moving-picture palaces of the present, was opened in 1914, and even more
luxurious emporiums were—in metaphor—just around the
corner. The movies were still rudimentary in content and
crude in technique; night scenes, for example, were shot in
bright daylight and then tinted in the studio to simulate darkness. But already Douglas Fairbanks and other Broadway
stars were deserting the theatre, and lesser-known actors, like
Lillian Gish, Mary Pickford, and Charlie Chaplin, were
achieving immense success in the new medium. Not the least
engaging of these was a certain Theodosia Goodman of Cin-
cinnati, who telescoped her given name, spelled Arab back-
wards, and emerged from obscurity as Theda Bara, the sinister vampire woman of *Cleopatra* and *A Fool There Was*. An
interviewer for the *Theatre* found her characteristically eat-
ing a luncheon of lettuce leaves and raw beef. Before many
years the moving pictures did practically kill the "road," oc-
casioning the Broadway producer more than one headache.
Little could he foresee at this time, however, the more severe
headaches of the future—the rise of the talkies, radio, and
television.

In the theatre itself a revolution was impending in which
the stage designer, the playwright, and the little theatres were
all preparing to take a hand. To understand more clearly the
nature of this revolution it will be advisable to survey briefly
the plays of the conventional theatre, the traditional entertainment of the Great White Way, which was increasingly threatened with attack from within as well as without. Many different genres were popular, the only common denominator being
their box-office appeal. Not the least successful type was the
tearful comedy, descendant of the sentimental play of the
eighteenth century, naïve, tender, poignant, with its perennial

Cinderella themes. *Peg o' My Heart* (1912) is an excellent
example. It was written by an English actor and author, J.
Hartley Manners, who was closely associated with the New
York stage during the last twenty years of his life. It was during this period that he married an American actress, Laurette
Taylor, who played the original Peg. In the play an Irish-
American girl, fiercely loyal to her unsuccessful father, is sent
by the terms of a will to the home of a stern English aunt and
her comic-strip son and daughter. In this unattractive household Peg suffers trials and humiliations, but eventually saves
her cousin Ethel from running off with a married man while
she herself agrees to marry an English nobleman, Jerry, who
has been kind to her. The play, despite or perhaps because of
its obvious characterization, has simple, direct emotional appeal, and it enjoyed a long run on Broadway and in London.

A play about a Scotch Peg o' My Heart, *Kitty MacKay* by
Catherine Chisholm Cushing, appeared in 1914, as did the
sentimental *Jerry* by the same author. While the latter was not
a success, it has some interest in the fact that Jerry, a young
girl who sets out to marry her aunt's middle-aged fiancé, was
played by Billie Burke, then a Frohman star, daughter of a
famous circus clown. One scene required her to play in pink
pajamas, but, says a contemporary reviewer, "There is no in-
delicacy in the pajamas, and the contentment of the audience
with this snug and simple attire is not discreditable to anybody, including the audience." Catherine Chisholm Cushing's
triumph of sentimentality, however, did not appear until 1916
with *Pollyanna*, a dramatization of the novel by Eleanor H.
Porter. Even the critic of the *Theatre* found it too sweet for his
taste and called it "peach melba drenched in syrup." This, if
anything, is an understatement. To the home of her frustrated
maiden aunt comes the orphaned Pollyanna, the Glad Girl,
with a sick kitten and puppy (Sodom and Gomorrah) which
she's picked up en route, as well as Jimmy Bean, a runaway
from the near-by orphanage. She finds her stern aunt and
three guests busy filling a mission barrel, and she exclaims:

(*Explosively, as she whirls around and sees the trio lined up, R.C.*)
LADIES' AIDERS! Oh, how Bee-you-ti-ful! (*Rushes toward them with
outstretched hands.*) Why—the Ladies' Aiders are the only mother
I have known since my *own* sweet mother died. (*Grips hands of all
as she beams and effervesces!*) I'm so glad to know you and I'm
going to LOVE you—every AIDER of you! (*Spies the barrel!*)
And my dear friend, Barrel! Oh, don't you know me, Barrel? I'm
Pollyanna—and you've furnished me with all my clothes since I
was hardly born! SEE! (*Shows her frock to the barrel.*) This frock
came out of your sister-barrel, and this lovely hat—and these
shoes! (*Indicates freakish hat and too-large shoes.*) And I thank
you, dear Barrel, for I love every stitch you've ever given me,
whether it fit or not! (*Hugs and kisses barrel.*) Dear—DEAR Barrel! (*Kisses barrel—*LADIES *gasp.*)

Unable to thaw out her aunt, Pollyanna teaches her glad game
to the neighborhood (if you break a leg be glad it wasn't your
neck, etc.) and soon meets the grouchy John Pendleton, who
had been in love with her "angel-mother." It isn't long before
Pendleton calls her "little Memory-Eyes" or "my Prism-Girl,"
and she persuades him to adopt Sodom, Gomorrah, and Jimmy
Bean. Later, she effects a *rapprochement* and eventually a
marriage between her Aunt Polly and Dr. Chilton, an estranged suitor of twenty years before. Badly injured in an accident, Pollyanna is a cripple for five years but recovers in time
to marry Jimmy Bean, now a Sophomore at Harvard, who is
discovered to be, not a waif, but one of "the Back Bay Wetherbys—the Quincey Wetherbys!" Misunderstandings bring complications in the final act, amid a welter of emotion, but the
ending is undeniably and tearfully happy. The Glad Girl was
played by Patricia Collinge.

Another orphaned Cinderella role, in 1914, had been assigned to the superb acting of Ruth Chatterton in Jean Webster's *Daddy Long-Legs.* Brought up in an orphan home, the
heroine, now eighteen, is assigned the task of caring for the
younger children but is a victim of unjust nagging and persecution. She is adopted and sent to college by one of the trus-

tees, whom she knows only as Daddy Long-Legs; she falls in love with a Mr. Jervis Pendleton only to discover that he and Daddy Long-Legs are the same, and she agrees to marry him —showing the preference of so many heroines of the period for older men.

It must not be assumed that the sentimental play was the exclusive property of the women dramatists. A variant of the ancient story was given in 1916 by Edward Childs Carpenter in *The Cinderella Man*, with Phoebe Foster and Shelley Hull. The hero, a struggling poet in the traditional garret, is desperately writing an opera libretto for a $10,000 prize. The compassionate daughter of a millionaire next door, pretending she is her own paid companion, comes over the rooftops to his room, bringing comfort and delicacies. Needless to add, the young poet, though he is kicked out of doors by a suspicious landlady, wins at last both the prize and the millionaire's daughter.

Most of the sentimental heroines of the time were incredibly uninformed and naïve, but the palm for innocence should perhaps be given to Marie-Odile, the young novice of Edward Knoblock's play of the same name. The author, a student of George Pierce Baker's 47 Workshop at Harvard, had settled in London under the assumption that the best way to have a play produced in New York was to have it appear in London first. In this work, meticulously staged by David Belasco in 1915, Frances Starr enacted the part of Marie-Odile, novitiate in an Alsatian convent at the time of the Franco-Prussian War of 1870. A drudge and slavey for the nuns, she has never been out of the convent and has seen no men except Father Fischer and an aged gardener. Her maturing emotional life is expended in the loving care of several pigeons, and she is profoundly disturbed when the Mother Superior demands St. Francis (one of the pigeons) for lunch. The Prussian Uhlans, however, are coming, and in the confusion, when the nuns depart in haste, Marie-Odile is left behind. When she sees her first young man in the person of Corporal Philip Meissner, she takes him for St. Michael himself and sinks to her knees "in simple, silent adoration." The other Uhlans also arouse her interest—"O what a queer smell— Your mouth is smoking," she says to one soldier smoking a cigar—but her favorite remains Corporal Meissner. When he starts to leave with the others and kissses her goodbye, she begs him to stay a few hours: "It —It is so sweet to be kissed—by a man." Her ignorance of sex and the brevity of her relationship with the Corporal do not prevent her from having a baby, to her own amazement and to the horror of the nuns when they return a year later. They are adamant about sending her and little Michael out into an inhospitable world, but Marie-Odile, though she does not yet fully understand what has happened to her, regards her experience of the last year as a precious and ennobling one. Whatever its merits or credibility to a present-day playgoer, the play struck a contemporary critic as "spiritual in the highest degree."

Closely allied to the sentimental piece was the romantic love play, perhaps best exemplified in Edward Sheldon's *Romance* (1913), relating the hectic but unhappy love affair between a young minister and an Italian prima donna, superbly played by William Courtenay and Doris Keane, respectively. A prologue shows the minister, now an old man and a bishop, impelled to tell his story to a grandson who is planning to marry an actress. This narrative is presented dramatically in three acts depicting a passionate and poignant love affair of years ago, which ends when the minister learns that Mme. Cavallina has had numerous lovers up to the time she met him. In a more sympathetic treatment than his profession was to receive at the hands of the playwrights of the twenties, the minister loses the opera singer but gains her moral reformation. In an epilogue the grandson still insists on marrying the actress, but the old bishop is reminiscently happy at having evoked romance from his bouquet of memories. The play is undeniably sentimental but it has much exotic color and obvious but forceful characterization. Its enduring quality is indicated by the many revivals it received.

Still sentimental but merging into witty comedy of character was Rachel Crothers' *Old Lady 31* (1916), her first popular success, concerning an old sea captain, Abe, and his wife Angie, who have been forced to sell their home, he to go to the poor farm, she to the old ladies' home. The thirty old ladies at the home, their sympathies aroused at this belated separation, propose that Abe become old lady 31 and remain with them and Angie. The old captain is not too happy in this feminine entourage in which at one point he excites a flurry of jealousy and later is mollycoddled into a state of invalidism. Finally he succeeds in making his escape for two days but returns to his Angie. In the meantime a letter has arrived announcing that some presumably worthless stock, purchased years before, has now a value of eight thousand dollars—enough to buy back their home and befriend a young couple who are planning to marry despite parental opposition.

Love and tears were not the only passport to Broadway fame. The neatly tailored farce-comedy, in which a clever idea was fully exploited with the aid of expert staging and popular juvenile leads, was a perennial favorite. This too, of course, could have tender and romantic moments, but the main emphasis was on plot and situation. Often the action began with some unusual wager. In *Believe Me, Xantippe* (1913) George MacFarland, played by John Barrymore (still a comic actor at this time), makes a bet that after committing a crime he will be able to evade arrest for an entire year. He has many narrow escapes, but all the complications do not prevent him from winning the cash and incidentally the daughter of a Western sheriff. This work, a Harvard prize play, was written by Frederick Ballard, one of many of George Pierce Baker's students to reach Broadway. Another bet initiates the action of James Montgomery's *Nothing but the Truth* (1916), in which a popular actor, William Collier, wins a wager that he will tell noth-

ing but the unadulterated truth for twenty-four hours. George
M. Cohan's *Seven Keys to Baldpate* (1913) likewise has a bet,
won by a writer of best sellers (Wallace Eddinger) in a clever
mixture of farce and melodrama.

Other forms of farce-comedy include the increasingly popular bedroom farces that were supposed to bring relaxation to
the "tired business man." One of this type, *Twin Beds* (1914)
by Salisbury Fields and Margaret Mayo, enjoyed a long and
successful run, with its usual mix-ups in beds and identities.
Madge Kennedy, a favorite ingénue, played a young wife
with a partiality for tango parties at a time when both twin
beds and tango were sufficiently new to be of topical interest.
A sentimental crook farce of 1916 with a bucolic twist, *Turn
to the Right!* by Winchell Smith and John E. Hazzard, showed
how a variety of popular themes could be shuffled into almost
any combination. A young man, accused of a crime he did not
commit, spends a year in prison but does not reveal the fact to
his mother, a paragon of maternal goodness. He returns home,
only to find that his mother is being swindled out of the farm
by a rascally deacon. Two prison companions arrive and employ their professional skill to foil the deacon. The two ex-
crooks are reformed, the son is proved innocent, the three men
acquire wives, and the entire group sets about marketing jam
made by the mother. This hodgepodge proved immensely
popular. Also popular were a series of business farces in Jewish
dialect by Montague Glass, of which *Potash and Perlmutter*
(1913) was the most successful.

Two other farce-comedies may be mentioned as examples of
simple themes expertly developed. Frank Craven's *Too Many
Cooks* (1914), in which he played the lead, offered the pleasant domestic theme of a young man who sets out to build a
suburban house for himself and his fiancée. Interruptions and
complications arise, however, including conflicting advice by
friends, relations, and future in-laws, a union strike by the
workmen, and a quarrel with the bride-to-be. The acts show
the house in different stages of construction and confusion, but

at the end the young couple are revealed on their front porch enjoying the suburban delights of mosquitoes, fireflies, and the whistle of a locomotive engine. The other play, which appeared the following season, was *The Boomerang* by Winchell Smith and Victor Mapes. A young doctor, played by Arthur Byron, has yet to encounter his first patient. When a girl enters, acted by Martha Hedman, a Swedish actress imported a few years earlier by Frohman, the doctor discovers to his surprise that she is looking for a job, not medical advice. He hires her as office girl. The first real patient (Wallace Eddinger) is found to be suffering from unrequited love rather than a more prosaic ailment. In effecting a cure the doctor tries jealousy, but is himself struck by the boomerang when he falls in love with his office girl. The comic possibilities of the situation were effectively realized in the direction of Belasco, who required the authors, after they had spent two years writing *The Boomerang*, to rewrite it completely three times. Both plays show the Broadway playwrights turning out thin but sprightly comic work of the escape variety.

Except for the plays of Shaw and other European importations, neither social comedy nor comedy of manners made much headway in the period under discussion. Broadway managers preferred sentiment to satire and they shied away from controversial questions. There were occasional attempts by playwrights like Rachel Crothers, William Hurlbut, and Chester Bailey Fernald to discuss feminism or trial marriage, but the time was apparently not ripe and the plays just did not "take." Near the end of the period, however, Clare Kummer in *Good Gracious, Annabelle* (1916) began a series of comedies, with some satire, that were at least touched by the comic spirit. Produced by Arthur Hopkins, with settings by Robert Edmond Jones, both comparatively new to Broadway, this madcap piece caused something of a stir. Arthur Hornblow of the *Theatre,** called it a "futuristic farce," comparable to the no-

---

* In 1917 this well-known periodical about actors and the stage changed its name to *Theatre Magazine.*

torious "Nude Descending a Stairway," and he liked neither the lines nor the sets. The play is actually very slight, and its success was largely due to a superlative cast, which included among others Roland Young, Edwin Nicander, Lola Fisher, May Vokes, and Walter Hampden. What distinguished the play from the more conventional product was the irrepressible verve of the lines; the burlesque of the big business man in his Long Island habitat with its usual complement of yachts, liquor, and servants; and the farcical idea of having several characters of cocktail society hire themselves out as servants on the Long Island estate. The real modernism of the play is clear in a reference in one of the lines to Freud, whose theory of association of ideas has been adopted by a hotel detective! A more conventional treatment of the same servant situation, by the way, had opened a week earlier in A. E. Thomas' *Come Out of the Kitchen*, based upon a story by Alice Duer Miller. A New York millionaire (the theatrical woods were full of them) rents a mansion from an impoverished Virginia family, with the proviso, however, that he must have a staff of white servants. These are impersonated by the family—two brothers and two sisters—with Ruth Chatterton as the cook. Conflicts arise between the New Yorker's disagreeable guests and the Southern "servants" until the play ends with a conventional declaration of love between the millionaire and the erstwhile cook. The play has none of the sparkling originality of *Good Gracious, Annabelle*, but there is significance in the fact that it ran twice as long.

Early in 1917 another play by Mrs. Kummer, *A Successful Calamity*, was produced by Hopkins with sets by Jones and a cast headed by William Gillette and Estelle Winwood. It also enjoyed a successful run. In good Shavian dialogue it told the fortunes of a millionaire, Henry Wilton, who tests the love of his wife and children by announcing that he is ruined, with happy results and reformations all around. Apparently the many performances and revivals of George Bernard Shaw in

New York were bearing fruit, for next season appeared *Why Marry?* by Jesse Lynch Williams, another play showing the influence of the Anglo-Irish vegetarian—a frank discussion of marriage and the new woman which won the first Pulitzer Prize. Jesse Lynch Williams and Clare Kummer both point to the future rather than to the past, however, and they are the exceptions that prove the rule that high comedy at this time was a negligible factor on Broadway.

To return to more popular fare, a protean variety of melodrama was always ready to thrill and delight the playgoer, usually with some twist or new wrinkle to clamor for special attention. Most important, perhaps, were the crime and crook plays. Of this type, two of the biggest hits were the work of Bayard Veiller, the first being *Within the Law* (1912), in which Jane Cowl rose to stardom. Sent to Auburn prison for three years for a theft she did not commit, Mary Turner (Jane Cowl) determines to get even with the world in general and her employer in particular. On her release she organizes a gang to operate blackmail and other schemes but always strictly *within the law,* under the supervision of a clever lawyer. When she traps her former employer's son into marriage, she feels that her cup of revenge is full, but in the unexpected entanglements that follow, resulting in a murder in which she had no part, she is brought to the realization that she really loves her husband. The shooting itself had an element of novelty in that the revolver was equipped with a Maxim silencer. Almost equally popular was Veiller's melodrama of 1916, *The Thirteenth Chair,* exploiting the interest in spiritualism currently aroused by the World War. The friend of a murdered man employs an Irish medium, played by the author's wife, Margaret Wycherly, to help identify the murderer. During the séance, at which a sizable group are present, he sits in the thirteenth chair and is himself murdered in the same way. The medium confesses to being a fraud, but when her daughter becomes seriously involved, she tries her occult powers again as a last resort and brings the criminal to light. Both plays are trivial as literature but are so skillfully constructed that they squeeze out the last drop of theatrical effectiveness.

There were other sensational successes in the field of crime. One was the previously mentioned *On Trial* (1914) by the young law clerk Elmer Reizenstein. Beginning in a courtroom with the final phases of a murder trial, it employed the cinema device of the flashback to reveal the story as told by witnesses and participants, thus giving a different slant to the murder and eventually freeing the defendant. A critic of the time called it a "talking motion picture" and much was written about its revolutionary technique, which should not be over-estimated but which had at least some influence in jolting dramatic technique out of its conventional rut. In the same year, an expensive necklace smuggled through the customs gave Roi Cooper Megrue the mainspring of the action in *Under Cover,* an elaborate high-society melodrama in which the heroine has to choose between her sister and the man she loves. Even more complicated was Max Marcin's *Cheating Cheaters* (1916), involving two gangs, one of them headed by Marjorie Rambeau as Nan Carey and Ruth Brockton, who is revealed at the end to be a detective but who hires the other gang as special detectives-because she has fallen in love with the leader.

With such plays, old-fashioned melodrama could not compete, though it appeared occasionally—in Augustus Thomas' *Rio Grande* (1916), for example, or in George Scarborough's *The Heart of Wetona* (1916), a joint production by Frohman and Belasco in which Lenore Ulric appeared as a half-Indian but a fully wronged woman. More up-to-date in theme was a sprinkling of war plays that started to make their appearance in 1915. One was Earl Derr Biggers' *Inside the Lines,* depicting a group of Americans at Gibraltar stranded without funds by the war. A sinister individual from India turns out to be a Gërman spy, and a supposed German spy—played by Lewis S. Stone, who enjoyed a successful career later in the movies—

is discovered, of course, to be an Englishman in the secret service. Far more replete with action was a war melodrama by Roi Cooper Megrue, *Under Fire* (1915), with the ubiquitous German spy, a scene in the trenches enlivened by a bomb explosion, and the final reunion in a hospital of the wounded hero and the heroine, now a nurse. It is amusing to note that the play aroused some objections because it was strongly pro-Ally and disregarded President Wilson's plea for neutrality.

In an age when American tragedy was practically non-existent, the real dramatic *pièce de résistance* became "the play with a punch," closely allied to melodrama but somewhat heavier. Like melodrama it had a more or less happy ending but was supposed to be strong dramatic meat. Designed largely for the proverbially tired business man, it did not pretend to seduce or captivate him, as did the girl shows and bedroom farces, but to deliver a thumping wallop in the solar plexus which would temporarily make him forget he was tired. What would be his emotional reaction if he chanced to enter a house of prostitution and found there either his wife or daughter? In real life such a situation might be rare, but he would enjoy a vicarious thrill from beholding it on the stage. Complete enumeration of the plays with a punch is impossible here, but a few samples will illustrate the type. *Polygamy* (1914) by Harvey O'Higgins and Harriet Ford, purporting to be an accurate exposé of conditions still existing in the Mormon church, shows a happily married man, Daniel Whitman, with the customary one wife and with two children. Unfortunately the Prophet decrees that Daniel must take Annis, a widow, as his second wife, despite the latter's passionate protest—"For God's sake let me save my body in my own way!" At last, in a series of dramatic scenes, the Whitmans foil the Prophet and avoid legal polygamy by the simple device of escaping from the State of Utah. More ordinary in theme is Cleves Kinkead's *Common Clay* (1915), another Harvard prize play, in which Ellen Neal (Jane Cowl) tries to forget her past by becoming a maid in the Fullerton household. She is not too successful, however, for she is recognized immediately by a guest as a habituée of Bender's Dance Hall and less savory places. Hugh Fullerton, the son in the household, takes advantage of this information and makes love to Ellen. When she has a baby, she does not demand that Hugh marry her but d. es want money to bring up the child properly, and is willing to take the fight to court despite the Fullertons' money and influence. In a dramatic courtroom scene Judge Filson, attorney for the Fullertons, discovers by chance that Ellen is his own daughter by a singer whom he had seduced and who had later committed suicide. He reveals his relationship to the girl and sends her to New York to study music. The last act, with much violence to probabilities, shows Ellen now a successful opera singer and Hugh willing to marry her and give his child a name. Although the plot is often ridiculous, it does succeed in uttering a strong protest against the established social system, based upon wealth and injustice, which makes possible the exploitation of girls like Ellen.

As a final example of the punch play Edward Sheldon's *The Song of Songs* (1914) may be mentioned, a piece based on a Sudermann novel but changed to an American locale. In it Lily Kardos (Irene Fenwick), a very young and exceedingly naïve girl of Greek extraction, poor and now alone in the world, is forever seeking the Song of Songs, which her father told her was love. She apparently falls in love with Dick Laird, but fright or ignorance or some other unexplained reason leads her to marry the old and lascivious Senator Calkins, who tries with mediocre success to have her tutored in English grammar and ladylike manners. She naïvely attempts to reform Dick, who has become involved with a Follies girl, but, though Lily is entirely innocent, Dick enters her room late at night via a ladder and the two are surprised by the Senator, who puts her out of doors at once and secures a divorce subsequently. Four years later, Lily, now twenty-one, is settled as Dick's mistress but still is trying to hear the Song of Songs—at this particular time with a young poet (Ernest Glendinning), who wants to marry her despite her past. Dick, in a rage, tell her she's "a damn little tart who sells herself to the highest bidder and then falls for every husky young chauffeur who's got enough hair on his chest." She leaves him, nevertheless, to marry the poet, but a short time later the poet's worldly uncle disillusions the lad by getting poor Lily drunk at a dinner party with the result that she recites risqué limericks (very mild ones) and behaves in a definitely unladylike manner. When she passes out and the poet leaves in horror, the uncle ships her back in a taxi to Dick, who truly loves her and expresses a desire to marry her. Lily is heartbroken, but a modern reader can only be glad, for her sake, that she escaped marriage to the priggish poet.

Whatever the demerits and ridiculous features of the play with a punch, it at least had the virtue—very well pointed out by Edward Goodman in 1914—of lifting some of the taboos in scene and situation which had so greatly restricted the American dramatists. Of serious realistic drama there was as yet very little, with the exception of Louis K. Anspacher's *The Unchastened Woman* (1915), in which the superior acting of Emily Stevens carried the play in spite of its unpleasant characterization.

A survey of the Broadway scene would not be complete without at least a glance at the musical shows, a distinctly American product which was to become one of our main contributions to drama. The period before April, 1917, was clearly one of transition. Victor Herbert was still active but giving way in popular favor to a former singer in East Side cabarets, Irving Berlin, whose "Alexander's Ragtime Band" and other songs had lifted him into the limelight and whose ragtime musical comedies—*Watch Your Step* (1914) and *Stop! Look! Listen!* (1915)—started the big parade from ragtime to jazz to swing. One of his early ambitions was to write a real American opera in syncopation. The old and the new were combined in 1916 in *The Century Girl*—a musical collaboration of Herbert and Berlin. John Philip Sousa, another old-timer, was still writing marches and playing occasionally in musical shows. Other favorite Broadway composers were the versatile George M. Cohan and Jerome Kern. The latter's *Very Good, Eddie* (1915) earned praise for its unconventional handling of lighting, costumes, and dances, as well as for a new type of chorus girl—now becoming popular under the tutelage of men like Ned Wayburn—a type that exhibited more modesty and refinement than her well-padded predecessors. Though the piece was not successful, a refreshing quality was noted also in *See America First* (1916), a comic opera of college origin by T. L. Riggs and Cole Porter, in whose cast was Clifton Webb. Earlier—December, 1915—*Ruggles of Red Gap* had appeared with incidental music by Sigmund Romberg. Dancing, too, was trying out new steps and rhythms—from the turkey trot to the tango, to the hesitation waltz, to the rhumba, the last described in 1916 as a new dance "not likely to win favor as a society pastime." In *The Sunshine Girl* (1913), imported from England, an English dancer, Vernon Castle, and Mrs. Castle (née Foote in New Rochelle, New York) became established as a famous dancing couple. A roster of stage dancers and singers would include many other familiar figures: Al Jolson, blackface comedian, and Ann Pennington, hula dancer; Ina Claire, who deserted the musical comedy stage in 1917 to play for Belasco, and Marilyn Miller, who graduated from vaudeville to *The Passing Show of 1914.* Many of them were luminaries of the annual *Ziegfeld Follies* or *Midnight Frolics* or *Passing Shows,* as were the zanies and comedians Bert Williams, Leon Errol, Ed Wynn, W. C. Fields, Frances White, and Fanny Brice. Another annual production, on a broader popular level, was the grandiose Hippodrome show, like *Hip-Hip-Hooray,* with the clown Toto, Charlotte, Annette Kellermann, and a plethora of spectacular effects.

Among numerous other theatrical events of the period was an American tour by the great French actress Sarah Bernhardt in 1916–1917, after the amputation of her leg, and a visit in 1916 of Diaghileff's *Ballet Russe,* with settings by Bakst and music by Stravinsky. Ten ballets were given in New York.

American audiences showed increasing interest both in ballet
and in aesthetic dancing. Pavlova was a frequent performer.
A young dancer from Brooklyn, Ruth Denis, who had been
given several dancing bits by Belasco, was advised by the
wizard to devote all her energy to her real love. Before long,
as Ruth St. Denis, she was giving recitals of oriental and classic
dances with the collaboration of Ted Shawn, a handsome as
well as athletic young man who later became her husband.
Other men were turning to the Dance with a capital D in defiance of the usual American prejudice against so aesthetic a
career. Paul Swan was one; it is also recorded that Marion
Morgan's Art Dancers, a troupe of college girls who made an
extensive vaudeville tour in 1916, were accompanied by one
Harvard man, Class of 1914, who took the part of a warrior.

For the older playgoer the names of actors and plays listed
in this rapid survey may have evoked memories occasionally
wistful and rarely unpleasant. Within its moral and commercial limitations Broadway, one must impartially admit, provided talent and entertainment of a h̦h professional quality.
The chief failure was the American playwright, but, as we
have seen, unless he was willing to conform he was beaten
from the start. To a vigorous minority of young men and
women, American drama was failing ignobly to fulfill its artistic and intellectual mission. They had aesthetic ideals reaching far beyond the commercialism of the "show business," and
they had a definite program of reform. At the same time America itself was experiencing a revolution in manners and morals
which was showing its influence in nondramatic literature and
must inevitably be reflected on the stage. The preliminary
stages in the metamorphosis will be the concern of the next
chapter. In 1917 it was possible for Rancholt Warsden, with
considerable justice, to rename Broadway the Great Trite
Way; only a few years later the pun would have been inexact.

Chapter 2

CHANGING MANNERS AND
THE NEW ART THEATRE

*T*HE BOX-OFFICE standards of Broadway rested upon the system of popular morality inherited from the nineteenth century. According to an unwritten but widely prevalent code, unpleasant subjects were barred from the theatre. Plays need not preach a sermon, but they should not run counter to conventional manners and morals. The criteria were the same in effect that govern the Hays censorship of the moving-picture industry or the acceptance and rejection of manuscripts by the popular magazines. How vitally these restrictions affected the stage is evident from contemporary reviews in newspapers and magazines, including the *Theatre*, edited by Arthur Hornblow, a publication considered by its enemies a mere trade journal for commercial Broadway. In 1913 two plays were stopped by the police, and their respective producers—Lee Shubert and William Harris—were haled before a magistrate. One play, George Scarborough's *The Lure*, was set with literal realism in a house of prostitution; the other, Bayard Veiller's *The Fight*, had one act in a brothel, exposing thereby the viciousness of a United States Senator. A strong moral purpose was claimed for both productions. In reviewing the case, the editor of the *Theatre* said:

A play should always teach a moral; a good play subtly does; a few successful plays do not. Precisely what we are to learn from a succession of plays based on the crusade against an unmentionable evil, remains to be found out. Perhaps we may venture the opinion that the stage is not the place in which to fight such crusades. To

make a drama—a poor, crude, mechanical drama of the subject—
it is necessary to take for protagonists types that are frankly exceptional. Now the drama, to be widely useful, cannot be confined to
narrow possibility; its types must be broad, its teachings general.
That is one good reason for putting the Red Light play out of the
theatre. Another is that the lesson it teaches is repulsive and immoral. The stage is no place for these distressing lessons. . . .
Have our dramatists no higher aim than to dramatize contemporary excitements?

With this prevailing dramatic theory it was little wonder that
Bernard Shaw's *Mrs. Warren's Profession* had been halted, or
that Richard Bennett had to move heaven and earth with the
providential support of the *Medical Review of Reviews* to get
Eugene Brieux's *Damaged Goods* (written ten years before)
on the stage at all. Bennett had intended to give a performance
of this piece at the Waldorf-Astoria, but this genteel hostelry
was shocked at the subject of the play, venereal disease, and
declined the honor.

The disapproval of the *Theatre* critic was not limited to the
treatment of prostitution on the stage. Praising the acting of
John Barrymore in Galsworthy's prison-reform play *Justice*,
the reviewer said: "He was one of the accidents, so to speak,
that make for this unexpected success of a play not adapted to
entertainment or even edification." Roberto Bracco's *Night of
Snow*, a one-acter dealing with the poverty and suicide of two
women who had led an irregular life, was described as "un-
suited, even to private performance." Guy Bolton's *The Rule
of Three* (1914), in which the child of a much divorced mother
has three fathers whom he calls respectively "father,"
"daddy," and "papa," was deemed a play with a subject not
proper for farcical treatment and one "that would hardly com-
mend itself to audiences of the kind managers should seek to
bring to the theatres." As for William Legrand's *The Smolder-
ing Flame*, which lasted about one night in 1913, the critic denounced it roundly: "What it did was to reduce to an absurdity
the desire of woman to motherhood." Nor did the *Theatre* ig-

nore peccadillos of impropriety. Of another play the critic
wrote: "One of the actresses emphasized childhood by appearing in bare legs. This was a touch of the much sought after
novelty." Of *So Long Letty* (1916), a show with music and
lyrics by Earl Carroll, he says:

There is a scene in a bathing house, in semi-darkness, in which the
nymphs of the sand disrobe in union suits. That is questionable,
according to the point of view, but not absolutely, for the vision is
momentary and not obtrusive. It is something in the nature of
pandering, but it belongs to the circumstances and is not inter-
jected without reason.

By 1916 theatregoers and critics were also becoming disturbed at an increasing verbal frankness on the stage, a problem discussed in an article by Alan Dale, one of the Broadway
reviewers. Apparently the profanity of these pre-*Tobacco
Road* days consisted mainly of "Hell" and "My Gawd." Despite all these disapprovals and limitations, however, it must
be stated that New York was liberal in comparison with
Boston, where one play was stopped merely because the
heroine, who has been "indiscreet" but whom the hero is willing to make an honest woman, refuses this proffer of marriage
as it is motivated by duty rather than love.

   Excessive as may seem the prudery of this prewar theatre,
the significant fact is that playwrights were at least trying to
break out of the bonds of convention. Dialogue was gradually
loosening up, as early as 1916 the flapper was making her bow
on the stage, and several daring plays were exploiting the
intimacy of the bathroom—first by means of running water
heard during the heroine's bath, then *via* an open door revealing for a second the girl's bare back glimpsed over the rim of
the tub. A number of plays, while not too successful, made
some attempt to discuss trial marriage, eugenics, and the new
woman. In 1913, for example, William Hurlbut's *The Strange
Woman* presented Elsie Ferguson as an emancipated woman,
former resident of Paris, who takes a trip to Delphin, Iowa,

with a young man to secure his mother's consent to their living together without benefit of church marriage. Of course, the heroine eventually yields to custom, but not without revealing the hypocrisy and secret immorality of the mid-western small town. Rachel Crothers, who had discussed the relations between the sexes in *A Man's World* (1910), showed realistically in *Ourselves* (1913) that reformatories for women are no solution for moral reform and in *Young Wisdom* (1914), with Mabel and Edith Taliaferro, presented two girls who wish to experiment with trial marriage, though the outcome is perfectly innocent.

Such themes, along with increasing freedom in speech and manners, were but mild reflections on the professional stage of a revolution in American life and letters—hastened by the First World War—which came to a climax in the twenties. Feminism and woman suffrage were part of this movement, as were the attacks on the business man and on puritanism. The novelists were already going to town in exposing Main Street and American Babbittry, with the aid of critics like H. L. Mencken and George Jean Nathan in *Smart Set*, who found perennial delight in taking potshots at the hinterlands. In Europe Gertrude Stein and James Joyce were trying out novel patterns and forms, cubism and futurism were revolutionizing pictorial art, and Freud's theories were undermining the whole foundation of conventional morality. Abroad and in this country unionism, socialism, anarchism, and the I.W.W. all pointed the way to political radicalism.

It was in these years that Greenwich Village, the shabby but picturesque section of New York in the vicinity of Washington Square, earned for itself a nationwide reputation quite out of proportion to its size. Here had settled a group of painters and writers, partly because rents were cheap, partly because they were attracted by the unfashionable charm of the neighborhood. Many of them, like John Reed and Emma Goldman, were social and political radicals. Most Villagers indulged in a rather blatant Bohemianism. Here congregated the short-

haired women in brightly colored smocks who shocked
bourgeois sensibilities by smoking countless cigarettes in
public and discoursing learnedly on free love and free verse.
They contributed to the creation of the early legend of the
Village as a "quaint" place abounding in arty restaurants and
tearooms—Polly's, the Samovar, the Black Cat—where one
might hear Bobby Edwards sing to the accompaniment of
homemade ukeleles constructed from cigar boxes. No doubt
much of the talk and behavior and "atmosphere" was a pose,
but the Village did nevertheless represent a community of
individualists—many of them serious and gifted—who placed
creative art above money-making, espoused radical causes,
and lived in happy promiscuity, free from snooping deacons
and gossipy neighbors. By the time the twenties and Prohibition came to the Village, many of the original denizens had departed and the neighborhood was left to earn its even more
lurid reputation as the home of bathtub gin and necking
parties. Whatever its transformations, however, it remained
a symbol of revolt against middle-class values and standards
and was to leave its mark on the new American drama.

The spirit of change, the eager search after new things, was
not limited to the world of manners and morals, but had been
at work in drama and the theatre for many years, slight as had
been its influence on commercial Broadway. Europe, long before America, had developed a new drama of distinction and
great variety, from the social problem plays of Ibsen to the
unorthodox comedies of Shaw, from the tortured psychological tragedies of Strindberg to the symbolic mysticism of
Maeterlinck. Excellent theatrical organizations—among them
the Moscow Art Theatre, the Abbey Theatre, the *Théâtre
Libre*, the London Stage Society—had brought to the stage
the work of these and other dramatists. Much of it was familiar
in America, either from special performances or from the
published plays, and Bernard Shaw, at least, was frequently
produced on Broadway. The American dramatist, when he

finally made his appearance, could not complain of lack of models and inspiration.

The strongest European influence, however, and by far the most dynamic of the revolutionary forces had to do with the "new stagecraft" and the concept of the "art theatre" which became increasingly dominant in the first two decades of the twentieth century. Prophet and leader in this new movement was the eccentric Gordon Craig, son of Ellen Terry and for a time an actor under Henry Irving. In 1897 he deserted the stage and in 1913 left England altogether to found in Florence his School for the Art of the Theatre. Among his influential publications were *The Art of the Theatre* (1905), *On the Art of the Theatre* (1911), and a periodical, the *Mask*, started in 1908. Very briefly, Craig's theories were formulated as a strong protest against realism, both of play and scenery. The new "art theatre" should instead be imaginative and poetic. At its best it would represent a synthesis of all the arts—music, the dance, painting, etc. In order to achieve unity and harmony of impression, the artist-director—the *régisseur*—should rule with an iron hand and be personally responsible for all phases of production. The actor, by contrast, would lose stature. Craig advocated the use of masks by the players and later proposed to do away altogether with the actors and the spoken word and to substitute the *über-marionette,* whose personality could in no way clash or interfere with that of the director. In stage designs, large broad masses and artistic simplicity would take the place of detailed realism. Craig proposed the use of tall, sweeping curtains and invented a set of large screens that could be arranged in different combinations for the presentation of almost any imaginative play. Costumes were to be considered part of the scenery and should have imaginative beauty rather than historical accuracy. Light, in the art theatre, would hold a place of special importance—not to imitate nature, as Belasco strove to do, but to create mood and arouse emotion. The desired harmony of all these elements could be achieved through "stylization," presenting the work in a certain individual style—permeating the designs, the direction, everything—which would be derived from the artist's concept of the inner or spiritual meaning of the play. In short, drama was to resemble a symphony or a ballet rather than what one ordinarily thinks of as a play. While in this extreme form Craig's views were rarely adopted, they had an immense influence on stage decoration and helped to establish the "artists" in the theatre.

Many other Europeans advanced the cause of the art theatre. Max Reinhardt, director of the *Deutsches Theater* and other Berlin theatres, showed how a practical man of the theatre could modify the theories of the extremists. Stanislavsky, director of the Moscow Art Theatre, developed an organization which showed a preference for realism but whose excellent repertory was an ideal model of ensemble acting. Jessner in Germany, Appia in Switzerland, Meierhold in Russia, Copeau in France, Granville Barker in England— these also were priests and prophets of the new movement. Among the more imaginative decorators were Leon Bakst, who used splashes of exotic color in his design for the Ballet Russe, and Joseph Urban, Austrian artist, who used a technique of *pointillage* or broken colors, borrowed from the French Impressionists. By painting his scenery in spots of different colors he could vary the color and shape of the design merely by playing different lights on it.

The ideals of the new decorators and of the art theatre had been made possible by a long series of mechanical devices and inventions tried out successfully in Europe and later America. Germany led the way in the installation of revolving, wagon, and other kinds of stages to facilitate quick changes of scenery. In that same country, also, were devised the different kinds of *Horizont* or cyclorama, particularly the *Kuppelhorizont*, a "sky dome" made of concrete which domed over the rear of the stage. Light which was played on the "sky dome" would give the illusion of distance and luminous atmosphere. In Germany, also, was invented the Fortuny lighting system, emphasizing the principle of reflected light in lieu of the glare and flat illumination of the traditional footlights and borders. Even the playhouse itself was to be shorn of its rococo decorations and designed according to the new ideals of functionalism and dignified simplicity.

In this ferment of theories and inventions from abroad, despite the clamor of American reformers, the Broadway producers were slow to be converted. Their ventures into the realms of imagination were uncommon to begin with, and they showed little interest in the new stagecraft. Their adherence to old methods and devices infuriated the devotees of the art theatre, men like Sheldon Cheney, who pointed scornful fingers at trembling scenery which combined real doors and windows with obviously canvas walls. The reformers expressed strong objection to the painted backdrop with artificial perspective and shadows. Especially bad, in their estimation, were the outdoor scenes, such as the traditional forest represented by an incongruous combination of plastic trees, painted cutouts, and a painted backdrop. Belasco had insisted on solid scenery and had established many other reforms, but the newcomers had just as strong a distaste for the minute and unimaginative realism of his settings—the overcrowded furniture, the broken wall space, the window showing a complete backyard scene, or the open door revealing another fully furnished room. They had little use for the famous Belasco "tricks"—the sleeping baby that woke up at just the right moment, for example—because they felt that such stunts called attention to themselves and drew it away from the play. All they demanded was simple, artistic scenery—making use of suggestion and symbolism rather than detailed accuracy— which would help to reveal the soul of the play.

Among the early American converts to the new stagecraft was Sam Hume, graduate of 47 Workshop, who worked for a time with Gordon Craig in Europe and who later became associated with the Detroit Arts and Crafts Theatre. Joseph Urban came to America, where he became designer for the

Boston Opera Company until he was later elevated to Broadway and the *Ziegfeld Follies*. Livingston Platt, another imaginative designer, staged many plays for the Boston Toy Theatre. Most important of the group was Robert Edmond Jones, Harvard graduate, student of 47 Workshop, who studied with Max Reinhardt at the *Deutsches Theater*. In 1915 he first attracted notice on Broadway by his unusual sets for Anatole France's *The Man Who Married a Dumb Wife*, produced by Granville Barker when the latter was invited to New York by the Stage Society. Jones soon became associated with a professional producer, Arthur Hopkins, for whom he designed settings for *The Devil's Garden, Good Gracious, Annabelle*, and other plays. The young designer's connections with the Washington Square Players and the Provincetown Players will be mentioned later. He rapidly became one of America's great decorators, as anyone will testify who saw *The Jest*, the Barrymore *Hamlet, Desire under the Elms*, or *Mourning Becomes Electra*.

Not everything connected with the professional theatre was anathema to the young men bent on reforming the stage. The producer Winthrop Ames—another member of Baker's English 47—had shown partiality to poetic and imaginative drama, including productions of *Prunella* (1913), a fantasy by Laurence Housman and Granville Barker, and of *Pierrot the Prodigal* (1916), a pantomime from the French. He had been managing director of the ill-fated New Theatre, which had put on Shakespeare and other poetical dramas, and he had built the Booth and the attractive Little Theatre, in contrast to the gilded playhouses of an earlier day. Another noteworthy event was Reinhardt's production of *Sumurun*, brought to New York in 1912. In the same year Harris and Selwyn produced *The Yellow Jacket*, a Chinese fantasy by George C. Hazelton and J. Harry Benrimo, and won at least an artistic success; the play proved financially more successful when it was revived by the Coburns in 1916. John D. Williams showed daring and imagination in presenting

Galsworthy's *Justice* with John Barrymore. Arthur Hopkins, another progressive producer, was converted early to the new stagecraft and with the aid of Robert Edmond Jones put on superior plays—Edith Ellis's *The Devil's Garden* for example, or Henning Berger's *The Deluge* (1917). The failure of these serious plays was more than compensated for a few years later, when with either or both of the Barrymore brothers as leads and Jones as designer he achieved such magnificent productions as *The Jest, Richard III,* and *Hamlet.* From these and other offerings it can be seen that, despite appearances, Broadway was not completely unprepared for a dramatic revolution.

The real revolution, however, came from outside Broadway, where influences from European drama and stagecraft were much stronger and more direct. For one thing, colleges and universities, departing from the traditional curriculum, began to offer courses in the history of drama and in actual playwriting. Best known, of course, was George Pierce Baker's English 47 (47 Workshop) at Harvard, which was rather timidly begun at Radcliffe in 1903. Later the course was expanded to include both elementary and advanced playwriting, and the students' best work was given experimental production in the Agassiz Theatre. Without being dogmatic about rules or techniques, New England enough to demand honest work and sincere effort, Professor Baker inspired his students' faith in the dignity of playwriting and in their own capabilities. Viewed in terms of the number and importance of his students who made their way in the theatre, his influence is truly colossal. Among the earlier graduates were Edward Sheldon, Edward Knoblock, and Percy Mackaye; more recent playwrights were Eugene O'Neill, Philip Barry, S. N. Behrman, Sidney Howard, and John Howard Lawson. Other students later became directors (Winthrop Ames, George Abbott, Theresa Helburn), critics (Kenneth Macgowan, Heywood Broun, Walter Pritchard Eaton, Robert C. Benchley, John Mason Brown), actors (Mary Morris,

Dorothy Sands, Osgood Perkins), and designers (Robert Edmond Jones, Lee Simonson, Donald Oenslager). In 1925 Baker was offered the chairmanship of the department of drama at Yale, where he also became director of the University Theatre, with better facilities and equipment for producing student work than at Harvard. Here he remained until his retirement in 1933. His real influence on the contemporary theatre, however, is more clearly identified with his earlier teaching at Harvard.

Outside the colleges, too, serious-minded groups felt the urge to put on unusual plays and promote the new stagecraft. One of the most prominent was the New York Stage Society, inspired by the celebrated London Stage Society, which organized one of the first subscription audiences in America. It was formed in 1912 by New York social leaders; at least two of its presidents—Mrs. William Astor Chanler and Mrs. Norman Hapgood—had been actresses at one time. It was this group that invited Granville Barker in 1915 to present four plays—A Midsummer Night's Dream was one of them—in the new manner. In the same year the Society promoted two performances of God and Company by H. Austin Adams, a parson turned playwright. This play dealt with the evils and hypocrisies of popular religion. In 1917 appeared the same author's 'Ception Shoals, a tragedy concerning sex ignorance in which Alla Nazimova played the daughter of a lighthouse keeper. This play (Theatre called it a "doleful obstetrical drama") was staged by Walter Wanger, a young Dartmouth graduate. Among other productions were Strindberg's Easter, Heywood's A Woman Killed with Kindness, and Ridgely Torrence's Negro tragedy, Granny Maumee. The Stage Society also sponsored exhibitions of stage designs by Hume, Platt, and others, and later helped the Provincetown Players to gain a foothold in New York.

Even audiences, larger and more general than the clientele of the Stage Society, were becoming organized. About 1910 an active Drama League of America was formed to encourage

the production and support of worth-while plays, sometimes
at special matinees. Books and articles about the insurgent
theatre flowed steadily from the pens of critics like Clayton
Hamilton, Walter Pritchard Eaton, Hiram K. Moderwell,
Sheldon Cheney, or Kenneth Macgowan. Lectures were given
before women's clubs and other organizations. The *Theatre*
was accused of championing the old commercial theatre, but
a rival made its appearance in Detroit in 1916—the *Theatre
Arts Magazine,* * published at the Arts and Crafts Theatre
under the editorship of Sheldon Cheney. Its aims and purposes appeared in the first issue in the form of a stirring man-
ifesto. In part these aims were:

To help conserve and develop creative impulse in the American
theatre; to provide a permanent record of American dramatic art
in its formative period; to hasten the day when the speculators will
step out of the established playhouse and let the artists come in;
such are the aims of THEATRE ARTS MAGAZINE. It begins modestly;
but there is a good fight to fight, and it intends to grow to the task.
It bespeaks your coöperation.
P.S.—We intend not to be swallowed by the movies.

Two years later, in time of war, the magazine ventured praise
of the German theatre and lost its local support. It moved to
New York, where it was better able to continue its campaign.

Closely related to all the forces of reform and revolution
was the little theatre movement, emanating from Antoine's
Théâtre Libre (founded in Paris, 1887) and other European
influences, which reached Chicago as early as 1906 but did
not become prominent throughout America until 1911. Among
the most famous of the small theatres that sprang up all over
the country were the Chicago Little Theatre, the Boston Toy
Theatre, the Detroit Arts and Crafts Theatre, and the
Wisconsin Players. The common characteristics of all these
various organizations were their true amateur spirit, their

* *Theatre Arts Magazine* changed its name in 1924 to *Theatre Arts Monthly*
and in 1939 to *Theatre Arts.*

experimentation with unusual plays and settings—particularly imaginative ones, their dependence on the one-act play, their practice of repertory, and their development of the subscription audience. It was not long before the little theatres —with these and other features—reached New York City.

Late in 1914 a few stage enthusiasts tried out a performance of Lord Dunsany's *The Glittering Gate* on a makeshift stage set up in the back room of the Washington Square Bookshop. Robert Edmond Jones arranged the simple décor. The success of this trial performance encouraged the group to organize as the Washington Square Players, under the direction of Edward Goodman, and to rent the small Bandbox Theatre for several bills. They leased this playhouse for the entire 1915–1916 season, and then—in a daring invasion of Broadway—moved uptown to the Comedy Theatre for the next theatrical year. America's entry into the war forced them to close shop, but in 1919, phoenix-like, they arose again as the Theatre Guild, destined to become one of the most important and successful producing organizations on Broadway.

The influence of the Washington Square Players was immediately felt; they did not, however, introduce the repertory of one-act plays to Broadway, for in 1913 the Princess Players under the direction of Holbrook Blinn had started the first of their three seasons at the Princess Theatre, patterned after the Parisian Grand Guignol. This company's bills included native as well as foreign one-acters, including one play by the editor and critic George Jean Nathan. The Washington Square Players attracted special attention because of the freshness and enthusiasm of their work, and by the time they reached the Comedy Theatre, with performers who have since become familiar to almost every playgoer—Helen Westley, Roland Young, Glenn Hunter, Katharine Cornell, for example —they had in part achieved professional standards without sacrificing their amateur spirit. Their bills included the work of both European and American writers; the only requirement was that it be out of the ordinary. They attempted heavy realism, historical satire, poetical drama, and fantasy. Occasionally they had a fling at the full-length play— Chekhov's *Sea Gull* or Ibsen's *Ghosts*. Much interesting work was contributed by Americans. One play was John Reed's *Moondown*, a tragic piece about love and poverty. Philip Moeller, later a director of the Guild, wrote several pseudo-historical satires in Shavian style. *Helena's Husbands* describes Menelaus as delighted to be rid of Helen of Troy and horrified only that he has to fight for her. *The Roadhouse in Arden*, another Moeller play, recounts an imaginary meeting between Shakespeare and Bacon. Zoë Akins' *The Magical City*, a free verse triangle involving an actress, her wealthy keeper, and her poet admirer, won much praise for Lee Simonson's superb setting revealing New York City at night through a studio window. Lewis Beach's *The Clod* shows a border woman, entirely ignorant of the issues of the Civil War, who shoots two Confederate soldiers because they have broken her dishes and upset her household. Most disturbing to the *Theatre* critic was *Another Inside*, dramatically presenting the interior of a human stomach attempting to digest pieces of lobster! Then there were Alice Gerstenberg's *Overtones*, Edward Massey's *Plots and Playwrights*, Eugene O'Neill's *In the Zone*, and numerous others. The main point is that here was an organization successfully presenting far more mature and unconventional drama than could be seen on traditional Broadway. When the Theatre Guild was formed in 1919 most of the six directors had been connected with the Washington Square Players and many other members of the original group had prominent parts in Guild productions. Though their first flight was not a financial success, it was a significant day in the history of the American theatre when Benavente's *Bonds of Interest*, staged by Philip Moeller, with settings and costumes by Rollo Peters, opened at the Garrick Theatre on April 19, 1919.

Equally spontaneous was the often-told beginning of another little theatre group at Provincetown, Massachusetts, in the summer of 1915, when two short plays—*Suppressed Desires* by Susan Glaspell and George Cram Cook, on the Freudian interpretation of dreams, and *Constancy* by Neith Boyce (Mrs. Hutchins Hapgood)—were given informally in the house of Hutchins Hapgood, one of the summer residents. Other members of the group were John Reed, Mary Heaton Vorse, George Cram ("Jig") Cook and Susan Glaspell, E. J. Ballantine, William and Marguerite Zorach, Wilbur Daniel Steele, and Robert Edmond Jones—writers and artists, most of them left wing. For a second performance an old fish wharf, owned by Mary Heaton Vorse, was transmuted into a theatre and two other plays were added: Wilbur Daniel Steele's *Contemporaries* and George Cram Cook's *Change Your Style*. Next year the pier was properly converted into the Wharf Theatre and several new productions were offered, including John Reed's *Freedom* and two plays by an unknown dramatist, Eugene O'Neill, who was fortuitously discovered on the Cape with an abundance of unproduced plays. The success of the venture impelled the group to continue operations in Greenwich Village, where most of them lived during the winter, and thus was born the Playwright's Theatre, remodeled from a brownstone house at 139 Macdougal Street. The twenty-nine original members took the name of the Provincetown Players and elected Cook president. Notable among them—besides the persons previously mentioned—were the radical journalists Floyd Dell and Max Eastman, and the latter's wife Ida Rauh, who was to play heavy dramatic roles for the company. With the help of the New York Stage Society, the first New York season proved successful, and in the next few years a host of Villagers and others took a hand in Provincetown productions, whether as authors, actors, scene shifters, or general factotums. Frank Shay, O. K. Liveright, Harry Kemp, Michael Gold (then assistant truck driver for Adams Express), Margaret Wycherly, Jasper Deeter, Lawrence Langner, Sherwood Anderson, Manuel Komroff—the roster provides a veritable cross section of arts, letters, and Bohemia.

A welcome newcomer, both as actress and playwright, was Edna St. Vincent Millay—author of *Renascence* and an enthusiastic Villager—whose first play, *The Princess Marries a Page,* and her later *Aria da Capo* were given by the Provincetown.

The Playwright's Theatre prospered in its cramped quarters and for the 1918–1919 season was encouraged and able to move to 133 Macdougal Street, a building, formerly stable and storehouse, which it converted into a small but improved playhouse. Susan Glaspell and Eugene O'Neill had been among its most constant and successful playwrights, and in 1920 George Cram Cook decided the forthcoming production of *The Emperor Jones* was worthy the construction of a "sky dome," useful for diffusing light, a common device in European theatres but one which had not found favor with Broadway producers. While this addition practically exhausted the Provincetown funds, the experiment proved eminently worth while in the tremendous success of Eugene O'Neill's play, which took New York by storm and later had to be moved to an uptown theatre. Glaspell's *The Verge,* Cook's *The Spring,* and O'Neill's *Diff'rent* and later *The Hairy Ape,* all were moved likewise to Broadway—the first three had mediocre success but the last was an immediate hit. Cook felt, however, that by competing with the professional theatre the Provincetown Players were sacrificing their amateur values and were failing in the mission of being a small, experimental theatre for the native playwright. It was decided to suspend operations for a while, and in 1922 with his wife, Susan Glaspell, George Cram Cook left for Delphi at Mount Parnassus in Greece, where two years later he died. When the theatre on Macdougal Street reopened in 1923, the old Provincetown Players had been formally dissolved, and the Experimental Theatre, Inc., under the direction of a triumvirate consisting of Kenneth Macgowan, Robert Edmond Jones, and Eugene O'Neill had taken its place. The new organization was still interested in experiment, but it was now more of a profes-

sional company, quite far in aims and ideals from the old Provincetown group. Like the Theatre Guild, however, it offered a
dramatic fare diametrically opposite to that of commercial
Broadway.

Unlike the Washington Square Players the Provincetown
Players, under "Jig" Cook's direction, refused to produce foreign plays and focused their attention on the native playwright. Eugene O'Neill's work for the Provincetown will be
discussed later. In Susan Glaspell, who wrote on her own as
well as in collaboration with George Cram Cook, another
promising dramatist was discovered. The feminine psychology
of *Trifles* has made it a favorite of many years on the amateur
stage. In *Tickless Time*—a playlet about a couple who substitute a sundial for their ordinary clocks—Glaspell and Cook returned to the light topical satire that made *Suppressed Desires*
so delightful. Susan Glaspell's *Inheritors* was a full-length protest against mob spirit. It brought a new actress, Ann Harding,
to instant fame. *The Verge,* with Margaret Wycherly, was an
interesting early experiment in presenting abnormal psychological states on the stage. After the demise of the Provincetown Susan Glaspell did not devote herself fully to the drama,
but some years later her *Alison's House,* suggested by the
career of Emily Dickinson, won the Pulitzer Prize, and in the
thirties she was active in the spectacular career of the Federal
Theatre.

Other little theatre groups operating in New York included
the perambulating Portmanteau Theatre, organized and directed by Stuart Walker, and the permanent Neighborhood
Playhouse, founded on Grand Street in 1915 by Alice and
Irene Lewisohn. Both organizations specialized at first in the
poetical melodramas by Lord Dunsany, the Irish writer, whose
work became very popular at that time. The Neighborhood
gave all kinds of productions, however, including Chester
Bailey Fernald's *The Married Woman,* which treated a marriage problem in an unconventional way. In an early cast it is
interesting to note the name of George Abbott, later writer and

producer of swift-moving, wise-cracking comedies. There
were also the Greenwich Village Players, organized by Frank
Conroy, another former Washington Square Player, who
opened a new theatre in 1918. How disturbed the old commercial managers became at the arrival of all these brash newcomers on the Broadway scene is evident from the attacks of
David Belasco, who unceremoniously called the little theatre
movement the "cubism of the theatre—the wail of the incom-
petent and degenerate."

But not even Belasco could stem the insurgent tide, and
with surprising ease and rapidity after 1917 the new theatre
won its battle against commercial Broadway. Joseph Wood
Krutch has very well pointed out, however, that the newcomers did not remain long an organized school or movement
in opposition to the institution they were deriding and attempting to destroy. Broadway became suddenly converted to
the new methods of decoration and staging, and the artists
themselves were móre than willing to turn professional. Already in 1917 Hiram K. Moderwell complained that the Washington Square Players had become high-hat and—forgetful of
earlier ideals and associations—were all accepting jobs on
Broadway. When the Guild became established, it became a
professional producing organization competing with, and in
some ways not too distinguishable from, its rival producers.
The commercial managers, on the other hand, welcomed the
newer playwrights, both American and foreign, and as producers found it good business to make their productions "artistic." The art theatre that had conquered Broadway was thus
itself swallowed by its victim. American drama of the twenties
represents a kind of fusion between the art and the professional
theatre, from which both were to profit.

In the creation of a new American drama the accent was
definitely on youth. Brief mention should be made of the rise of
eager young actors and actresses, scornful of the old star system, who stressed naturalness on the stage and were willing to
conform to the ideals of ensemble acting. Often their perform-

ance, even in a realistic play, would be capable of lifting dialogue to a high poetical or imaginative level. Pauline Lord,
first noticed on Broadway in 1912, gave notable performances
for Arthur Hopkins in *The Deluge, Anna Christie,* and others.
Katharine Cornell, making her debut for the Washington
Square Players, soon became one of the finest actresses in the
art theatre. A London player, Lynn Fontanne, came to America in 1916 to join Laurette Taylor. In J. Hartley Manners' *The
Harp of Life* she won praise from the critics in her depiction of
a pure girl who knows none of the facts of life; she seems to
have corrected this deficiency some years later when she
played Nina Leeds in *Strange Interlude.* Her future husband,
Alfred Lunt, after a childhood in Finland and a fling in John
Craig's stock company in Boston, was asked by Margaret
Anglin to tour the country as her leading man, and in 1919
rose to stardom in *Clarence.* John Barrymore, after his success
in *Justice,* was willing to sacrifice his earlier fame as matinee
idol in escapist drama to play in *Redemption* or *The Jest* or
Hamlet. These players and a host of others were ready for the
coming of a new theatre and helped to create it.

From 1912 through the early years of the Theatre Guild only
one important element was lacking, the native playwright, and
at first the insurgent theatre had to borrow heavily from European dramatists—Dunsany, Shaw, Maeterlinck, Benavente,
Molnar—so that the movement became more than ever an
international one. When Eugene O'Neill emerged from the
Provincetown and rose to splendor on professional Broadway
with *Beyond the Horizon* in 1920, the reformers had good
cause to believe that the Great American Playwright had at
last arrived. To their delight he was joined before long by
Maxwell Anderson, Sidney Howard, Robert Sherwood, and a
dozen others.

Chapter 3

EUGENE O'NEILL

*I*N voicing a strong plea for poetic and imaginative plays, suitable for production by the new art theatre, the insurgent forces cast admiring glances at the drama of the past, uncorrupted by the realism of the nineteenth and twentieth centuries. They were forced to concede some merit to sincere realism and to social drama, but they found their true ideal in Greek and Elizabethan tragedy. Why not revive poetic prose, if not actual poetry, and bring back the tragic muse to Broadway? One of the strictest rules of the conventional theatre demanded the "happy ending," whether or not it was required by the logic of the situation. No dramatist was more responsible for the revival of the unhappy ending and the triumphant return of the tragic spirit than Eugene O'Neill, the little theatre's gift to American drama.

In the many critical works about him Eugene O'Neill has been called variously realist, poet, mystic, seer, and plain writer of highbrow melodrama. These designations all fit to a certain degree, for, regardless of his eventual reputation, O'Neill remains a many-sided figure. Much of his work was undeniably realistic, but even in his depictions of life in the raw the insurgents found something that was grandiose and poetic, that had power to stir the imagination. Furthermore, his plays were experimental—in style, in treatment, in the use of ingenious devices—and thus lent themselves readily to imaginative production.

O'Neill was twenty-six when his first work, *Thirst and Other One-Act Plays*, was published in Boston at the expense of his father. Born in New York of Catholic parents, son of James

O'Neill, romantic actor of the old school, Eugene spent much
of his childhood close to the stage and the odor of grease paint.
After a varied, erratic, and interrupted education, he entered
into a series of occupations and wanderings, not unmixed with
dissipation, which led him eventually to employment as seaman on merchant ships to South America, Africa, and England.
The first of his three marriages, in 1909, ended in divorce three
years later. For six months in 1912 he worked as reporter and
columnist on a newspaper, his first attempt at professional
writing, but he had obviously not yet found his real talent. In
the same year a brief stay in a tuberculosis sanitarium gave
him an opportunity to take stock of himself and of life in general. His final decision was to write plays, a task to which he
then applied himself assiduously. In 1914, the year of the
Thirst volume, he attended Baker's 47 Workshop at Harvard.
O'Neill at this time was thus no neophyte in the theatre; to his
childhood recollections had been added practical experience
with his father's road companies and two years' apprentice-
ship in the writing of plays. His variety of adventures on sea
and land had provided him with interesting characters and situations, some of them quite novel to the stage. Finally, the
maladjustment indicated by the abrupt termination of his college career, the failure of his first marriage, and the confusion
about finding himself was bound to have a profound effect on
his philosophical outlook and the nature of his drama.

The journeyman work of famous dramatists, while usually
mediocre, is always revealing. O'Neill himself, in a letter to
Richard Dana Skinner, selected *Bound East for Cardiff*, written before his course with Baker, as most important in including the germ of his later work. Equally significant, however,
are the five plays of the *Thirst* volume, despite their lack of
merit. All are melodramatic and unhappy in ending. The title
play, for instance, presents three persons—a girl in dancing
costume, a gentleman, and a West Indian Negro—tortured by
thirst on a raft in tropical seas until they become raving mad
and die or kill off one another. Here we find already romantic

setting and characters, exploitation of the sea, and a sense of
malevolent destiny. The West Indian is interesting as the first
of many Negro characters, and his humming of a song during
most of the action shows O'Neill's experimentation even then
with unusual sound effects.

Three other plays combine realism with melodrama. *The
Web*, about a woman who decides to go straight only to be
cheated a final time by fate, has the sentimentalized conception of the prostitute which was to recur in plays like *Welded*
and *Anna Christie*, and we find in Tim Moran, with whom the
prostitute falls in love, a sort of prototype of the Hairy Ape.
Warning shows the tragedy of a radio operator, father of a
large family, who learns that he is on the verge of deafness but
is persuaded by his nagging wife to keep his job aboard ship,
with fatal results. *Recklessness* deals with a sadistic husband, a
wealthy business man, who discovers that his wife is having
an illicit affair with her chauffeur; with diabolical cunning the
husband sends his rival to death and goads his wife into suicide. The plays reminds one of later works, such as *Welded*,
which deal with tortured relations between husband and wife,
and it holds some interest also in offering a few modest samples
of the strong language which was soon to startle New York
audiences.

Most significant of future development, perhaps, is the one-
acter *Fog*, in which the author first assumes the mantle of poet
and mystic. From a lifeboat lost in fog off the banks of New-
foundland come two Voices discussing the death, the day before, of the child of a Polish immigrant woman, who is still in
the lifeboat holding the dead body. As the fog lifts, one speaker
is revealed as a typical American business man, brash, unfeel-
ing, aggressively optimistic, conventional, patriotic, blind to
any values except those of money. The other man is a typical
O'Neill hero—dark, with oval face, large eyes, black mous-
tache and hair, a high forehead—in short, a Poet. In contrast
to the other passenger, he is sensitive, sympathetic, melancholy, unselfish; he describes himself as a humanist rather than

a socialist—a believer in justice who hates poverty and other ills of society. Later in the play the lifeboat is picked up by a passing steamship, but the big moment is the revelation that the rescue party was just now directed to the scene by the cries of the Polish child, who has been dead for twenty-four hours. The successful business man was to reappear later in *Marco Millions* and *The Great God Brown;* the dark Poet in numerous plays; mysticism and religious feeling in *Lazarus Laughed* and *Days without End.*

Only one of O'Neill's earliest plays was actually presented on the stage—*Thirst,* by the Provincetown Players. But in the collection as a whole, to summarize, are already discoverable many of the ingredients of his great successes: novelty of characters, realism of scene and language, romantic and unusual settings, interest in experimentation, use of melodramatic situations. Also we find O'Neill's identification of himself with the dreamer and the poet, tired of the world but looking with scorn upon the American business man, the pre-Sinclair-Lewis Babbitt. Finally, while fate appears as a tricky and ironic jade, O'Neill did not rule out in life the possibilities of mysticism and the religious spirit.

O'Neill's chance encounter with the Provincetown Players in 1916 has already been related. In the next few years, both in Provincetown and in Greenwich Village, this group presented over a dozen plays by O'Neill, most of them one-acters. One other play, *In the Zone,* had its first production by the Washington Square Players in October, 1917. There is no denying that Eugene O'Neill, as Bernard De Voto and others have pointed out, came on the scene at a singularly opportune moment, and on the impetus of the little theatre movement and the new stagecraft he was carried to rapid prominence.

Taken as a whole, the one-act plays of this period from 1916 to 1920 are interesting and theatrically effective. They continue, with greater skill and power, the blend of romance and realism characteristic of his first published work. They are melodramatic, with violent and unhappy endings, dramatic

irony, and occasional sentimentality. While most are about the
sea, others deal with New England and several with Negro
life. Four of the best-known sea plays are set on the same
British tramp steamer and, as a matter of fact, were presented
together in 1924 under the general title *S.S. Glencairn*. Revived in later years by the Federal Theatre, they were brought
up to date and given extremely effective production in motion
picture form in 1940. In them O'Neill has caught very well the
dialect and local color of the fo'c's'le, with the ubiquitous complaints about food, the smutty bragging of sailors, their drinking and wenching, their sentimental pessimism about the
seafaring way of life. *Bound East for Cardiff* (1916), which
O'Neill found so significant in relation to his later work, deals
with the affecting death at sea of Yank, a member of the crew.
"It's hard to ship on this voyage I'm goin' on—alone!" he concludes, and as he dies, his pal Driscoll, to the amazement of the
fo'c's'le, kneels at the side of his bunk and prays. The play
shows O'Neill's latent if unorthodox concern with life after
death and with religion, his fine conception of friendship, and
his common theme of "not belonging." Among many sound
effects, incidentally, are snoring, the music of an accordion,
the ringing of the ship's bells, the fog horn, and the "a-a-l-l's
w-e-e-e-l-l-l" call by the lookout. *In the Zone* (1917), the most
popular of the one-acters both in America and abroad, dramatizes the sudden hysterical belief in the fo'c's'le that Smitty is a
German spy. What the men later find in a black box which
aroused their suspicion is merely a package of love letters revealing Smitty's unhappy love affair. The piece is sentimental
but does not ring so false when we consider the time of its writing, when spy scares were commonplace and sentimentality
more in vogue. *The Long Voyage Home* (1917) tells the tragic
and ironic story of a sailor who decides to give up the sea and
return to his native Sweden, only to be drugged in a London
dive and shanghaied on a windjammer going round the Horn.
The Moon of the Caribbees (1918), probably the most interesting of the group, is a study in mood and setting. The S.S.

Glencairn is in a tropical port; several black girls come aboard with forbidden rum; they drink and make love with the sailors; there is a sudden brawl in which a seaman gets knifed; and the girls are put off without their money. Throughout the scene a mournful Negro chant comes from shore, a dramatic elaboration of the humming of the West Indian in *Thirst*. Here, also, one of the sailors calls a companion "a 'airy ape"—an epithet employed later by the author for the title of his famous play about Yank.

Of the other one-act plays special mention must be made of *Ile* (1917), a dramatic study of a whaling captain who chooses to let his wife go insane rather than bear the disgrace of returning to port without a full quota of oil. In melodramatic force this must be held one of O'Neill's best. *Where the Cross Is Made* (1918), showing the contagious madness that results from a quest for buried treasure, is amateurish and theatrical, although interesting for its presentation of ghosts on the stage. The same situation and characters were later employed with even less success for a three-act play entitled *Gold*. *The Rope* (1918) deals only incidentally with the sea. It is an unpleasant New England story of hatred, cunning, stupidity, and covetousness, without a single character to engage our sympathy. As the play ends with the senile, Bible-quoting grandfather being tortured to reveal the hiding place of his money, little Mary, who has found the gold pieces in the barn, tosses them into the sea to make them skip. An equally realistic piece, *Before Breakfast* (1916), is a Strindbergian tour de force in which only one character, a nagging wife, speaks, while her husband commits suicide in the next room. One more short play may be mentioned here, *The Dreamy Kid* (1919), O'Neill's first play completely about Negroes. Old Mammy Saunders is dying; her grandson, the Dreamy Kid, has been persuaded to come to her, although he is in hiding for murder. There is still a chance for him to escape, but Mammy, now delirious, threatens him with a curse if he leaves. Forced to remain, he prepares to shoot it out with the police as they are heard coming up the stairs. The situation is melodramatic, to be sure, but theatrically effective.

Had O'Neill written nothing further, he would still have achieved some reputation as a dramatist of exciting short plays with unusual features and effects. Luckily, however, he was not content with the limitations of the one-act form. On the basis of what he had done there were several possible courses he might follow. He might exploit his natural bent for realism. More likely, he might devote himself to the romantic, imaginative drama that had brought him success already and had so appealed to the devotees of the art theatre. Then again, he might try his hand at the psychology of the passions, an interest early indicated in *Restlessness* and now supplemented by a study of Freud. Or he might revert to the poetical and mystical tendencies of *Fog* and write philosophical drama dealing with God's inhumanity to man. Two points at least were quite certain: his work would remain melodramatic and experimental. A brief consideration of his later plays shows that he followed not one but all the courses indicated, sometimes combining them, with rather odd results.

O'Neill's first full-length play, *Beyond the Horizon*, produced by John D. Williams in 1920 with Richard Bennett in the role of Robert Mayo, revealed both the author's dramatic growth and Broadway's receptiveness to the new drama. For here was a grim, modern tragedy of New England, intensely realistic yet not without poetic beauty, a play of frustration and irony that ended in wholesale disaster. Two brothers on a New England farm near the sea are of diametrically opposite character: Robert Mayo is poetic, restless, curious about what lies beyond the horizon; Andrew is matter-of-fact, practical, unimaginative, perfectly content with his lot as farmer. Fate intervenes with a typical O'Neill trick. As Robert is about to realize his life-long ambition to travel the seven seas on a sailing vessel, he discovers and reveals his romantic love for Ruth, Andrew's sweetheart. She accepts him and he immediately forsakes his dream, with the result that it is Andrew who goes to sea and Robert who stays at home to tend the farm. The inevitable outcome is frustration and tragedy for the three principals, who discover that they have made an irrevocable mistake. The tragic impetus of the play proves truly affecting, though one must admit that the cards are stacked pretty heavily against the characters, especially Robert, weak to begin with, who suffers successively the death of his parents, the nagging of his mother-in-law, the discovery that Ruth does not love him, the death of his infant daughter, and his own final demise from tuberculosis. The play has faults of construction and characterization, but in opposition to the escapist pabulum of Broadway it won an enthusiastic hearing and a significant victory for the art theatre as well when it was awarded the Pulitzer Prize. Some symbolism was intended in the use of two scenes in each act—one indoors and one outdoors—designed to suggest a tidelike rhythm in the lives of the characters, a device which probably escaped the notice of O'Neill's audiences. In the employment of many scenes, however, the play did prepare the way for the then unconventional technique of *The Emperor Jones* and *The Hairy Ape*.

The former of these two plays opened at the Playwright's Theatre, specially equipped for the occasion with its new "sky dome," in November, 1920. It included a total of eight scenes, not divided into acts, and had as its most striking feature continuous use of the tom-tom offstage during practically the entire action. O'Neill's departure from conventional form, the exotic theme, and the brilliant action of Charles S. Gilpin as the Emperor assured the success of the piece, and before long it moved uptown to the Princess Theatre. Deriving his inspiration from the career of Henri Christophe and of President Guillaume-Sam of Haiti, O'Neill develops in the play the colorful and dramatic career of Jones, former Pullman porter, now self-styled emperor of an island, who claims he is invulnerable to any but a silver bullet. Fully prepared for an uprising of the people he has tyrannized, he escapes to the tropical forest as the sound of tom-toms in the distance indicates that the revolt is gathering strength. But night has come sooner than he expected and he loses his way in the forest, where in a series of terrifying visions he recapitulates not only the main events of his life but also the primitive history of his race. He ends by killing himself with his own last silver bullet after finding that he has traveled a wide circle during the night, while the beat of the drums becomes faster and more menacing. With his racy dialogue and superb strutting Jones possesses epic grandeur, so that we can only regret his downfall and concur with the last line of the play, when Smithers speaks: "Silver bullets! Gawd blimey, but yer died in the 'eighth o' style, any'ow!" *The Emperor Jones* is the high-water mark, up to that time, in O'Neill's drama of imagination, although one must not overlook the essential realism of its characterization and dialogue.

Almost immediately O'Neill returned to straight realism in a two-act play, *Diff'rent*, which opened in Macdougal Street and in February, 1921, joined *The Emperor Jones* at the Princess Theatre, where it ran daily at matinees. Though harmless enough, it marks O'Neill's first encounter with censorship. In the first act a romantic young girl of 1890 thinks she and her fiancé, a sea captain, are "diff'rent," and hence breaks off the engagement when she learns that he has had a casual affair with a native woman in the South Seas. The second act, set thirty years later, reveals her as a pathetic and repressed old maid, overdressed and coquettish, victimized by an utterly worthless young whelp who is interested merely in getting money out of her. The play has one of the usual O'Neill endings, with the woman's old sweetheart, Caleb, hanging himself and Emma going to the barn apparently to do likewise. Except for its violent and unconvincing conclusion the piece has excellent characterization, effectively brought out in the acting of Mary Blair and Charles Ellis, but it did not prove popular on the stage.

Of four O'Neill plays which reached the boards during the 1921–1922 season all were predominantly realistic and only one was experimental in form. First and perhaps best was *Anna Christie,* revised from an earlier play which had failed in a wretched production in Atlantic City. Now presented by Arthur Hopkins with an excellent cast, it became one of the theatrical events of the year and received the Pulitzer Prize ˆɔr 1922. The story is a realistic one about old Chris Christophei-son, captain of a barge, who sentimentalizes over a daughter he has not seen for fifteen years; Anna, the daughter, who becomes regenerated from a career of prostitution as a result of her new life on the barge; and Mat, a loquacious Irishman, who falls in love with Anna and is tortured to drink and madness when he learns of her past life. From such a set of characters only tragic irony and suffering can result, and we find Anna voicing the theme of this as well as other early plays by O'Neill: "Don't bawl about it. There ain't nothing to forgive, anyway. It ain't your fault, and it ain't mine, and it ain't his neither. We're all poor nuts, and things happen, and we yust get mixed in wrong, that's all." Throughout the play old Chris continues raving about "dat ole davil sea," on which he blames all tricks and calamities. The supremely ironic moment comes at the end when Chris and Mat, who intensely hate one another, discover that they have both signed on the same ship. In spite of some uncertainty of purpose *Anna Christie* makes good "theatre," and the original performance of Pauline Lord as the bewildered and tragic Anna was one not easily to be forgotten. She, along with the colorful settings and the dramatic, almost poetical dialogue, helped to lift the play, sordid as it was in substance, into an inspired and imaginative realism.

A far more pedestrian naturalism pervades *The Straw,* a minor production at the Greenwich Village Theatre. Based partly, no doubt, on O'Neill's recollections of sanitarium life, it presents one truly sympathetic character beset by disease and other people's selfishness. Eileen Carmody, abandoned by her family and the man she expected to marry, falls in love with a fellow patient in a tuberculosis sanitarium, a disillusioned and maladjusted newspaper man whom she encourages to write short stories. He does not return her love and after he leaves the institution her malady grows steadily worse. When her case has become hopeless, he returns for a visit and, at the suggestion of a nurse, pretends a love he does not feel. Now that it is too late, he suddenly discovers that he has loved her right along. This final moment of realization offers O'Neill his usual opportunities for dramatic irony and a sense of frustration.

This play was followed, early in 1922, by a domestic tragedy, *The First Man,* which appeared at the Neighborhood Playhouse. Entirely conventional in form and uninspired in its naturalism, it deals with the marital conflict between an archeologist and his wife, and in addition it castigates the malicious gossip and pious smugness of the man's family, a group of Connecticut philistines. In one scene a baby is born off stage with realistic sound effects; because of its interference with his plans the husband has prayed for its death, but with O'Neill's customary irony it is the mother who dies and not the child. The author has presented a good Strindbergian theme with regard to the struggle between the sexes, but the play must be regarded as a failure.

A far more important play of 1922, *The Hairy Ape,* was immediately termed expressionistic, although O'Neill denied any direct influence from the expressionism of German writers like Kaiser, whose *Morn to Midnight* was offered in New York the same year. Expressionism may be defined in simple terms as an attempt to portray inner reality in nonrealistic terms by the use of abstraction, symbolism, and distortion. This method, "the shorthand of expressionism" as Kenneth Macgowan called it, was an excellent medium for satire and social comment and at the same time offered an excellent opportunity for imaginative stage designs and production. It was employed more effectively by other American dramatists and more completely by O'Neill himself in *The Great God Brown* and later plays. *The Hairy Ape,* tolerably clear in its symbolism, relates in a

series of short scenes the story of a man who (in the words of
O'Neill) loses his old harmony with nature. Yank, a stoker on a
transatlantic liner, has always gloried in his work and in his
brute strength until he is startled and infuriated when Mildred
Douglas, spoiled daughter of a millionaire, visits the stokehold. Driven to thought and unable to rationalize his place in
the scheme of things, Yank is obsessed by the idea that he
"doesn't belong." He is clapped into jail for starting a riot on
Fifth Avenue, and he is even thrown out of the I.W.W. as an
unwelcome intruder. Finally he attempts to shake hands with a
gorilla at the zoo but is crushed to death by the animal—
O'Neill's symbolism for his inability to get back to a lower
order of existence. The play, obviously, is concerned not so
much with Yank as with Man and his struggle to find himself,
and to bring out the symbolism O'Neill has departed from
naturalism, as in the famous Fifth Avenue scene where the
passers-by are represented as mere walking automatons. Reality is still present and recognizable, however, especially in the
salty speech of the stokehold, and the play might very well be
called another example of imaginative realism. The excellent
production by the Provincetown Players, in which Louis Wolheim took the part of Yank, soon moved uptown to Broadway.
The Hairy Ape proved popular not only here but also in Europe, the Orient, and Australia. It achieved particular success
in Russia, where an anticapitalistic rather than a philosophic
message was read into it.

It is not necessary to dwell at length on *Welded* (1924), a
melodramatic and amateurish study of the passions which succeeds merely in sounding artificial. The inability of a married
couple to separate in spite of the torments resulting from their
bondage of passion has possibilities as a dramatic theme, but a
lighter hand than O'Neill's would be required to treat it successfully.

Eugene O'Neill's second play of 1924, *All God's Chillun Got
Wings*, opened on Macdougal Street, having earlier appeared
in print in the *American Mercury*. While such plays as *Diff'rent*

had shown considerable interest in abnormal psychology, this play represents the author's first extensive invasion of Freudian territory. *All God's Chillun* is a clinical study of miscegenation and racial hatred, handled with restraint and yet with dramatic power. Of all the author's works this has had the most widespread success in Europe, South America, and Russia. This far-flung success, however, took place without the intent or cooperation of the New York police, who, alarmed at the storm of protest which the theme of miscegenation had aroused before the opening of the play, did their best to stop the production. They succeeded in keeping from the stage the children who were to act in the first scene, but the parts were read by James Light, one of the Provincetown directors, and the rest of the play went on without difficulty. Later, the work was banned in Boston, as were many of O'Neill's other plays.

Still showing preference for relatively short scenes, O'Neill divided his material into two acts with a total of seven scenes. Jim Harris (Paul Robeson) and Ella Downey (Mary Blair) are shown as childhood sweethearts, quite unconscious of the fact that he is black and she is white. As they grow older, they become increasingly estranged until Ella's tragic and sordid love affair with a young tough of the neighborhood comes to an end. She starts going around again with Jim, "the only white man in the world," and agrees to marry him. After the wedding they go to Europe, only to realize some time later that this attempt to escape has not worked out. On their return Ella, obsessed with a feeling of degradation about her marriage, soon becomes a violent maniac, maliciously doing her best to keep Jim from passing his bar examinations and ready at any moment to kill him. When the news comes that he has failed again, Ella plunges a carving knife into a Negro mask from the Congo, thus ridding herself of her desire to kill, but she suffers a reversion to childhood and it is clear that she and Jim will live henceforth only as children. This moving story is told expertly and sympathetically, with no attempt at propaganda on the subject of race. Rather is O'Neill's interest his usual question of the relations of man to God. "Maybe He can forgive what you've done to me," says Jim to Ella in the last scene; "and maybe He can forgive what I've done to you; but I don't see how He's going to forgive—Himself." The author's use of the Congo mask may have been suggested by contemporary discussion of Craig's theories or by articles in the *Theatre Arts Monthly* on the subject of masks; the topic, in any case, was in the air, and O'Neill was soon to exploit it further. *All God's Chillun* is far from being the best of O'Neill's plays but it remains one of the most interesting in his realistic vein.

The fall of 1924 saw the production of only one new play by O'Neill, the well-known *Desire under the Elms*, which like its immediate predecessor won an international hearing. It opened at the Greenwich Village Theatre and later moved uptown in spite of the efforts of the police to close it. Some symbolism is apparent in the stage settings with the malevolently brooding elms, but otherwise the play is a starkly realistic portrayal of a New England farm tragedy. Old Ephraim Cabot, seventy-five years old, stern and Bible quoting, has just taken to himself a third wife, Abbie. Partly because she wants an heir to insure her possession of the farm, she seduces Eben, Ephraim's son by an earlier marriage. From this illicit relationship a child is born which old Ephraim proudly believes to be his own. Eben and Abbie, however, have found themselves caught in a passion stronger than they. In a desperate attempt to prove her love Abbie smothers the infant and reveals its true paternity to old Cabot. Eben, who in his first horror has rushed to call the sheriff, realizes the depth of his love for Abbie, and the two lovers face the uncertain future with a sense of exaltation. It is this closing note that keeps *Desire under the Elms* from being merely sordid and endows it, according to various critics, with something akin to the catharsis of Greek tragedy. A novelty at the time was the use of a single set to represent the exterior of the Cabot farm, scenes within the house being shown in one room or another with the outer wall removed. Noteworthy also was the acting, with Walter Huston as

Ephraim Cabot, Mary Morris as Abbie, and Charles Ellis as the youthful Eben. This was one of several productions under the combined direction of Kenneth Macgowan, Robert Edmond Jones, and Eugene O'Neill—the triumvirate that took over after the breakup of the original Provincetown group.

The same partnership was responsible for the presentation of *The Fountain* (1925), in which O'Neill cast realism entirely to the winds and plunged into romance and fantasy. The play offers an imaginative and literary treatment of the remote past, dealing with Ponce de Leon and his quest for eternal youth and employing characters and situations that are almost entirely fictitious. Ponce, characterized as "soldier of iron—and dreamer," a mixture of two conflicting selves, has become governor of Puerto Rico. The arrival of his ward, the young and beautiful Beatriz de Cordova, with whom he falls in love, again spurs him on to seek the fountain of youth. Ambushed by Indians, he is severely wounded. During his convalescence he receives a visit from Beatriz, who in the meantime has fallen in love with his nephew, and in the love of the young couple, despite his personal disappointment, he begins to understand eternal youth. This romantic plot requires eleven scenes, a large cast in picturesque costumes, and much singing and dancing, especially in a scene representing Ponce's delirium. The play offers a series of pretty pictures but never comes to life.

It would have been rash at its opening to predict commercial success for O'Neill's next play, *The Great God Brown* (1926), and yet it ran in New York for almost a year. The author here abandoned both the stark realism of *Desire under the Elms* and the romantic mood of *The Fountain* and plunged boldly into symbolism, employing the ancient device of masks, which the players took off or put on or even exchanged to indicate changes in personality. The play, which almost defies analysis, deals with the fortunes of William Brown (William Harrigan) and Dion Anthony (Robert Keith), both in love with the same girl at the time of their graduation from high school. It is the artistic and erratic Dion, however, and not Billy Brown, that Margaret prefers and later marries. After college Brown becomes successful as builder and architect, but finds that he needs the aid of Dion's artistic genius. Dion, however, is maladjusted and unhappy, in spite of his love for the faithful Margaret, who has borne him three sons. He is driven to drink and gambling, and finds his main solace with the town prostitute, Cybel. Eventually Dion dies in the house of Brown, who takes his mask (hence his personality) and poses sometimes as Dion, sometimes as himself, until his death in the arms of the sympathetic Cybel. This unusual plot becomes more intelligible when O'Neill explains that Dion Anthony represents a combination of Dionysus and St. Anthony, "the creative pagan acceptance of life, fighting eternal war with the masochistic, life-denying spirit of Christianity as represented by St. Anthony"; that Brown stands for the demigod of the materialistic American myth of success, "building his life of exterior things, inwardly empty and resourceless"; that Margaret is the eternal girl-woman, modern descendant of Marguerite in Goethe's *Faust;* and finally that Cybel personifies Cybele, the Earth Mother of Greek mythology. In his note to the Wilderness edition of his plays O'Neill states further that the play "attempts to foreshadow the mystical patterns created by the duality of human character and the search for what lies hidden behind and beyond words and actions of men and women. More by the use of overtones than by explicit speech, I sought to convey the dramatic conflicts in the lives and within the souls of the characters."

Confusing as are the theme and symbolism, as well as the use and exchange of masks, *The Great God Brown* remains an artistic success. Nowhere else is O'Neill's dialogue more charged with emotion and lyrical beauty. Even where we are uncertain about the meaning of the words, they offer at times sudden glimpses of the ineffable mystery of human life—something he never succeeds in doing in his more "philosophical" plays, such as *Lazarus Laughed*. Whereas most of O'Neill's prostitutes are unconvincing and juvenile, Cybel becomes much more than the personified abstraction she was meant to be. The other characters are equally well realized. It is only when Brown seizes the mask from the dead Anthony and starts putting it on and removing it at frequent intervals that the audience, not to mention Margaret, is lost in bewilderment. The play bogs down at this point, but perhaps a more conventional treatment would have meant a loss of vividness and dramatic power. O'Neill's growing dependence on literary sources and material rather than on experience is worthy of note in this period of his drama.

The Great God Brown may be characterized in a sense as realistic, but in *Marco Millions*, written at about the same time but not produced until two years later, O'Neill returned to fantasy with a pseudohistorical background, adding only the new element of satire. In an ironical foreword he states his intention of whitewashing the soul of Marco Polo, which he proceeds to do by revealing him as a glorified traveling salesman, a true Babbitt—shrewd, aggressive, materialistic, uxorious, entirely devoid of sensibility. In aiming at the American business man of the Harding and Coolidge eras, O'Neill is returning to the point of view of the early *Fog*. Marco descends like a plague on the placid and philosophical life of the East, at first amusing the great Kublai Kaan and later filling him with disgust. Only the little Princess Kukachin thinks he has a soul and loves him, but although he is directed to kiss her daily during a two-year journey to Persia, Marco remains blind to her love and vulgarly materialistic. O'Neill indulges in some satire of conventional religion and reveals his usual preoccupation with the deity. "My hideous suspicion," reflects Kublai Kaan, "is that God is only an infinite, insane energy which creates and destroys without other purpose than to pass eternity in avoiding thought. Then the stupid man becomes the Perfect Incarnation of Omnipotence and the Polos are the true children of God." *Marco Millions* was the first production of O'Neill by the Theatre Guild, with Alfred Lunt as Marco and

Margalo Gillmore as the Princess, and no expense or pains were spared to put on a magnificent spectacle. Nevertheless the play as a whole remained a pictorial museum piece, a pageant rather than drama, and it proved only mildly successful in New York.

With *Strange Interlude* (1928), however, which ran seventeen months on Broadway, the Guild found itself with a real success. The novelty of attending a performance which started at 5:30 and was interrupted later for dinner no doubt contributed to the success of the play, as well as O'Neill's revival of the ancient aside and soliloquy to express the inner thoughts of the characters. So completely were these last two devices used that one might almost say that O'Neill employed the regular dialogue to supplement the asides, rather than vice versa. This was an attempt, of course, to adapt in drama the stream of consciousness method of contemporary fiction, and except for slowing up the action it proved fairly successful. The nine acts of *Strange Interlude* represent the intimate relations of Nina Leeds, daughter of a college professor, to several men who affected her life, especially to three. Emotionally upset because of the death in France of her fiancé, Nina hates her father, whom she considers responsible for preventing their marriage. She leaves home to become a nurse and returns only at her father's death. She is then prevailed upon to marry Sam Evans, diffident and good-natured, and feels almost happy at the discovery of her pregnancy until she learns of a strain of insanity in Sam's family. She resorts to abortion, but unhappy and maladjusted once more, she takes as her lover Dr. Darrell, who lives up to his bargain of supplying her with another child. As little Gordon grows up, he feels instinctive hatred for his real father but, ironically enough, loves Sam, his ostensible one. Later Nina goes through the maternal torture of losing Gordon, now grown up, to the girl he loves, and after the death of Sam Evans she decides to marry Charlie Marsden, a spinsterish childhood admirer, whom she has come to associate psychologically with her father. This fragmentary synopsis may suffice to indicate O'Neill's invasion of the novelistic medium and his dependence on Freudian psychology—the Oedipus complex and the father-daughter fixation, for example—in such manner that the soliloquies and asides become almost imperative to indicate inner motives, loves, hates, and by-plays. The device, however, did not win the unreserved approval of the critics. Alexander Woollcott maliciously called the play "the *Abie's Irish Rose* of the pseudo-intelligentsia," and objection was made to its oversimple interpretation of Freud. But nothing could halt its popularity, attributable in part to the excellent interpretation of Nina Leeds by Lynn Fontanne, with Glenn Anders, Earle Larimore, and Tom Powers as the three principals in her sex life.

One of the best-known passages—the one that provides the title—shows O'Neill still concerned with the mystery of human life. In the last act, referring to Nina's association with the Gordons, Marsden suggests that they "forget the whole distressing episode, regard it as an interlude, of trial and preparation, say, in which our souls have been scraped clean of impure flesh and made worthy to bleach in peace." And to this Nina replies philosophically: "Strange interlude! Yes, our lives are merely strange dark interludes in the electrical display of God the Father!"

With the usual inability of authors to judge their own work O'Neill, we are told, considers *Lazarus Laughed* as his most successful play. Physically impossible for Broadway to produce, it had the good fortune to receive a hearing in California, in April, 1928, at the Pasadena Community Playhouse, whence it proceeded to the Music Box in Hollywood. In color and pageantry *Lazarus Laughed* outdoes *The Fountain* and *Marco Millions,* but no more than these does it succeed in giving the impression of life. It provides another imaginative excursion into the past, with religious and philosophical implications. A moment after his return from death Lazarus laughs—as a profound assertion of joy in living, "the Eternal Life in Yes." This laughter proves strangely contagious and Lazarus soon acquires many followers. At the command of Caesar he proceeds to Rome, where he discomfits Caligula and Tiberius and even converts some of the Roman legions. Later, when his wife Miriam has been poisoned and when he himself is being tortured and burned in the arena, he still reaffirms dramatically his assertion that there is no death but only life. The theme obviously gives O'Neill plenty of opportunity for striking scenes and mass movements of the chorus, and he has taken full advantage of them. To reinforce his symbolism he returned in this play to masks and half-masks, but made them twice as large as in *The Great God Brown* and conventionalized them so the audience, as he says, could get the idea at once. As an experiment *Lazarus Laughed* is undeniably interesting and it is only fair to mention that the California reviews were enthusiastic, but it labors under the faults of being prolix, overlong, cumbersome in structure, and occasionally ridiculous. The vast amount of laughter required, for one thing, must have proved trying to both cast and audience. In the Pasadena performance Irving Pichel, said to have been excellent as Lazarus, laughed uninterruptedly on one occasion for four minutes.

Although not a success on the stage, O'Neill's next play, *Dynamo,* produced by the Theatre Guild in 1929, makes absorbing reading. Here O'Neill returns to realism and abnormal psychology. His hero is, in fact, psychopathic, suffering from an Oedipus complex (a recurrent theme with O'Neill) combined with religious mania. When Reuben Light loses his faith as a result of a practical joke by the atheistic Fife, he leaves home recognizing no God but electricity—a line that recalls Nina's speech in *Strange Interlude.* On his return he finds that his mother has died. He gets a job in the power house, where, becoming gradually insane, he transfers his mother-complex into a mystical and passionate love for the electric dynamo. Feeling degraded by his sensual affair with Fife's daughter, Ada, he eventually kills her in the power house and then expiates his sins by committing suicide on his beloved dynamo. A plot of this sort is obviously too special and abnormal to enlist very wide and enthusiastic response, but the realism comes as a relief after the pompous inanities of *Lazarus Laughed.* Quoted in Barrett H. Clark's biography is a statement by O'Neill that he wrote the play as a "symbolical and factual biography of what is happening in a large section of the American (and not only American) soul right now. It is really the first play of a trilogy that will dig at the roots of the sickness of today as I feel it—the death of an old God and the failure of science and materialism to give any satisfactory new one for the surviving primitive religious instinct to find a meaning for life in, and to comfort its fears of death with." The second play in the proposed trilogy appeared in 1934 as *Days without End.* In *Dynamo* O'Neill employed once more the aside and he went *Desire under the Elms* one better by having two houses on the stage with a garden between. The neurotic hero was played by Glenn Anders with Claudette Colbert as the unhappy victim of his mania.

What most critics consider O'Neill's masterpiece, *Mourning Becomes Electra,* was next produced by the Theatre Guild, on October 26, 1931. O'Neill had kept the general idea in mind for some years but the writing itself was not begun until 1929 in France and finished in the Canary Islands in 1931. Dedicated to Carlotta Monterey, his third wife, *Mourning Becomes Electra* is described as a trilogy; the three parts, with a total of thirteen acts, were entitled respectively *Homecoming, The Hunted,* and *The Haunted.* This mammoth performance was given, like *Strange Interlude,* with an intermission for dinner. In the new play O'Neill attempts to reinterpret the old story of Agamemnon, Clytemnestra, Orestes, and Elektra in terms of modern psychology. The result is a New England tragedy, not particularly Greek, but remarkably effective and moving. The main incidents of the classic plot have been preserved. General Mannon, returning from the Civil War, is murdered by his wife Christine with the aid of her lover, Captain Brant. Vinnie, the daughter, insanely jealous, succeeds in arousing the suspicions of her brother Orin, who has returned from the war mentally unbalanced because of a head wound. These two trail the mother to Brant's ship, where they later kill Brant himself. There remains nothing for Christine but suicide. After these tragic events Vinnie and Orin set out on a long voyage to the South Seas, but they cannot escape the Mannon destiny. Orin becomes more and more violently insane and he too commits suicide, but only after sowing the germ of suspicion into the mind of Vinnie's fiancé. Realizing at last that a normal, happy life is impossible for her, Lavinia retires into the old Mannon house and orders the shutters nailed close to keep out the sunshine. In Seth, the gardener, who is most important of the minor characters, O'Neill has employed the trusty old servant and confidant of Greek drama, and in the townspeople who appear at the beginning of each part he has attempted to revive in a modern way the ancient chorus.

Giving force and direction to this tragic plot, the Freudian concepts of the subconscious are employed freely to suggest a twentieth-century version of fate. Christine, having felt nothing but revulsion on her wedding night, hates both Mannon and her eldest child, Lavinia. The latter, on the other hand, starved for affection in childhood, is jealous of her mother and in love with her father. Her secret passion for Captain Brant, her mother's lover, who resembles her father, adds to this jealousy—her hatred being rationalized into a sense of duty to avenge her father's murder. After Christine's death Vinnie temporarily blossoms out and, interestingly enough, begins to affect her mother's dress and manner. But Orin, victim of an Oedipus complex, transfers his incestuous love to Vinnie and becomes insanely jealous of her attentions to other men. "Can't you see," he exclaims, "I'm now in Father's place and you're Mother? That's the evil destiny out of the past I haven't dared predict! I'm the Mannon you're chained to!" Orin's rantings in the third part of the trilogy become a little tedious but nevertheless the underlying psychological motivation works out extremely well. It will be noted that the emphasis of the Greek story has been changed somewhat and made to fall heavily on Vinnie, the last of the Mannons—a part superbly played by Alice Brady. In fact, the Guild casting came as near as possible to perfection. The exotic and tragic loveliness of Christine was given life by Alla Nazimova in an unforgettable performance. To Christine, O'Neill entrusted his usual complaint about the deity: "Why can't all of us remain innocent and loving and trusting? But God won't leave us alone. He twists and wrings and tortures our lives with others' lives until —we poison each other to death!" It might be added that Robert Edmond Jones designed for the play sets of startling beauty —from the exterior of the Mannon house to the inside cabin of the "Flying Trades." A share in O'Neill's success must be ascribed to the collaboration, which he always enjoyed, of the best possible directors, actors, and designers.

Up to this point a dominant note in O'Neill's plays—even to some extent in *Lazarus Laughed*—had been a sense of futility at the tragedy of human life, finding expression in dramatic irony or in the unhappy ending. At least, no one would have accused the playwright of philosophical optimism. Man might have an essential nobility of character, but Fate or God or his own self was always getting him "balled up." Lazarus expresses positive affirmation in the goodness of life, but in spite of his optimism his wife was poisoned and he himself burned at the stake. It came, therefore, as a distinct shock to find the author suddenly turned kindly, wistful, reflective, and reminiscent in his first comedy, *Ah, Wilderness!*, produced by the Theatre Guild in 1933. The selection of George M. Cohan to play the main role in New York and of Will Rogers in San Francisco should prove sufficient commentary on the change. *Ah, Wilderness!* is a homely, bourgeois comedy of "the American large small-town at the turn of the century," with a charming dedication to George Jean Nathan "who also, once upon a time, in peg-top trousers went the pace that kills along the road to ruin." The protagonist here is really the entire family, typical American and upper middle-class, with the kindly father, the adolescent child, the maiden aunt, the family drunkard, and so on. All are depicted graphically with the faithfulness of portraits in a family album. What plot there is concerns Richard, the adolescent boy, who has been reading radical literature and sending erotic poetry to his high school sweetheart. When he is reprimanded by the family and—as he thinks—spurned by Muriel, he seizes the opportunity to get even by making an assignation with a "college tart." The only damage he suffers is intoxication, but when he finally reels home reciting poetry the household is plunged into consternation. The next day Nat Miller, the father, stammers out some advice on the facts of life to Richard, who is later brought back to bliss when he makes up with Muriel. The portrayal of young love is pleasant and humorous, and the entire production—excellently acted and directed—earned a deserved success.

Whatever the surprise of the Broadway critics at O'Neill's venture into domestic comedy, it could not equal their bewilderment and shock at the presentation of *Days without End* by the Guild in January, 1934. Here was a modern "miracle play" (to use the author's own designation) in which the hero's split personality becomes whole again through a return to the Catholicism of his childhood. To represent John Loving's dual self in a dramatic way, O'Neill assigned the part to two actors appearing concurrently on the stage—one to act John, the actual hero, to whom the other players address their remarks, and the other to act Loving, the cynical, rational other self, unseen to the others but always hovering near John and chiming into the conversation. This rather cumbersome device is reminiscent of the Good Angel and Bad Angel of medieval drama. The plot itself is far simpler and less melodramatic than is O'Neill's wont. In writing an autobiographical novel John is in reality trying to solve his own psychological problem. His devoted wife, Elsa, is recovering from influenza. John knows that his affair with Lucy, an old friend of Elsa, will be found out sooner or later. Elsa's death is the only solution, and under pretense of discussing the plot of his novel with his wife and his uncle, Father Baird, that solution is exactly what John, prompted by Loving, suggests. Elsa, now understanding the situation, deliberately walks out in the rain, as a result contracting pneumonia. Hovering between life and death, she loses the will to live until John, tortured by conscience and despair, has prostrated himself before the crucifix and confessed his faith—upon which Loving, his cynical alter ego, expires and the hero becomes integrated once more as John Loving.

Nothing is more uncertain than the attempt to read autobiographical experiences into fiction or drama, but nevertheless it was immediately suggested that John Loving's spiritual development had certain parallels to O'Neill's own. John, brought up by devout Catholic parents, is described as having lost his childhood faith at the time of their death. In turn, after this, he becomes an ardent atheist; takes up successively socialism, anarchism, and bolshevism; returns to religion via the "defeated mysticism of the East"; and falls again into scientific mechanism until his marriage to Elsa. Father Baird's comment upon all this is that John is always thinking himself the Antichrist and running away from the truth in order to find it. A consideration of O'Neill's work from the tortured beginnings to the changed outlook of *Ah, Wilderness!* and *Days without End* lends some color to the belief that O'Neill and John Loving are the same. Apparently reaching this conclusion, Soviet Russia, which had espoused the author's earlier plays with zeal and enthusiasm, finding in them a defense of exploited classes (the prostitute, the worker, the Negro), now turned upon him with considerable bitterness. "Thus O'Neill shows his real face," wrote A. Abramov in the *Literaturnaia* of Moscow, "the face of a churchman and an obscurantist, who has found his life-ideal in the garb of a Catholic priest. And this is not a chance happening. Catholicism is becoming today an outpost, around which the active elements of the bourgeoisie are gathering in their struggle against Communism." The weakness of the Soviet point of view, as thus expressed, lies in the assumption that O'Neill was ever a revolutionary propa-

gandist. While he showed sympathy for certain groups championed by communism and was intellectually influenced for a
time by Marxian ideology, at no time do his plays attempt direct social propaganda. As was pointed out earlier, O'Neill's
main interest lay in the individual's struggles with the universe
and particularly in his relations to a supposed deity whose
ways are normally obscure and mysterious, if not downright
malignant. O'Neill deals with individuals, not economic
classes. Much unconscious humor is evident in A. Abramov's
further assertion that "Anna Christie is not a prostitute but a
human being, a personality used as a symbol of society's destruction of women. *Emperor Jones* is the tragedy of the out-
cast whom capitalistic civilization has excluded from society."
A similar propaganda slant had always guided the productions
of O'Neill in Russia. For example, Tairov's production of *Desire under the Elms* for the Kamerny Theatre interpreted the
play, not as personal tragedy, but as an exposé of the degeneration of capitalistic society. American leftists reacted even more
violently than the Russians to Eugene O'Neill's apparent conversion; a typical attack in *New Theatre,* in an article by
Charmian von Wiegand, berated O'Neill as the "dramatist
of the petty bourgeois intelligentsia, lost between the heaven
of the upper classes and the earth of the proletariat" and compared him to the Emperor Jones in the forest, who came out at
the same place where he went in. Whether or not O'Neill
should be considered a traitor to radical doctrine, it was pre-
mature on the part of Communists or Catholics to take *Days
without End* as a literal confession of the author's faith in the
Catholic cross. Later plays would throw light on this point, and
there was danger in the meantime, as suggested by Joseph
Wood Krutch, of giving undue weight to plays like *The Straw*
and *Days without End* while minimizing the importance of
others like *Mourning Becomes Electra.* Not worrying about
possible autobiographical implications, New York audiences
found *Days without End* dull and stayed away from it.

Twelve years elapsed before playgoers had the opportunity

of seeing a new play by O'Neill, *The Iceman Cometh* (1946), produced by the Theatre Guild with sets by the author's old friend and associate, Robert Edmond Jones. During this hiatus O'Neill had been writing steadily on an ambitious project of long plays but had been delayed by ill health and by mental distress over the state of the world. In addition to several other plays scheduled for production, O'Neill is reported to have completed in 1940 a dramatic work, *Long Day's Journey into Night,* not to be published until twenty-five years after his death.

O'Neill's return to the theatre shows him concerned philosophically with the mystery of human illusion. Employing the bare yet leisurely simplicity of *Days without End*—in contrast to the more luxuriant and melodramatic style of his earlier work—he exhibits in *The Iceman Cometh* a group of down-and-outers that frequent Harry Hope's West Side saloon in 1912. The place is described sardonically by one of the characters as the No Chance Saloon, Bedrock Bar, the End of the Line Café, the Bottom of the Sea Rathskeller. And yet its habitués are far from unhappy; they manage somehow to remain drunk and they delude themselves "with a few harmless pipe dreams about their yesterdays and tomorrows." There is Harry Hope, for example, the proprietor, who looks back with maudlin sentimentality on the period of his marriage to Bessie. He has not ventured out into the street since her death twenty years ago, but he promises himself some day to take a walk around the ward and see his old friends. Another contented wreck, Jimmy Tomorrow, rationalizes his alcoholism as the result of his wife's infidelity many years ago; once a newspaper man, he is confident that tomorrow he will set forth and get his old job back. Several others, including a Harvard graduate, similarly entertain the pleasant delusion that they can and will return to their onetime vocations. The night bartender, who has two streetwalkers under his management, genially maintains that he is not a pimp but a bartender with a sideline. The two girls accept this premise and in turn he encourages them

in the gratifying fiction that they are tarts, not whores.
There are other characters with the same capacity for rational-
ization, most complex of whom is Larry Slade, former Syn-
dicalist-Anarchist, who serves as *raisonneur* of the piece. His
main delusion is that he is now in the grandstand, observing
life dispassionately, waiting only for death. Another of Larry's
pipe dreams is that he left the Movement because of disgust at
human greed and stupidity and not because of the unfaithfulness of a famous radical with whom he once lived, a woman
who loved him but who felt she had to have many lovers in
succession to prove to herself how free she was. This woman's
son now comes to Larry for help—the young man has betrayed
his mother and sent her to jail—an act of treachery to which
Larry does his best to remain indifferent. With these and other
frustrated guinea pigs in Hope's saloon O'Neill is ready to start
his ethical, psychological, and philosophical inquiries.

As the play opens, the entire group of derelicts is waiting
for the arrival of Hickey, a hardware salesman, who never fails
to appear with plenty of money and jovial talk to celebrate
Hope's birthday party. In the past Hickey has enlivened the
occasion with comic gags, the favorite one being that he has
just left his wife in the hay with the iceman. This time, however, he is no longer the life of the party—he even refuses to
drink with the gang. As he tells them, he no longer needs alcohol; he has faced the truth about himself and now, being at
last without illusions, he is completely at peace. This peace he
insists on bestowing on his comrades by the process of destroy-
ing their pipe dreams of yesterday and tomorrow. The task of
thus saving them is both difficult and painful, resulting in quarrels and burning hatred. Inexorably Hickey forces Hope to
admit that Bessie was "a nagging old bitch," and Tomorrow
that his wife's unfaithfulness was the result—not the cause—
of his drinking and merely offered him a welcome excuse to
keep on drinking. By next day Hickey has driven most of his
companions out of the saloon in an effort to bring their pipe
dreams to the test of actual realization. They all rush back in

panic, as he knew they would, but he believes that the shattering of their final illusions will bring them the peace that he has
himself attained. But to Hickey's surprise they are completely
licked; even when they drink they find the whiskey has lost its
kick. In spirit and appearance they are dead. To convert them
by his own example Hickey then tells them the sordid story of
his marriage to Evelyn. In spite of his many moral lapses she
always forgave him, deluding herself into thinking that this
was the last time and that he would reform. The only way to
free Evelyn from this pipe dream of reformation, to give her
the peace she always wanted, Hickey tells the startled group,
was for him to kill her. He insists he committed the murder
with love, not hate, in his heart. But suddenly, in the course of
his recital, Hickey comes to the unexpected realization that he
too has been deluding himself, that he really killed Evelyn because he hated her. The revelation is too much for Hickey to
face, and he says he must have been insane. Pouncing avidly
upon this straw of Hickey's insanity, which would nullify the
cogency of his persuasive arguments, Hope and most of his
cronies regain their composure and their illusions, ending the
play in a good old drunken brawl. Two individuals, however,
have been touched by Hickey's words. Realizing that he was
motivated by hatred in betraying his mother, the young radical—with Larry's help—learns that only by killing himself
can he ever become free of her. Larry, too, has lost his pipe
dreams. Helping the young man has proved to him that he can
never be a success, even in the grandstand; until his death he
will remain a weak fool betrayed by pity and fatally condemned to see all sides of a question. He is the only real convert to Hickey's drastic treatment.

It is evident that *The Iceman Cometh* presents an O'Neill
sobered by experience, a step further in philosophical disillusionment, concerned for the moment not with the inhumanity
of God but with the mystery of man's own soul. Is it possible
for mankind to live without pipe dreams, illusions? The answer
seems to be no. In the course of the play Larry identifies the

Iceman with Death, and Hickey's attempt to strip life of all
rationalizations results in death—for his wife, for the young
radical, for Larry perhaps, for the others temporarily; Hickey
deceives himself that he has found peace, but it is the peace of
insanity or maybe of the electric chair. The play does not lack
O'Neill's innate religious feeling, implicit in his work from the
early days of *Fog* and *Bound East for Cardiff*, here most apparent in his deep compassion for the derelicts of Hope's saloon, but at the same time the piece shows no evidence of
church doctrine or of the conversion suggested by *Days without End*. In a sense, it is true, the play is an assertion of faith,
but a scarcely orthodox faith, in lies and pipe dreams without
which man cannot exist. As in earlier plays, O'Neill writes
much about tortured marital and filial relationships, but
though Freud looms in the background, the language and the
technique are no longer the professional psychologist's. In
fact, *The Iceman Cometh* gives rather the impression of being
a modern morality play with its symbolism disguised in grimly
realistic terms. As in the past the author makes no concessions
to popular appeal, the play's theme, its characters, its length
all militating against its acceptance. In deliberately avoiding
the dramatic cohesion and sweep of his earlier work, O'Neill
often makes his action seem slow and repetitious. Yet, if *The
Iceman Cometh* falls short of his highest dramatic achievement, no one can deny on the other hand that it has a depth
and power rarely found on the Broadway stage.

   An accurate estimate of Eugene O'Neill's place in American
drama cannot with justice be given until his work is complete.
Almost from the start criticism has differed sharply on his
merits, though the bulk of it has been favorable. In the late
thirties his reputation began to suffer, partly because of his
long silence after *Days without End*, partly because of the
confusing change of mood and point of view in *Ah, Wilderness!* and *Days without End*, partly because of the rise of new
dramatists like Odets and Saroyan with different themes and
techniques. Nevertheless his preeminence in the early days of

the insurgent movement remains unquestioned and his historical place is secure. He received international recognition in 1936 when he was awarded the Nobel Prize in literature. His main contributions to American drama, very considerable ones as we have seen, belong mainly to his first ten years on Broadway. They may be summarized briefly as (1) revival of tragedy and the unhappy ending; (2) romantic novelty of scene; (3) realism of situation and character in the depiction of sailors, prostitutes, farmers, Negroes, and others of humble station; (4) use of profanity and realistic diction on the stage; (5) experimentation in form, including the use of multiple scenes and acts; (6) interest in symbolism, leading to unnaturalistic scenery, revival of masks, and other devices; (7) adoption of Freudian psychology with ingenious revival of the soliloquy and aside to represent the stream of consciousness; (8) development of historical fantasy, tending toward the masque form in such plays as *Marco Millions* and *The Fountain;* (9) passionate absorption in the problem of man's rapport with himself and with God, leading at various times to frustration, to dramatic irony, or to conversion. The enumeration may be incomplete but it will at least indicate the variety of O'Neill's interests and experiments. He was of particular significance as a pioneer, even when his innovations were considerably modified by subsequent writers. *Desire under the Elms,* for example, in local color and realism of speech foreshadowed the hillbilly play of later years. *The Hairy Ape* and *All God's Chillun Got Wings,* while not meant as communist propaganda, prepared the way for leftist drama. O'Neill's tortured questionings about God and fate must have had some influence upon later philosophical and religious plays, and of course his exploitation of Freudian psychology found immediate imitation. He had, in short, the genius to select timely themes and techniques, and if some of his plays appear dated, the reason is partly that his innovations were so widely adopted that we no longer recall how revolutionary they once were. O'Neill's experimental boldness helped to establish his position as the first great dramatist of the art theatre and as a poet, but from the start he was also a realist and will probably best be remembered for those plays that show an ideal fusion of realism and imagination.

Chapter 4

POETRY AND IMAGINATION

$\mathcal{E}$UGENE O'NEILL'S plays were the first and perhaps the best fruits of the insurgent movement to come to maturity on professional Broadway. With their success much of the new American drama was committed to the expression of poetry and imagination. It soon became evident, however, in the work of other writers as in the O'Neill plays, that it was impossible for the art theatre to divorce itself from the everyday world, its people and its problems. Imaginative plays could not live in a romantic vacuum and the best of them included a strong admixture of realism. Without making academic distinctions which are too fine it is possible to segregate and consider together the plays that show a preponderance of imagination over realism. Serious drama in verse would belong in this category, also historical, biographical, or costume plays, regional and folk drama, fantasy, or any combination of these types. The finest examples would come from the pens of dramatists like Maxwell Anderson and Saroyan who thought of themselves primarily as poets.

Their welcome on Broadway was made easier by theatrical events and developments between two world wars. While the little theatre movement soon lost its vitality, devoting itself more and more to the production of the previous season's Broadway successes, its mission had been accomplished and its influence lived after it. The imaginative and poetical play was taken over by progressive producers like Arthur Hopkins and by the Theatre Guild, which after a shaky start was becoming established and was developing an ambitious plan of subscriptions and road tours. The Guild's success encouraged nu-

merous other groups and organizations, among them the
Equity Players, Eva Le Gallienne's Civic Repertory Theatre,
the Group Theatre, the Playwrights' Company—widely different in aims but with a common dislike of the commercial
play. After 1918 Broadway awoke with pleased surprise to find
itself the theatrical center of the world, to which, drawn by a
powerful financial magnet, gravitated a host of theatre no-
tables from other countries—Balieff, Duse, Reinhardt, Noel
Coward, Mei Lan-fang, the Moscow Art players. Some of
them proved disappointing, but their names were magic and
they contributed prestige and a new feeling of self-confidence
to the art theatre. After the rise of the Nazis Elisabeth Bergner
led a parade of refugees to the new world, many of whom became permanently settled on Broadway and supplemented
the already impressive list of native players capable of bringing poetic fervor to the theatre.

By 1920 the stage designers, the new artists, were firmly in
the saddle. Sometimes their experiments seemed extravagantly
romantic and imaginative. Of particular interest were Robert
Edmond Jones' sets for *Macbeth* (1921) with three huge
masks staring impassively down at three hooded scarlet figures below to represent the witches, and with Macbeth's castle
pictured symbolically by what the reviewers facetiously described as a large bicuspid at a rakish angle. Unexpected inspiration from the movies came in the form of a German expressionist film, *The Cabinet of Dr. Caligari,* and American
experiments in expressionism offered ample opportunity for
nonrepresentational designs. As early as 1921 these tendencies
were delightfully satirized in a scene at the Neighborhood
Playhouse showing the Bronx Art Theatre of the future with
no actors but only scenery and lights. Undaunted, the designers adopted constructivism from Russia—the use of func-
tional, skeleton sets with many steps and playing levels,
designed to be completely nonrepresentational. Other experimental scenery included what Sheldon Cheney called the
"formal permanent architectural stage"; the darkened scene

where the actors were spotted by brilliant light; the completely bare stage (as in *Our Town*) revealing the backstage
radiators. Some of the aims of these experiments were to focus
the interest on the actors, to provide several playing levels as
in the Elizabethan theatre, to avoid long waits between scenes,
and to abandon completely the realistic "peep show" stage.
The same impulse to freshness and originality of treatment ac-
counted for the many novel productions of Shakespeare—
Hamlet in modern dress with young Hamlet smoking a cigarette during his famous soliloquy and shooting Polonius with
a revolver, or the Orson Welles *Julius Caesar* interpreted as an
anti-Fascist propaganda play. It is certainly possible that the
ghost of Shakespeare, leaning back in the unaccustomed luxury of an orchestra seat, found more enjoyment and truer
Elizabethan spirit in these interpretations than in the more
ponderous and pontifical productions, let us say, of Sothern
and Marlowe. Be that as it may, the designers went on with
their bold experimentation. It must not be assumed that all
their scenery, especially for modern plays, was fanciful or nonrepresentational. Like the dramatists they soon found a balance between extremes, and were satisfied with realism of design as long as it was treated with simplicity and imaginative
beauty.

The crusading zeal for nonrealistic plays, suitable for artistic
décor, could not at first be satisfied by American playwrights,
and after the First World War the theatre turned eagerly to
Europe. Perhaps the high-water mark in this imported drama
of imagination was reached by Benelli's *The Jest* (1919) and
Molnar's *Liliom* (1921). The former, adapted by Edward
Sheldon, was produced by Hopkins with Jones as designer.
Here was a lurid Renaissance melodrama of passion and revenge, with John Barrymore as a sardonic weakling who secures his revenge on two bullies, devoted brothers, played by
Charles Kennedy and Lionel Barrymore. Weaving a Machiavellian web with the fishmonger's beautiful daughter Gi-
nevra as lure, John Barrymore as the protagonist eventually

drives his antagonist Lionel—who boasts that he picks his teeth with a two-handed sword—into fratricide and madness. Few spectators of the original production will forget John's cunning wiles or Lionel's three hops in a moment of angry passion or the dazzling beauty and terror of the Jones sets. More fantasy and tenderness were apparent in the Guild's *Liliom*, the story of a roughneck barker at a merry-go-round (Joseph Schildkraut) who mistreats Julie (Eva Le Gallienne), the servant girl who loves him in spite of his occasional brutality. Sixteen years after his death the heavenly magistrate sends him back to earth as a beggar to show that he can do something good for Julie and his daughter Louise, born posthumously. He brings Louise a star, but in a dispute that follows, his old self returns and he strikes her. Aware of the underlying tenderness, Louise is surprised that a blow can be delivered hard and not hurt at all. *Liliom* proved both an artistic and a popular event; it was occasionally revived and in 1945 transformed into a musical play, *Carousel*, with an American locale.

Molnar's work proved highly successful in America, as well as the plays of the Czech writer Karel Čapek, whose most striking drama, *R.U.R.*, a philosophical fantasy, dealt with the problems of modern science and man's eventual destruction by the machines he has created. Then there was Pirandello, whose *Six Characters in Search of an Author* illustrates his particular brand of intellectual fantasy. In competition with these brilliant and original plays what did Broadway—in addition to O'Neill—have to offer?

From the beginning the art theatre felt a great romantic pull toward the poetical drama of Greece and a special inclination toward the drama of the Renaissance. Shakespeare and his fellows of the Mermaid Tavern were writers of heroic mold whose work was never stultified by the demands of petty realism, who could cascade their emotions in flaming poetry, whose plays could be staged and costumed with imaginative color. The Arthur Hopkins revivals of Shakespeare with sets

by Robert Edmond Jones and with John Barrymore sardonically poetic as Richard III and Hamlet seemed a glorious realization of everything the new theatre stood for. It was only
natural that some contemporary writers should wish to return
to dialogue in verse. Unfortunately the conventions of the
modern stage called for prose and few playwrights could qualify as poets. Several men nevertheless tried their hand at verse
drama, though only one, Maxwell Anderson, had any substan-
tial success in its practice. The use of verse seemed to demand
a noble or romantic subject, preferably from the past. At its
best it would take the form of tragedy with historical, pseudohistorical, or merely fictional characters.

The first attempt chronologically was a costume melodrama
in verse by Sidney Howard, *Swords* (1921), a play on the
order of *The Jest* set against the medieval background of the
struggle in Italy between the Guelphs and the Ghibellines.
The action and interest center on the trials of Fiamma, played
by Clare Eames, later the author's wife, who is held as hostage
in the castle of Ugolino. In Fiamma the author offers a highly
romantic and idealized conception of womanhood, designed
to suggest the medieval idea of the Virgin Mary. The melodramatic climax occurs when the villainous Canetto forces her
to agree to be his mistress. "Come when you will," she says, entering her room. Later Ugolino, jealous, forces the door open
and the body of Canetto falls out, his throat cut. The villagers,
who have worshipped her, all conclude that it was not Fiamma
but God himself who murdered the villain. The play is juvenile
and sentimental, with rhetorical dialogue; though it had some
good dramatic moments, it is clearly inferior to Howard's later,
realistic work.

He abandoned poetry, but two years later there appeared
another first play in verse by a young journalist, Maxwell Anderson, which also failed on Broadway. This was *White Desert*, a tragedy set in modern times and concerned with the fortunes of a homesteading couple. Writing sometimes with the
collaboration of Stallings and sometimes without, Anderson

then proceeded to build up a dramatic reputation in realistic drama, of which *What Price Glory?* was the most sensational example because of its antiwar message, though it had its romantic side too. Two failures of 1925, *The Buccaneer* and *First Flight*, about the pirate Morgan and Andrew Jackson respectively, showed Stallings and Anderson now attempting pseudohistorical costume drama in prose. In the meantime Anderson was evolving a formula for the writing of tragic drama, which was later outlined in *The Essence of Tragedy*, a paper read before the Modern Language Association and published with other essays in 1939. Starting with a reexamination of Aristotle's *Poetics* and other treatises, he concludes, briefly, that tragedy requires some "recognition" by the hero —a discovery of "some element in his environment or in his own soul of which he has not been aware—which will affect him emotionally and alter the direction of the play." The hero, as in the Aristotelian conception, must not be a perfect man, so that the change after the "recognition" must be for the better, working in him a spiritual awakening or regeneration. This last principle readily leads to Anderson's credo "that the theatre at its best is a religious affirmation, an age-old rite restating and reassuring man's belief in his own destiny and his ultimate hope." Other essays in the volume express the opinion that in drama the best prose in the world cannot come up to the best poetry, and that the dramatic poet must be "prophet, dreamer and interpreter of the racial dream." A later essay in *The Bases of Artistic Creation* (1942) restates in detail Anderson's belief in the fundamentally ethical nature of drama: to be truly great a play must stress moral excellence in the character and fortunes of the protagonist, concern itself with the struggle between forces of good and evil, and make of the theatre "a religious institution devoted entirely to the exaltation of the spirit of man."

These and other theories of Anderson obviously were arrived at gradually and are more completely illustrated in his later work. Beginning in 1930 he temporarily abandoned real-

ism and wrote a series of plays in irregular blank verse inter-
mingled with prose, most of which were tragedies on historical
subjects. Two of them dealt with Renaissance England. In
Elizabeth the Queen (1930), produced with great success by
the Theatre Guild, we have—in verse with a few prose scenes
—an imaginative interpretation of the famous love affair between Elizabeth (Lynn Fontanne) and the Earl of Essex
(Alfred Lunt). The mercurial and headstrong hero is brought
by the stratagems of his enemies into a successful revolt
against the Queen. As soon as she becomes his prisoner, he
chivalrously returns her kingdom and surrenders to her, after
which she immediately sends him to the Tower on a charge of
treason. Distraught by the conflict between love and queen-
ship, she sees him before his execution and offers to pardon
him, but he insists on dying, for he realizes that he has a weakness for being first wherever he is, and would later take the
kingdom from her. This last she now offers to him, but he refuses the crown because he feels that England will be better off
if it is ruled by Elizabeth. As he goes to his doom, Elizabeth
realizes that, although she is still queen, and England has been
saved, she will be "queen of emptiness and death." The play
thus ends with a double "recognition," by Essex and by Elizabeth.

It is evident that Anderson followed both the mold and content of Elizabethan tragedy, not only in the prose-verse combination and the multiplicity of scenes but also in the stock
characters of sixteenth-century drama—the punning jester,
the outspoken lady-in-waiting, the low-life soldiers and
servants, the hypocritical courtiers. To add to the verisimilitude, Richard Burbage and other Elizabethan players are
brought in to enact before the Queen several passages from
Shakespeare. While the play is thus intentionally imitative,
it succeeds because of its color and pageantry, its strikingly
dramatic scenes, and the audience's familiarity with the subject. Compared with Shakespeare's the verse seems inevitably
thin and the characterization somewhat artificial, but the

production found an enthusiastic audience and seemed an excellent start in the revival of poetical tragedy.

Mary of Scotland (1933), Anderson's other play built on English history, deals with even more dramatic material. Bringing to poetic life the familiar figures of John Knox, Bothwell, Darnley, and Rizzio, the play attempts a vindication of Mary as an idealist who tries to rule with tolerance and mercy, therefore falling an easy prey to the machinations of the unscrupulous Elizabeth. Mary refuses to marry Bothwell because she feels that he would lead her to rule by wrath and violence instead of wisdom and gentleness. It does not take her long to realize her mistake, and after Darnley's murder she marries Bothwell, though she can enjoy only a fleeting happiness with him. The big scene comes at the end, in Carlisle Castle, when the two queens meet and Elizabeth tries to induce her prisoner Mary to abdicate the Scottish throne. Here Mary first realizes that Elizabeth is the evil that has touched her life at every turn. To her assertion that in spite of lies and forgeries history will vindicate her, Elizabeth replies cynically:

> It's not what happens
> That matters, no, not even what happens that's true,
> But what men believe to have happened. They will believe
> The worst of you, the best of me . . .

Mary still feels that she will win eventually, for she has a child, an heir who will inherit both Scotland and England, and she bravely prepares to face suffering and persecution from Elizabeth. While the play, like the earlier one, makes free with strict historical accuracy, it shows considerable advance in depth and power over *Elizabeth the Queen*. Not only is the plot better integrated, but it also has more good scenes and characters. *Mary of Scotland* marks the height of Anderson's achievement in the historical play, and perhaps also in poetical tragedy. In production it enjoyed an excellent cast—Helen Hayes as Mary, Helen Menken as Elizabeth, and

Philip Merivale as Bothwell. Like O'Neill, Anderson was fortunate always in having the best actors available.

Another historical tragedy, this time about Austrian royalty, *The Masque of Kings* (1937), gives Anderson's interpretation of the famous double suicide of Prince Rudolph and Mary Vetsera at the Prince's hunting lodge, Mayerling. In picturesque and melodramatic scenes the author shows the struggle between the autocratic and Machiavellian old Hapsburg emperor, Franz Josef, and his weak, democratic, idealistic son, a struggle which is bound to end in the latter's failure. Rudolph's final disillusionment comes with the discovery that even his mistress, Vetsera, whom he hopes to make his wife, at first had been one of his father's spies hired to report on all his movements. The abortive revolution against Franz Joseph is considered at length, with Rudolph's sudden realization that to be successful a revolutionary movement must give up all ideals of justice, mercy, and freedom of speech, something the young Prince refuses to do. Through all the episodes the Emperor senses, although he is victorious, that his world is fast disappearing and that kings are obsolete. Heartbroken after Rudolph's suicide, he retains his political astuteness and self-possession long enough to make arrangements to blame the deaths of his son and Vetsera on a hunting accident. Here, as in some of the other plays, Anderson shows a fine sense of dramatic rhetoric and a keen interest in the expression of ideas, but his characters remain shadowy and unconvincing as human beings. The narrative is prolix and involved and, as indicated in the author's protest in the printed play, was considerably cut for stage production. In the Guild production Dudley Digges played the aged emperor, with Henry Hull as Rudolph and Margo as Vetsera.

Mary of Scotland and *The Masque of Kings* had employed historical themes to show the failure of the idealist in a wicked world. In several plays concerned with American history Anderson continued to express both his passionate convictions in favor of idealism and his hatred of business and political materialism. First in this group, *Night over Taos* (1932), was presented by the Group Theatre with a cast including several young and as yet unknown players—Franchot Tone, Clifford Odets, and Burgess Meredith. Retaining the general form of Elizabethan tragedy, it dealt with the end of the regime of General Pablo Montaya in New Mexico in 1847 before the isolated and autocratic community was taken over by the hated Americans, who are represented throughout as treacherous peddlers and barbarians, ready to do anything for profit. Pablo Montaya, a dictator to the end, if a patriotic and paternalistic one, does not flinch at killing his eldest son for treason and is about to administer poison to his younger one for daring to fall in love with a girl of twenty whom Pablo has decided to marry, regardless of her opposition. But realizing at last that he represents an old and dying civilization, a lost cause, that his people are doubtful of his system and would rather surrender to the victorious North, Montaya ends by drinking the poison himself. The play has melodramatic moments and excellent rhetorical declamations, but the plot is long and involved and the entire result too remote and artificial to make for first-class drama. It is interesting in illustrating two of Anderson's favorite themes, the basic nobility of man in supporting lost causes and the lack of idealism of the Yankee peddler, the Marco Millions of Eugene O'Neill.

In the realistic *Both Your Houses* Anderson had delivered a scathing attack on Congress and its hypocritical politicians. A historical play, *Valley Forge* (1934), resumed the onslaught on both the merchants and the politicians, representing George Washington at Valley Forge in the darkest days of the Revolution, when his starved troops were deserting, when his officers were plotting against him, when Congress was shipping rotten meat, if any at all, to the army and simultaneously carrying on secret negotiations with General Howe. Washington's trials increase when Mary Philipse, now Mary Morris, with whom he had once been in love, comes through the lines from Howe to induce him to make peace. But through

all ordeals he is kept going by an intense belief in the right
of freeborn men to govern themselves in their own way, an
ideal for which he is willing to die and one which he is able
to communicate to his independent and unstandardized
soldiers. In contrast to the ill-fed, ragged Americans with their
rough, salty speech we are given a view of a resplendent ballroom in Howe's headquarters at Philadelphia, where a mas-
querade composed by Major Andre is being given before an
elegant audience. Later, with evident allusion to the twentieth
century, Anderson has one of the American officers suggest
that Washington make himself a dictator, but the General
replies that the war is being fought against usurpation of
power and that if he should usurp the powers of Congress,
from which he derived his power, he would have nothing
left to fight for.

The bitterest satire comes when two commissioners from
Congress come to visit the camp, representing the merchants
who want profits, not freedom, and reckon their lives in dollars. Washington, at the end of his patience, literally kicks
the commissioners out of the room and declares that he will
end the war in his own way. Later, as he is about to discuss
peace terms with Howe, he derives new courage from the
bravery of his men; he admits that by all the rules of the
game he is beaten but realizes that his soldiers are not seeking a trade advantage but following a dream which is destined
to win. He therefore refuses to make peace. Skillfully combining humor with drama and satire, the play is interesting as
an expression of Anderson's idealism without any hint of the
conventional Fourth of July oratory. Unfortunately it was
uneven in production and not very successful on the stage.

Valley Forge is interesting as an early attack on dictatorship and a defense of democratic ideals. The play had lambasted the "fat-backed Puritans screaming over taxes" and
not unwilling to commit treason in order to save their money
and their skins. In *The Wingless Victory* (1936), a period
tragedy in verse, he returned to the attack on the score not

only of materialism but also of religious bigotry and hypocrisy. Nat McQueston, who left Salem as a penniless sailor, returns as captain and owner of a five-master. His Puritan family, however, is disagreeably shocked at the discovery that he has brought back a Malay wife, a princess in her own country, and two children he has had by her. The McQuestons are glad to use Nat's fortune and they permit him to bring his native family ashore, although they and the entire town make it a point to treat Oparre and the children like lepers. By borrowing and trickery the townspeople soon get control over Ned's money and forthwith trump up charges against him which force him to agree to send Oparre and his children back to the Orient, although he knows that as half-breeds they must necessarily become prostitutes. Though he loves Oparre, his return to Salem has changed him, the New England spirit and atmosphere having made his relations to her now seem shameful and obscene. Oparre, who had taken the Christian doctrine seriously, calls in the townspeople "with your white witless faces" and announces that she has been misled by their Christ "and his beggar doctrine, written for beggars." She turns to her old gods, and after being sent to a cabin aboard the "Wingless Victory" administers poison, according to native custom, to her Malayan servant, her children, and herself. At this point, however, she reconsiders the ideals of Christianity and concludes that Christ came too soon and that men will not be ready for his teaching for another hundred thousand years. Nat rushes in before her death, realizing he cannot live without her, but of course, too late. This colorful and melodramatic play is obviously not so much a colonial story as an attack on intolerance and racial hatred with an eye on Nazi doctrine, as indicated in the line that "in sheer asininity the Aryan tops the world." With Katharine Cornell to play the dusky Oparre *The Wingless Victory* was well received on Broadway. The poetry is irregular, as usual, and rather thin, but adequate for dramatic purposes, and one must admit that it gives a certain elevation to the dialogue of which prose is not normally capable.

After writing historical and period plays with present-day reference Anderson's next logical step was to attempt tragedy in verse on a modern subject. In so doing he explained in an introduction to the printed version of *Winterset* that he was establishing a new convention, for in the past poetic tragedy had never been successfully written about its own time and place. Two unusually interesting plays resulted from this experiment. The first one, *Winterset*, was produced in 1935 with a splendid cast that included Richard Bennett, Burgess Meredith, and Margo. Although the characters are differently named, the play is a kind of poetical sequel to *Gods of the Lightning* (1928) by Anderson and Harold Hickerson, a journalistically realistic work based upon the Sacco-Vanzetti case and its flagrant injustices. With the aid of striking sets representing a city river front under the arc of a bridge and a miserable cellar apartment close by, Anderson's modern tragedy centers on the ᵔᵔⁿ of the executed radical Romagna, young Mio, now seventeen, whose single, all-consuming desire is to clear his father's name. Mio has come East to investigate new evidence, and now chance brings him to the bridgehead, where he meets and falls in love with Miriamne, young sister of Garth, who had been implicated in the Romagna affair but had never been allowed to testify. Later Mio meets the gunman Trock Estrella and his henchman Shadow, one of whom committed the murder for which Romagna was executed. To the bridge and to the cellar apartment also wanders old Judge Gaunt, cloudy in mind and broken in spirit. He, too, has heard of the new investigations of the case and to everyone he meets he seeks pathetically to justify himself and his decision as trial judge. In the cellar apartment, when he learns the truth about Romagna's innocence, he defends himself by saying that the common good of humanity, through its faith in the courts, was worth more

than a "small injustice." Though revenge is within his grasp,
Mio is cheated of it by Miriamne's equally strong desire to
save her brother, and suddenly he realizes that it does not
really matter:

> I've lost
> my taste for revenge if it falls on you. Oh, God,
> deliver me from the body of this death
> I've dragged behind me all these years! Miriamne!
> Miriamne!

He thus gives up his mission, but the star-crossed lovers are
still denied happiness; Mio is killed by Trock's gunmen and
the girl purposely gets shot by them also, to prove to Mio that
she did not send him to his death. In considering their sad
fate, Miriamne's father finds in their lack of fear, in their
defiance of death, something noble and heroic.

The play is less imitative of the Shakespearean form than
Elizabeth the Queen, but it should be obvious, even from
this sketchy summary, that Anderson has absorbed much of
the spirit and substance of the bard of Avon. Mio's mission
of revenge for the murder of his father reminds us of *Hamlet;*
Judge Gaunt's incoherent ravings during a thunderstorm offer a clear reminiscence of King Lear; Shadow, who comes
back drenched and bloody from the river, is a modern counterpart of the Elizabethan ghost; the love at first sight of Mio
and Mariamne and their tragic situation call to mind *Romeo
and Juliet*. The play has its origin, therefore, in literary tradition rather than in observation or experience, even as its
dialogue is artificial and conventionalized, though it has moments of power and beauty. The catastrophe is Elizabethan in
its violence but not logically convincing. In the matter of
Romagna's legal murder the issue is obscured by the compli-
cation of Mio's love affair, and the two themes—the righting
of injustice and romantic love—are not combined too happily.
The personal tragedy of the two lovers is affecting, however,
and *Winterset* proved successful on the stage, receiving the

new Drama Critics award as the best play of the 1935–1936 season.

Winterset was an attack on a social wrong which was strangely cast in poetical form with dramatic reflections of the past. Anderson's other verse tragedy on a modern theme offered a far broader assault on what the author had come to consider one of the great ills of the modern world—scientific materialism. *Key Largo* (1939), produced by the Playwrights' Company, was a philosophical and analytical play dealing with the mental and spiritual problem of King Mc-Cloud, who has led a small group of American volunteers to Spain to fight for the Loyalist cause. Learning that this cause is desperately lost and that his group is to be sacrificed in a hopeless rear-guard action, King, disillusioned about the whole crusade, advises the others to desert. Inspired by the idealism of Victor d'Alcala, one of the group, who asserts that only by staying can he keep faith in himself and what men are, the others choose to remain and are killed during the night. After clearing out alone, King falls in with the Franco forces and is forced to abandon his principles to the extreme of fighting on the other side, but he saves his life and eventually reaches the United States. He finds, however, that he cannot rationalize or justify his action, and he wanders about telling his story to the families of his dead companions, hoping thereby to do penance and to find at least one person to agree that he did right in running away. Last of all he comes to Key Largo in Florida, where d'Alcala, Victor's blind father, and Alegre, Victor's sister, are running a tourist camp. They are themselves in a difficult situation, for they are wholly in the power of a gangster and gambler, Murillo, who has taken over one of the cabins and is operating under the protection of the crooked Sheriff Gash. Murillo announces his intention of possessing Alegre, by force if necessary. In this situation King is of no great help to Alegre and her father, who pity him but are utterly shocked and revolted by his story. King's real

struggle lies in the fact that, in spite of other people's disapproval, his mind tells him that he was right in deserting in
Spain; now in Florida he promises to do what he can to
oppose Murillo

> —But, God, how can I explain?
> If it comes to dying I don't trust my brain,
> my busy, treacherous, casuistic brain,
> presenting me with scientific facts
> and cunning reasons. It's separate from myself,
> separate from my will—a traitor brain,
> an acid eating away at all the faiths
> by which we live, questioning all the rules,
> and leaving us bare—naked white animals
> without poetry or God.

Later, denying the validity of such virtues as justice, honor,
love, and friendship, he is almost ready to sacrifice two innocent Seminole Indians for his own safety, until he discovers
that Alegre has secretly idealized and loved him from Victor's description and letters. The girl declares that she no
longer loves him, but "the portrait of one dead" shows him
what to do and he finally arrives at the main thesis of the
play, that

> A man must die
> for what he believes—if he's unfortunate
> enough to have to face it in his time—
> and if he won't then he'll end up believing
> in nothing at all—and that's death, too.

He clears of blame the Seminole Indians and has the pleasure
of shooting Murillo, though he himself is killed at the same
time.

Dealing with so much soul-probing and discussion on the
conflict between scientific materialism and idealism, the play
tends to be wordy and sometimes confusing on the stage,
though it makes excellent reading. To obviate this difficulty
Anderson was obliged to use many melodramatic situations
and devices, but neither the melodrama nor the excellence of

Paul Muni as King McCloud could make the play entirely successful. In ease of verse, originality of form, and sincerity of theme it surpassed the more popular *Winterset* and might easily be considered Anderson's most interesting—if not his best—experiment in poetical tragedy.

Still concerned with spiritual ills of the modern world, Anderson in 1940 wrote a verse play on a religious subject, *Journey to Jerusalem,* showing Jeshua (Jesus) at the age of twelve on his visit to the temple in Jerusalem. Anderson selected biblical history because of its resemblance to the present day, the period being one when despair and unfaith gripped the "slave state" of the Jews under the iron rule of materialistic Rome. The author's purpose is given in an introductory note as the desire to show the problem of unfaith as it presented itself to Jesus in youth. Faith of some sort, he feels, is an absolute prerequisite to any successful opposition to Hitlerism, based as the latter is eventually upon a scientific and materialistic conception of the universe, with man demoted to mere animal. In the play the journey to Jerusalem of Joseph, Mary, and Jeshua and their meeting with the bandit-prophet Ishmael are presented colorfully, yet devoutly. At the gate of the city Jeshua escapes death, and later in accordance with scripture story he confounds the priests in the temple by his clever answers. At this point he feels that the Messiah will be known on earth by his armies and his magnificent victories. This illusion is subsequently dispelled by Ishmael, who persuades Jeshua that the Messiah will stand alone with no help from heaven or from men. For centuries his wisdom will be ignored or ridiculed, although eventually his "words will catch and move among men like fire." He will have to die in agony. When Jeshua admits his fear of death, Ishmael explains that if he were afraid and ran, then Herod would surely win. At this moment and later Jeshua comes to the realization that he is the Messiah, and in spite of Herod's persecution there comes already among his family a nascent feeling of faith. The subject matter causes Anderson to write more simply and concisely than usual, with less dependence on melodramatic situations. *Journey to Jerusalem* is readable, but like most biblical plays it was not a success on Broadway, the devoutness, the message of faith, the unaccustomed costumes and beards all proving difficult for modern audiences to accept. It holds considerable interest, however, in showing Anderson, like O'Neill in *Days without End,* turning to faith for some solution to the confusion of the modern world.

Maxwell Anderson's fantasies, occasionally in verse, and his realistic plays in prose will be considered later. On the subject of his historical tragedies and other serious poetical plays critical opinion has been sharply divided. Edith J. R. Isaacs, editor of *Theatre Arts,* has found particular delight in the historical plays. In a critical article in the *South Atlantic Quarterly* Homer S. Woodbridge—welcoming the growth of an audience for poetical drama—has high praise for *Mary of Scotland* and *The Masque of Kings* and finds that Anderson compares very well with Shakespeare's second-best. The critic Edmund Wilson, on the other hand, asserts that Anderson's plays offer "the most striking confirmation of the obsolescence of verse technique." Anderson's poetry has suffered attack from other quarters as well, usually on the score of outworn poetic imagery incongruously blended with colloquial realistic diction, and the Broadway reviewers have frequently called attention to the occasional pompousness of his style. The historical tragedies, one must admit, often seem involved and pretentious, with good theatrical moments but shadowy characterization and unconvincing dialogue. Yet the plays undeniably have romantic color, and even when not fully successful, they offer a sharp and welcome contrast to the run-of-the-mill Broadway play. They are never trivial. No modern playwright has written so passionately in defense of his convictions or held so high a conception of drama as a kind of religious affirmation of the ideals of the human race. This lofty belief in the theatre's mission coupled with a crusading spirit has given Anderson his particular significance in American drama.

Broadway saw a scattering of other plays in verse, none of them successful except for T. S. Eliot's *Murder in the Cathedral*, a historical tragedy by the celebrated Anglo-Catholic poet. It was more English than American in authorship since it was written by the expatriate after he had become a naturalized British subject. First performed in England, the play was presented in New York by the Federal Theatre in 1936 and by an English company two years later. More individual in form than Anderson's plays and superior in poetry, *Murder in the Cathedral* combines devices of Greek tragedy with features of medieval drama in imaginatively depicting the murder of Thomas à Becket in 1170. A herald and a chorus of Women of Canterbury show borrowing from the Greek, whereas Four Tempters who assail the Archbishop with subtle argument, as well as the general tone of a church service, suggest the medieval religious play. There is a scene in prose when four knights, the murderers of Becket, step out front and address the audience in robust, matter-of-fact speech explaining the reasons for the murder. Becket is revealed as a sincere, devout churchman, resisting the multiple temptations of conviviality, power, ambition, and pride in the glory of martyrdom. The play has power and beauty, and is one of the few examples of effective drama by a poet not professionally connected with the theatre.

The renaissance of verse drama, interesting as it was, remained limited to a handful of writers, inspiring no wide acceptance or imitation. Of course, any prose play might be deemed poetical if it possessed certain characteristics of style and imagination. For poetical content most of O'Neill's plays would surely qualify, or works as different as Robert Turney's *Daughters of Atreus* (1936), a retelling in elevated and sometimes turgid diction of the classic story of Agamemnon's fated brood, and Dan Totheroh's *Wild Birds* (1925), a tale of idyllic love on a prairie farm ending in brutal tragedy.

Poetic or not, the more imaginative plays of the twenties and
thirties leaned heavily on the past and made free use of
costume, historical, or biographical material. The English
showed special aptitude for this type of drama, as evidenced
by *Victoria Regina* and *The Barretts of Wimpole Street,* but
there were many American attempts which showed a wide
range of purpose. A modern bedroom farce was given a
strange Renaissance setting in Edwin Justus Mayer's *The
Firebrand* (1924), in which Joseph Schildkraut indulged in
much bravado posturing and love-making as Benvenuto
Cellini. Flippant sophistication was coupled with romance in
The Pursuit of Happiness (1933), a delightful colonial
comedy by Lawrence and Armina Langner on the subject of
bundling. While not as lofty in intent, these were better and
certainly more successful than serious plays like Totheroh's
Distant Drums (1932) about the covered-wagon era of the
West and Totheroh's and George O'Neil's *Mother Lode* about
early San Francisco. A romantic costume play of 1926, *Capon-
sacchi,* was an adaptation by Arthur Goodrich and Rose A.
Palmer of Browning's *The Ring and the Book.* Biographical
pieces were numerous though not often successful. They
treated such diverse personages as the Brontës (*Moor Born*),
Richard Steele (*Yr. Obedient Husband*), Emily Dickinson
(*Brittle Heaven*), and Jesse James (*Missouri Legend*). Drink-
water's *Abraham Lincoln* initiated a series of plays dealing
directly or indirectly with the Emancipator: E. P. Conkle's
Prologue to Glory (1938), Philip Van Doren Stern's *The Man
Who Killed Lincoln* (1940), Arthur Goodman's *If Booth Had
Missed* (1932)—an ironical historical fantasy—and Robert
Sherwood's superb *Abe Lincoln in Illinois* (1938), first production of the Playwrights' Company. It is worth noting that
historical and biographical drama abandoned increasingly the
blood-and-thunder histrionics of the Bulwer-Lytton school,
becoming less romantic, more scholarly and realistic. Often
the author's treatment of the past had specific application
to the problems of the present. This practice was seen in An-

derson's tragedies. It may be observed in the popular *Harriet* (1943), a play by Florence Ryerson and Colin Clements about Harriet Beecher Stowe suggesting a modern social message, or in Sidney Kingsley's *The Patriots* (1943), a dramatic statement of the conflicting views of Hamilton and Jefferson with allusion to present-day political philosophies. This trend toward realism and contemporary reference appears at its best in *Lincoln in Illinois*, a historical play which is decidedly not a romantic period piece. By the time this play was written Robert Sherwood, famous already as an author of high comedies of devastating wit, had become converted to the New Deal and to the writing of propagandist drama in favor of American democracy. *Abe Lincoln in Illinois* gives us a brilliant analysis of a maladjusted, unhappy man forced into unwilling action, partly by the persistent single-mindedness of Mary Todd, partly by his acute awareness of the social and moral ills of the time. A brilliant scene shows Lincoln on the night of the 1860 election desperately hoping that he will not win, fully conscious of what victory would mean. The play's effectiveness comes partly from this realistic characterization but mainly from pointed application to the late thirties, when again the United States faced the issue of property rights versus human rights, and when the confused liberal was struggling against inertia and attempting against his will to derive a positive faith and a course of action. With great astuteness Sherwood shows Lincoln debating with Stephen A. Douglas in 1858 and quotes liberally from the actual speeches. Well-contrived also is the play's final scene revealing Lincoln's dejected departure from Illinois for the White House in 1861, with the President caring nothing about his personal safety. In a calm speech he asks his fellow townsmen to believe that the ideals of liberty and equality are not decadent or doomed. The audience's knowledge of subsequent history gave tragic irony to this quiet ending. The play is not without poetry or imagination, but it scarcely belongs to the same species as *Richelieu* or even *Elizabeth the Queen*, and indicates again the encroachment of realism on the favorite forms of the art theatre.

The writers of imaginative drama found a natural haven in the past, but they did not disregard the present or the near present. This, in good romantic fashion, they discovered in the byways of America, rich in local color and folk traditions, home of the unusual and the picturesque. New York in their opinion was too ingrown and sophisticated, prone to consider itself the whole of America. Regionalism and folkways provided them with a kind of contemporary costume drama, not without possibilities of poetical treatment. Under the leadership of men like Frederick Koch in North Carolina, E. C. Mabie in Iowa, and Alfred Arvold in North Dakota the university theatres eagerly encouraged the dramatic exploitation of local material. In Paul Green the educational theatre discovered at least one first-rate dramatist who could write successfully for Broadway as well as for the Chapel Hill campus.

Regionalism showed a normal tendency to become entangled with other elements—realism, social significance, fantasy—and some examples of it will necessarily be considered elsewhere. Regardless of the exact form employed, the seekers after the picturesque left few parts of the country untouched. Local speech and manners provided the main attraction for pleasant if inconsequential comedies like Patterson Greene's *Papa Is All* (1942) about the Pennsylvania Dutch. New England rarely struck the playwrights as quaint but merely as disagreeable—as witness the plays of O'Neill and Owen Davis—but the West received pleasant regional treatment in the work, for example, of Lynn Riggs, whose *Green Grow the Lilacs* (1931), original of the popular *Oklahoma!*, gave a breezy love story of the Indian Territory with Franchot Tone and June Walker and a wealth of cowboy songs. Riggs' *Cherokee Night* was not produced on Broadway, but his *Russet Mantle* (1936), comedy about a radical poet who secures employment on a Santa Fe ranch and becomes seriously involved in a love affair, derives much of its charm from local color. Regionalism is incidental also to much of the Western drama of Dan Totheroh and John Steinbeck. But it was the South that offered the widest opportunities for rural themes and folkways, especially among mountaineers, poor whites, and Negroes.

The hillbilly play, inspirer of a thousand jokes and cartoons, came to town early with Lulu Vollmer's *Sun-up* (1923) and with Hatcher Hughes' *Hell-Bent fer Heaven* (1924), Pulitzer Prize winner for that year—though not without argument. The former play derives its humor and quaintness from the Widow Cagle's conception of the First World War as a mountaineer feud in France, a place located forty miles east of Asheville. Her son Rufe has been drafted—as she thinks—to fight the Yankees. Widow Cagle's opinions on revenue officers and corn liquor are equally unorthodox. Though interesting, the play ends in melodramatic absurdity. Widow Cagle is about to kill the son of the revenuer who shot Rufe's pappy when suddenly there comes a message with music from the spirit of Rufe (he's been killed in France) explaining the obsolescence of feuds. She reluctantly lets her victim go but is herself arrested by the Sheriff. *Hell-Bent fer Heaven,* also set in the North Carolina mountains, likewise brings in feuds and the First World War but has the new element of mania arising from "that camp-meetin' breed o' religion." Rufe Pryor, hypocrite and liar, is disturbed when Sid returns from war because Rufe will now lose his job in the country store as well as his chances of courting attractive Jude Lowry, engaged to Sid. Rufe stirs up fights, revives an old feud, dynamites a dam, and during a thunderstorm declares his erotic passion to Jude with much religious symbolism, until his eventual exposure brings the play to a happy conclusion. Later plays by the same authors—*The Dunce Boy* and *Trigger* by Lulu Vollmer and *Ruint* by Hatcher Hughes—lost the advantage of novelty and were far less successful. As suggested earlier, the

mountaineer play may have had some indebtedness to
O'Neill's *Desire under the Elms* and the type later developed
into *Tobacco Road* and other works of social significance. At
the start it depended mainly upon quaint speech and local
color.

The change from superficial regionalism to serious treatment of the South with its manners, folk lore, and social
divisions is seen in the drama of Paul Green, a Southern farm
boy who received his college education at North Carolina—
where he was active in the Carolina Playmakers—and later
at Cornell. At the conclusion of his graduate work he returned
to Chapel Hill to teach in the department of philosophy. As a
dramatist he first attracted notice in 1924 with his one-act
play *The No 'Count Boy,* prize winner in the Little Theatre
Tournament of that year. Of his many subsequent plays about
the South some half dozen were produced on Broadway.
Green's work may best be described as poetic realism inclining
to tragedy, with a side interest in folk fantasy. His first Broadway production, *In Abraham's Bosom* (1926), a Pulitzer Prize
play, showed in a series of tragic scenes the problem of the
ambitious Negro in the South, held down by the bondage of
his race and his own rebellious temper. Abe McCranie (Jules
Bledsoe), half white and unafraid to speak his mind, struggles
to set his people free by teaching, but meets constant defeat
from both blacks and whites until he is finally driven to kill
his white half-brother and to face the shots of the mob that
comes after him. For all its tragic intensity and beauty of style
the play is mainly realistic. More originality and experimentation are displayed in *Roll, Sweet Chariot* (1934), called by
the author "a symphonic play of the Negro people," a play
which unfortunately failed on Broadway. It reveals the teem-
ing, varied life of a small settlement called Potter's Field (originally the play's title) which is casually torn up because it
lies in the path of a road under construction. With the incidental aid of music and song Green records not only the
tribulations of the black race but also its laughter and gaiety.

The community centering at the boardinghouse of Quivienne Lockley and her feeble-minded husband includes laborers, servants and cooks for the white folk, a barber, an abused wife, Quivienne's son by a white man, a bogus minister who prospers on the superstitious credulity of the others, a fugitive from a chain gang who reclaims his wife, now mistress of another man, and is later killed by his rival. The play ends with tremendous power in a chain-gang scene, the convicts digging on impassively at the same even pace after one of their number has been whipped to death by a guard. "Dig on the road to heaven! Digging towards the sun!" they sing. "Dig on to Jesus," "Coming to set man free"—expressing in somber music their stoic acceptance of the present and their sole hope for the future. Poetic or not, such drama obviously has a strong vein of social significance and it is not surprising to find Green protesting passionately against injustice in the one-act *Hymn to the Rising Sun* and—in collaboration with Richard Wright—in *Native Son*.

Though Green, like O'Neill, was a pioneer in the drama of Negro life, he employed other themes as well. *The Field God* (1927) traces the tragic downfall of a white farmer, Gilchrist—healthy, strong, pagan, a veritable field God—married, however, to an invalid, bigoted, pathologically religious wife. When her niece Rhoda, young and healthy, comes to the farm, the girl and Gilchrist are attracted by each other's strength and fall in love. Venomously jealous, the wife dies, cursing her husband and Rhoda. The two marry, but malicious neighborhood gossip and revivalist meetings to save their souls drive them apart and break down their strength until at the very end they are liberated spiritually from the shackles of a revengeful God.

The Field God did not succeed on Broadway, but Green enjoyed at least an artistic success in *The House of Connelly* (1931), a study of social changes in the South. Handled freely as poetic realism, with the aid of dance and serenade and with two ancient sibyl-like Negresses serving symbolically as a Greek chorus, the play showed the decay of the proud and aristocratic Connelly family as the consequence of poverty, weakness, and the sins of their fathers. Tate, one of the Connelly tenants, is on the rise, however, and it is his daughter Patsy who, in the face of vicious family opposition, marries young Will Connelly and gives him strength to overcome the past. The struggle is a bitter one, for Will's mother, his decadent Uncle Bob, and his two spinster sisters do their utmost to preserve their dead traditions and to break up Will's romance with a "poor white" girl. Unofficially the Connelly family includes a goodly number of Negroes and mulattoes, a living tribute to the prolific ardor of the late General Connelly and of Uncle Bob. The play was the first offering of the Group Theatre, which persuaded Paul Green to change the original tragic ending to a final victory for Will and Patsy. The production with Franchot Tone as Will, Margaret Barker as Patsy, Morris Carnovsky as Uncle Bob, and the Group's future dramatist—Clifford Odets—in a small role was a triumph for the company's experiment in communal living and rehearsing. In the play's description of decadence in the old South, of course, *The House of Connelly* was not without social significance.

Green's *Johnny Johnson*, though experimental in form, will be considered more logically among the antiwar plays. His work designed specifically for regional production is likely to show more extreme imagination than his Broadway productions. We may note in passing, for example, his *Tread the Green Grass*, a folk fantasy with music, pantomime, cinematic interludes, and masks—a wild and incoherent piece about a country girl who is magically touched by creatures of the wood and in the end goes completely mad. There is also *The Lost Colony*, a "symphonic drama" commemorating the first English settlement on Roanoke Island, presented first in 1937 and for some years thereafter with financial assistance from the state of North Carolina. Good or bad, these pieces show Paul Green's complete independence from Broadway, a freedom which permitted him to develop his natural bent for regionalism and imagination, and yet to conquer New York through the force and excellence of his best work.

Negro life and manners in the South provided material for other writers who knew the subject. One of the most popular folk plays was the well-known *Porgy* (1927) by Dorothy and DuBose Heyward, a Guild production staged by Rouben Mamoulian with special attention to dramatic lighting and mass effects. The stage represents Catfish Row in Charleston, South Carolina. Porgy (Frank Wilson), a crippled peddler, has given refuge to Bess, whom he loves, the woman of a rambunctious longshoreman now hiding for murder. Her efforts to remain with Porgy and go straight are prevented by the reappearance of the longshoreman at a picnic. She is then victimized by Sportin' Life, bootlegger and dealer in drugs, who tempts her with "happy dust" and persuades her to go with him to New York. Porgy, doggedly patient and still in love with Bess, sets out after her in his goat cart, heading north, confident that he will find her in the distant city. The effective use of spirituals suggested the possibilities of musical treatment, and in 1935 the play was refurbished as a folk opera, *Porgy and Bess,* with a score by George Gershwin. The Heywards were responsible, also, for another melodramatic Charleston play, *Mamba's Daughters* (1939), presented with Ethel Waters, Canada Lee, José Ferrer, and Anne Brown.

Folk material, as we have seen, could easily slip into fantasy. The two elements were superbly fused in Marc Connelly's *Green Pastures* (1930), based on stories by Roark Bradford, one of the finest of the Negro plays. Voltaire's remark that man created God in his own image comes immediately to mind in connection with Connelly's masterly telling of the biblical story as seen through the eyes of a Negro preacher and a group of Negro children in Louisiana. Opening realistically with a Sunday school scene, the play turns swiftly into delightful fantasy—essentially realistic in dialogue and characterization—recording such events as a

fish fry in heaven, complete with "seegars and biled custard."
De Lawd, played by Richard B. Harrison, r'ars back to pass
a miracle—more firmament is needed for the custard—but the
trouble with a miracle is that you always have to r'ar back and
pass another. There's been too much firmament, and to drain
off the excess he creates earth and man. Pleased at first with
his handiwork, he soon becomes irritated by man's orneriness
and habitual sinfulness. Not even the Flood can stop man's
fighting, his dissipation, his lechery. De Lawd tries a different plan, directing Moses to lead his people from Egypt to
the Land of Canaan, but even that doesn't work. An amusing
scene represents Babylon as a Negro night club in New Orleans, which the King enters accompanied by five chippies.
At last God renounces man completely, closing his ears to all
pleas and suffering. But during the siege of Jerusalem he cannot resist going down once more. "Even bein' God ain't a bed
of roses," he tells Gabriel. Here De Lawd learns from man
that the old concept of a God of wrath and vengeance is outmoded, replaced by Hosea's idea of a God of mercy. Later, as
the Crucifixion is about to take place on earth, he comes to the
realization that mercy comes through suffering and that even
God must suffer. The miracle is that the play succeeds in being
both humorous and affecting, with spiritual sincerity and no
trace of ridicule. It well deserved the season's Pulitzer award
and was later capably done in the movies, a medium well
suited for the presentation of fantasy.

Green Pastures managed to tell fundamental truths about
Negro character—not to mention God and humanity—without having recourse to a literal transcription of reality. Holding up to nature the mirror of imagination, suggestion, fable,
symbolism—rather than of photographic realism—had been
one of the prime aims of the art theatre, and from the start
the drama of fantasy was its favorite child. The type could be
successful on many levels and for many moods or purposes;
at its worst it could be distressingly bad, at its best it gave

us some of the finest plays of the modern theatre, worthy of comparison with *Liliom, R.U.R.*, and other European models. Fantasy might be represented in the theme itself, as in plays of the supernatural; in the method of presentation, as in the earlier *Yellow Jacket* or in *Our Town;* or in both, as in *The Skin of Our Teeth.* Like regional drama it was not usually practiced by the professional Broadway scribblers but by poet-philosophers like Wilder and Saroyan. An examination of the principal examples will show the interests and techniques of the dramatists addicted to its use.

The simple type of fantasy—on the level which a mass audience could understand—is pleasantly represented by Marc Connelly's *The Wisdom Tooth* (1926), about a young man whose years in business as a clerk have made him conservative and servile, afraid to speak his mind. In a dream his grandparents and a fairy called Lalita show him how pugnacious an individual he was as a boy, when everyone called him Skeeter, and they restore his independent spirit. He promptly loses his job but gains the love of a fellow boarder who had discerned the man under the carbon copy.

Connelly's play, while not an immediate hit, made a respectable showing on Broadway. A more abstract message and satirical intent proved too heavy a burden for popular acceptance of another comic fantasy of the same year, Philip Barry's *White Wings,* his first attempt in the genre. The play interprets the struggle between conservatism and progressiveness in terms of the battle between Mary Todd, whose father had invented a horseless carriage, and Archie Inch, last generation of a family of aristocratic street cleaners who have followed their proud calling since they came over on the Mayflower. Most amusing of the characters is the horse Joseph, who senses intuitively that Mary is an enemy and gives a cynical horse laugh after biting her. Only after Archie's occupation is doomed by the success of the automobile does the hero give in to his love for Mary. *White Wings* has imagination and wit, and deserved a better fate.

At least two fantasies were concerned with the concept of time, also a favorite theme of the English dramatist J. B. Priestley. The first, *Berkeley Square* (1929), was written by John L. Balderston, an American residing in London, where the play was first produced. The American hero (Leslie Howard) becomes so thoroughly immersed in old letters and documents found in an ancient house in Berkeley Square that in defiance of the ordinary workings of time he finds himself living in two centuries, the eighteenth and the twentieth. In the former he assumes the physical identity of Cousin Peter, an American colonial come to visit the Pettigrews in London, and falls in love with his cousin Helen. As a result, in the twentieth century, he curtly dismisses his American fiancée, Marjorie, giving her and his friends the impression that he has gone mad. Unfortunately he cannot find contentment or adjustment in the past, and Helen Pettigrew, in her deep love for him, persuades him to return to his own world. Now he seemingly is cured of his madness, but finding from a tomb-stone inscription that Helen died unmarried three years after his departure from the eighteenth century, he refuses to have anything more to do with Marjorie. The mysterious shifts in time are handled with an appropriate sense of wonder, and the romance with the long-dead Helen seemed theatrically convincing.

The other time play was Maxwell Anderson's *The Star Wagon* (1937), produced by Guthrie McClintic. The action starts in the present with a quarrel between Stephen—an elderly, gentle, unworldly inventor—and his wife Martha, who complains of her lifelong drudgery and his failure at money-making. It would have been much better, she says, if he had married instead, thirty-five years before, the wealthy Hallie Arlington and if Martha had become the wife of Reiger, a banker's son. When Stephen loses his job at the factory, he and an old crony decide to try out a time machine with which they have been experimenting on the quiet. They are successfully transported back to July, 1902, so that

Stephen has the opportunity to live his life once again without Martha. The outcome is far from pleasant, with Stephen
wealthy but cynical and disappointed, bereft of ideals, unhappy because he is spending his time in an office trying to
cheat people out of their money. His wife, Hallie, is "growing
old hysterically" in the throes of a cheap love affair with
Duffy. Nor is Martha happy with her husband Reiger. In
short, Stephen is overjoyed at being able to return to the
present and to Martha, who agrees that they had been right in
their marriage all along. With their reconciliation a little later
in the play comes also realization of Stephen's worth by the
president of the rubber company, who rehires him with the
salary and promotion he deserves. Anderson's usual picture of
business men trying to get all they can for nothing is not a
pleasant one, but the play has otherwise a good deal of sentimental and reminiscent charm, especially in its 1902 scenes,
and it brings out very well the idea that happiness and human
life are at bottom an insoluble mystery. The nostalgic, sentimental quality of *The Star Wagon* was enhanced by the selection of Burgess Meredith and Lillian Gish to play the parts
of the inventor and his wife. Except for the device of the time
machine, of course, the play is developed in straight realism.

Anderson's most ambitious attempt at fantasy, *High Tor*,
had appeared earlier in 1937 in a combination of verse and
prose. The scene is High Tor, a lofty mountain top overlook-
ing the Hudson River, owned by an eccentric young man,
Van Horn (Burgess Meredith), who prefers a meager, haphazard, but free existence on his mountain to the usual ways
of American life. As he remarks to Judy, who loves him, the
Chevrolet factory and Sing Sing, as they appear in the distance from High Tor, look very much alike. Judy has a normal
desire for home, children, and money, and she urges Van to
sell his land to a company that intends to dig out the mountain
for commercial purposes. Because of Van's refusal the girl
decides to break off their love affair. But Van is not left alone.
On the mountain resides a very aged Indian, friend of Van,

who is merely waiting to die. A group of bank robbers come
to divide their loot before making an escape. Two vulgar,
double-dealing lawyers—Biggs and Skimmerhorn—come to
cajole and cheat Van out of his property at a ridiculously low
price. Finally, a series of ghosts—the crew of the old Dutch
ship, the "Half Moon," and Lise, the captain's wife—also
wander about High Tor, where they have waited for two or
three centuries for their spectre ship to take them home to
Amsterdam. In the weird episodes that follow, these various
groups get intermixed: the robbers are caught, the rascally
lawyers are discomfited and later arrested in connection with
the robbery, Lise and Van Horn engage in an idyllic love
scene, and the Indian announces that he has selected the spot
for his grave. When Judy comes back to Van, the Indian now
advises selling the mountain, for High Tor is not worth keeping. As for the consequent despoiling of nature, the Indian
asserts philosophically that everything made by man eventually ends in good ruins. Altering his decision not to sell, Van
holds out for fifty thousand dollars and makes plans to move
West with Judy. This unusual plot offers opportunity for
arresting and amusing scenes. The mood of fantasy—on several levels as in *A Midsummer Night's Dream*—is established
very well and is sometimes enlivened with rare humor, as
when the low-brow lawyers attempt to explain the night's
supernatural experiences to a state trooper and the elder
Skimmerhorn, who conclude the two men have been on a
drinking bout. Throughout the play Anderson's contempt of
crooked lawyers, his hatred of machines and commerce, and
his love of natural beauty are evident. His scornful view of
modern civilization is shown by the ghostly DeWitt, who is
overjoyed at finally departing for home. Anderson's Catskill
fantasy, like his historical tragedies, provoked widely diver-
gent reactions as to the worth of the play.

   Anderson's fantasy in *High Tor* may be described as romantic. Among other possible moods or themes traditionally
associated with the form, the weird and the supernatural

hold a prominent place. Moon madness was the burden of Martin Flavin's *Children of the Moon* (1923), an unearthly, somber play about the Atherton family in whom lunacy—in its literal derivation—is an inherited characteristic. During the war the son of the family has crashed his plane by flying in the path of the moon, and now the daughter, flying from home with her aviator lover, disappears forever in the fog in quest of the same celestial body. In building up his atmosphere of weirdness Flavin relied upon poetical rather than clinical treatment. Another unearthly play, this time based on folk superstition, was a free dramatization of the old Barbara Allen ballad, detailing with music and dance the tragic fate of a young woman and her witchboy lover. This fantasy, *Dark of the Moon* (1945) by Howard Richardson and William Berney, a Maxwell Anderson prize play at Stanford University, turned out to be surprisingly successful on Broadway.

Death has always held a strange fascination for the writers of serious fantasy. The subject aroused popular interest on Broadway in the thirties, partly because of the troubled times, partly because of the success of Alberto Casella's *Death Takes a Holiday* (1929), an Italian play adapted by Walter Ferris in which the heroine, enamoured of Death, abandons her earthly life to depart with him as her lover. Death, personified as Mr. Brink, appeared later in Paul Osborn's *On Borrowed Time* (1938), based on a novel by Lawrence Edward Watkin, another popular success. The piece shows how Gramps (Dudley Digges) is unwilling to die and leave his grandson in the unsympathetic hands of the boy's aunt. He traps Mr. Brink in an old appletree and by means of a charm prevents his descent. Without the ministration of death the entire world suffers, finding no surcease from its miseries, but Gramps holds out until the boy also dies and the two are happily united in the other world. As pointed out by the psychologists, the popularity of such glorifications of death may have indicated a mass impulse to suicide in times of depression and Nazi aggression, in an effort to find wish-fulfillment in fantasy. By contrast a less sentimental view of death was presented in John Hayden's *Lost Horizons* (1934), a play about a young woman who takes her life after being disappointed in love. From the heavenly Hall of Records she discovers that the remaining portion of her life held much in store for her and that by living she would also have aided a number of persons as yet unknown to her. These plays are arresting even though they are sometimes obvious in fantasy and negligible in their philosophy.

Another fantasy, Albert Bein's *Heavenly Express* (1940), interestingly combined the theme of death with hobo legend and song. Granny Graham, patroness of hobos, is dying. She is visited by the Overland Kid, legendary "bo" and now advance ticket taker for the Heavenly Express, which is also about to pick up Granny's vagrant and long-separated son. At Granny's boardinghouse the Kid again meets his old friend Ed Peeto, a famous engineer. As Granny is being told of the joys of Hobo Heaven and of her selection by the Almighty Vagabond to "mudder du boys an' mak 'em hot meals," the Heavenly Express arrives off stage with much noise to receive her. In the course of the play the Overland Kid sings various hobo classics—"The Wabash Cannonball," "Gila Monster Route," and "Hobo Convention"—and there is much allusion to customs and superstitions. For all its local color and authenticity Bein's fantasy lacked direction and dramatic cohesion, and lasted only briefly on Broadway, but it had at least the virtue of originality.

From death it was only a step to religious and philosophical fantasy. Among milder specimens we find *Father Malachy's Miracle* (1937), the dramatization of Bruce Marshall's novel by a Canadian writer, Brian Doherty. Humorously it shows the consternation of a priest when he unexpectedly performs a miracle by removing a dance hall twenty miles from his church. *Family Portrait* (1939) by Lenore Coffee and William Joyce Cowan is a simple, realistic portrayal of the family of Jesus which—because of its subject—might also be listed as

fantasy. On a grandiose scale Eugene O'Neill, it will be re-
called, served out large portions of pseudo philosophy in spectacular fantasies like *Marco Millions, The Fountain,* and
Lazarus Laughed, not by any means his dramatic forte. For
the capable handling of religious or philosophical themes in
the form of fantasy he was outdistanced by two other dramatists—Philip Barry and Thornton Wilder. The former's *Hotel
Universe* (1930) attempted to sustain its dramatic mood by
continuous performance without intermission. In this unusual
play the audience is introduced to a set of frustrated and
unhappy guests at the villa of Ann Field in the south of
France, where she is living with her aged semi-insane father,
formerly a scientist. The guests have all at some time con-
templated suicide, and Ann realizes that Pat, whom she loves
and who once loved her, is planning to take his life. Between
her and Pat stand an Oedipus complex and the suicide of an
English girl with whom he became involved. The frustration
of Lily, an actress, results from fixation on her father, a ham
actor of the old school. The other characters are also slaves
to something—Norman to business, Alice to her unrequited
passion for him, Hope to her overdeveloped maternal instinct,
and so on. Ann's father joins the group, and because of his
mystical awareness of several aspects of life knows all their
unconscious thoughts and difficulties. By inducing the guests
to reenact their past he brings the cause of their frustrations
out into the open. Impersonating Lily's father, with the actress
reverting to a scene in her childhood, he shows her that the
father she worships was actually a drunken bum. The old
scientist helps others as well, and before his death from a
cerebral hemorrhage he straightens out Pat's difficulties.
The guests are liberated from their frustrations, and Pat,
losing the impulse to suicide, will remain with Ann. *Hotel
Universe* of necessity relies on conversation rather than on
action and its message was too complex for wide popular appeal, but the suggestion of the weird, halfway world between
sanity and insanity proved effective and moving. The title in-

dicates that the play's message is not restricted to the characters, and the play holds interest as a dramatization of Freudian
analysis in nontechnical terms with perhaps a suggestion of
the Catholic confessional.

More bitter in tone, Barry's next fantasy—*Here Come the
Clowns* (1938)—took up the perennial problem of misery and
evil in the world. Here we have another assortment of baffled
and tortured characters, gathered together in the backroom
of the Café des Artistes run by Ma Speedy, a retired female
impersonator. The café, representing a small cross section of
the world, is connected with the Globe Theatre, a vaudeville
house operated by James Concannen (God), a benevolent
old gentleman who hasn't been around very much of late.
Among the patrons in the café are Major Armstrong, a
midget; Michael Clancy, a half-crazed stagehand; Connie,
chief usher at the Globe; her sister Nora, who was married
to Clancy but left him to live with another man; Jim Marble,
a ventriloquist, and his wife; Lew Cooper and Fay Farrell,
a vaudeville team. There is much discussion of Michael
Clancy's misfortunes—the loss of an eye in an accident, the
death of his young son, and the departure of his wife—and
also of Clancy's strange behavior in interrupting an act in
the Globe Theatre on Saturday night to call for someone in
the audience, presumably God. A newcomer arrives, Pabst
(the Devil), an illusionist who owns a share or two of Globe
stock. Asserting his interest in the truth and acting as master
of ceremonies, Pabst cynically gets some of the miserable
characters to put on their real acts. The ventriloquist, joking
with his dummy, reveals the tragic problem of his wife's lesbianism. The midget's cross in life is shown to be his wife's
bearing of a normal child, who became necessarily estranged
from his parents and ran away. Lew Cooper next is made to
run through the paces, and Pabst brings out that he is the
midget's son, a fact which accounts for his unresponsiveness
to the love of Fay Farrell. Clancy's wife then is induced to
reveal her affair with the other man and to confess that the

son whom Clancy loved so dearly was really fathered by her
lover. Crushed temporarily, Clancy still insists on finding
God and learning the reason for evil. Pabst, disguised as old
Mr. Concannen, gives him the stock answers, but Clancy
finally sees through him and at the end, when he is accidentally shot in trying to save his tormentor, he knows that he
has found God in the free will of man, which "can as easily
be turned to Good as to Bad" and which has the power to
overcome even death. This unusual play achieved a respectable run, partly through the excellent acting of Eddie Dowling as Clancy, and it indicated the existence at least of an
audience for religious and philosophical drama.

From the author of *The Bridge of San Luis Rey* one might
reasonably expect philosophical fantasy. *Our Town* (1938),
Thornton Wilder's most popular play, combines realism of
content with imaginative treatment. Played on a bare, curtain-
less stage, with Frank Craven as a homespun stage manager
and narrator with pipe and battered hat, it deals with as
universal a theme as does Gray's *Elegy:* the simple annals of a
village community; the lives, loves, and deaths that form the
pattern of existence in a small New England town. Wilder's
approach is expository and philosophic. His stage manager not
only gives the facts about Grover's Corners, New Hampshire,
but also interprets them; halts the action to show how something started or how it ended; raises questions about life or
marriage or immortality. In addition he arranges the simple
properties—tables, chairs, ladders—and plays several roles
himself, explaining carefully whom he is interpreting. Most
of the stage business is handled in pantomime—cooking
breakfast, picking beans, stroking a horse. Two ladders, which
the characters mount, represent the second story of the Gibbs
and Webb houses; several rows of chairs indicate the graves
of a hillside cemetery; actors planted in the audience ask questions or make comments. The real protagonist is the town of
Grover's Corners between 1901 and 1913, but several threads
of narrative emerge, mainly concerned with George Gibbs

(John Craven) and Emily Webb (Martha Scott), who go to school, fall in love, marry, and set out to run a farm. Emily dies in childbirth, and the poignant scene where she joins Mother Gibbs and other townspeople in the graveyard gives ample opportunity for philosophical comment. The dead are shown as indifferent to human affairs, waiting patiently for "the eternal part in them to come out clear." Their main conversation is about the weather. The presence of living persons in the cemetery brings only discomfort, and the dead take funerals and the grief of relatives quite casually. Emily, against the advice of Mother Gibbs, decides to go back—as she can do—among the living and recapitulate the events of her twelfth birthday. But she cannot bear the experience for long and returns to the graveyard—in life things happen too fast, and her knowledge of the future gives tragic irony to the most simple conversation. The earth is too wonderful, she concludes; human beings cannot fully realize life while they live it, they are blind and lacking in understanding. Only saints and poets, admits the stage manager, have a faint realization of what life is. The play ends with Frank Craven pulling the curtain across the stage; it is eleven P.M. and everyone in Grover's Corners is asleep. *Our Town*, it should be evident, offers a highly idealized conception of a New Hampshire village, free from the mean spirit and malicious gossip which are sometimes part of the picture. The sweetness and light of the author's attitude, however, made for a moving and stimulating performance on the stage and the play deservedly received the Pulitzer Prize for the season.

Less sentiment and more fantasy characterize *The Skin of Our Teeth* (1942), Thornton Wilder's tribute to man's genius for escaping destruction by the skin of his teeth in spite of such assorted dangers as the Ice Age, the Deluge, the evil in himself, war, and occasional discouragement. As long as he has his family and, more important, his books, he can find courage to go on and to rebuild, confident that he has learned much and is still learning. The main characters in this pano-

ramic saga of human indestructibility are Mr. George Antrobus of Excelsior, New Jersey, inventor of the wheel and the
lever, on the verge of completing the multiplication table and
the alphabet (he has just separated *em* from *en*); his wife,
Mrs. Antrobus, "every inch a mammal," inventor in her own
right (the apron, the gusset, the gore, frying in oil), who has
just celebrated her five thousandth wedding anniversary and
whose single purpose in life is to maintain her home and pro-
tect her children; and Lily Sabina, the perennial seducer of
man who is always overcome by the wife, however, and
eventually demoted to the kitchen. The Antrobuses have two
children, Gladys and Henry; the latter, formerly known as
Cain, represents the whining, unsocial tendencies in man.
Attractive minor characters include a mammoth and a dino-
saur, Judge Moses, a fortune teller (Florence Reed), and
several music teachers of a sort—the Misses E. Muse, T. Muse,
and M. Muse. The most entertaining act shows the Boardwalk at Atlantic City, where the Ancient and Honorable Order
of Mammals, Subdivision Humans, are holding a convention
and have just elected Mr. Antrobus president. George is temporarily seduced by Miss Lily-Sabina Fairweather, hostess of
the Boardwalk Bingo Parlor, to whom he has awarded the
prize in a beauty contest; but when the Deluge actually starts
it is not of her but of his wife and children that he thinks
first. Act I is concerned with man's survival of the Ice Age,
and Act III of devastation by war, with Mr. Antrobus—battered but still eager to build a new world—concluding that
in the struggle for existence all good and excellent things must
be fought for.

The unusual form of the play, the novel staging, the inspired
acting of Fredric March and Florence Eldridge as the Antrobuses and especially of Tallulah Bankhead as Sabina, all contributed to the spirit of playful spoofing which gave zest to
the performance. Beneath the fooling, of course, lay much
serious meaning for those who cared to look. To bring out his
points Wilder employed one or two devices of the Living

Newspaper—the voice of the announcer and the projection of films or lantern slides. In an attempt to disarm the audience of any hostility or lack of cooperation he has frequent humorous interruptions, as when Sabina steps out of character to tell the spectators that she hates the silly play and doesn't understand a word of it. "Oh—why can't we have plays like we used to have—" she asks; *"Peg o' My Heart,* and *Smilin' Thru,* and *The Bat,* good entertainment with a message you can take home with you?" The entire play is treated with humor and imagination. When fuel is needed to combat the Ice Age, there is a call for wood from the audience. Immediately the ushers rip up chairs and bring them down the aisles, giving Sabina the delightful first-act curtain line: "Pass up your chairs, everybody. Save the human race." Later, when a symbolical scene has to be prepared for, the stage manager interrupts the performance, announces the illness of seven actors from food poisoning, and proceeds to hold an impromptu rehearsal with the wardrobe mistress, the dresser, the captain of the ushers, etc. With regard to the symbolism the stage manager says confidentially to the audience: "I don't suppose it means anything. It's just a kind of poetic effect." Enough has been said, it is hoped, to suggest the high intellectual level of the play, enhanced by the pretense of not taking itself seriously. The fantasy is as freshly original as Saroyan's with this difference, that its ideas are not infantile.

The Skin of Our Teeth was sufficiently symbolic and nonrealistic to drive more than one spectator from the theatre in bafflement and infuriation. Nevertheless the play was clear as crystal in comparison with Gertrude Stein's opera, *Four Saints in Three Acts* (1934), which remained completely nonrepresentational in words and staging. The author's main premise was that saints weren't expected to do anything, only converse a little. This they did fluently in Miss Stein's musical, mannered style ("Pigeons on the grass alas") through four acts designated respectively: "*Avila:* St. Theresa half indoors and half out out of doors"; "Might it be mountains if it were not Barcelona"; *"Barcelona:* St. Ignatius and One of Two literally"; and "The Saints and Sisters reassembled and re-enacting why they went away to stay." The opera was sung and acted with great expressiveness by a cast of Negro singers before startlingly beautiful sets of translucent cellophane with a few palm trees in the foreground. The designs, the acting, the choreography, the direction, the music of Virgil Thomson all helped to create an unusual and delightful experience in the theatre—in many ways superior to the sterile patterns and arid conventions of ordinary opera. Here, perhaps, was the closest approximation to the ideals of Craig—purely aesthetic drama, divorced from realism, depending for its effects upon a fusion of the arts.

The general theatre public might ignore Gertrude Stein, whose opera attracted but a scant following of the *cognoscenti,* but it could scarcely disregard the loudly heralded appearance of a new poet on the dramatic horizon whose own claims of excellence were almost rivaled by the blare of critical comment pro and con. Already celebrated as a fiction writer, William Saroyan now became a Peter Pan among the dramatists, bringing unabashedly his ideals of perennial childhood to the theatre and delighting in tossing into the ash can the most venerable of dramatic conventions. The newcomer's Armenian background, his racial mysticism, his meager formal schooling but vast reading in the Fresno Public Library, his paradoxical admiration for Bernard Shaw, whom he called the strongest influence on his drama, his years as Postal Telegraph messenger and in other unliterary occupations on the West Coast, his inexhaustible creative energy, his boundless sentimentality, all help to explain the character and content of his dramatic fantasies, which differ materially from those of his predecessors. They have properly been called dream or symphonic plays, stressing mood rather than plot, for Saroyan abandoned the playwright's usual objectivity to give us himself and his ideas in a whimsically elaborate symbolism, as clear to him as it was obscure to the average theatregoer.

His work, as a result, was almost as nonrealistic and non-representational as Gertrude Stein's, despite his insistence that he is a realist.

The voluminous introductions and appendices to Saroyan's printed plays provide clear statements of his dramatic theories, which are based upon self-confidence and extreme individualism. A cardinal point in his dramaturgy is form-lessness. One of his own plays (*Sweeney in the Trees*) he describes as "anything you like, whatever you please" and another (*Love's Old Sweet Song*) as "literally a song." His main advice to young playwrights is emphatically not to take Professor Baker's course but to eat simple food, drink one's favorite liquor, and smile at a pretty face. Saroyan's natural distaste for stage tricks and technique finds its pet aversion in fluffy drawing-room comedy. In view of this scorn of conventional structure it is not surprising to learn that six acts were planned for *The Time of Your Life*, one for each day in the week, though the number was later changed to five. Few playwrights have given the public so many arcana or attendant circumstances about the creation of their work: the last-mentioned play, we are told, was composed in the Great Northern Hotel, the author ate at the Automat, his beverage was Scotch; *My Heart's in the Highlands* was dramatized from a short story he wrote when he was "feeling lousy" just before an emergency appendix operation. While Saroyan works rapidly, he has a passion for revision. An extreme example of this was seen during the run of his own production of *The Beautiful People* when he had to leave New York and the members of the cast received long daily telegrams suggesting changes in dialogue. As a playwright Saroyan states that he is not addressing "that collective non-entity" called the public, but the individual in the audience. With this in mind he arranged during the Pasadena Community Playhouse production of *Across the Boards on To-morrow Morning* to repeat the play immediately after the regular performance for any spectators that wished to see it again.

A closer view of Saroyan's plays will reveal the charm and novelty of his fantasy. His first Broadway production, *My Heart's in the Highlands* (1939), put on by the Group Theatre, returned—perhaps unconsciously—to the technique of the medieval miracle play by showing on the stage simultaneously a Fresno house and Mr. Kosak's grocery store. The time is August to November, 1914, and no act divisions are indicated. The occupants of the house are Johnny, a newsboy of nine, overwhelmed at the glory of ice cream in the world; his father, inveterate but unsuccessful poet who receives his poems back from *Atlantic Monthly* in a sad scene of the play; and the old grandmother who speaks only Armenian. To them comes Jasper McGregor, a very old man, once a Shakespearean actor and now a runaway from the Old People's Home. His heart is in the Highlands, however, and when the neighbors hear his bugle solo they all gather at the house with offerings of fruits and vegetables, including one eggplant. When he is taken back to the Home by guards eighteen days later, McGregor tells Johnny and his father that never before has he "communed with souls loftier, purer, or more delightful" than theirs. Three months later the little family must leave their home for nonpayment of rent. The grocer Mr. Kosak graciously cancels all bills, but Johnny's father insists on paying by giving his poems to little Esther Kosak, aged seven, who weeps and sobs because they are so beautiful. Just before leaving home the family are cheered by the sound of McGregor's bugle solo, "My Heart's in the Highlands"; the old man has run away again. The guards come after him, but after delivering some jumbled dramatic speeches from *Lear*, McGregor dies, though the sound of his bugle reverberates in the distance as the boy, the poet, and the grandmother turn the house over to the new tenants. Considering the fact that they have no place to go, Johnny ends the play by remarking, "I'm not mentioning any names, Pa, but something's wrong somewhere."

Simply and naïvely but with emotional force Saroyan not only shows the tragic lot of the poet or artist in a materialistic world but also emphasizes his real worth because he is lowly and pure in heart and courageous. Johnny's father consoles himself by saying, after denouncing the outbreak of war in Europe, "There will always be poets in the world." The innate graciousness of the grocer, the delicate understanding between father and son, the independent spirit of old McGregor are well brought out, but with the addition of considerable whimsy as when Johnny's father tries a somersault to keep up with his son. Defining a classic as "simply a first work, the beginning of a tradition," Saroyan expressed his belief that *My Heart's in the Highlands* was a classic and would have a profound influence on the new American theatre.

His next work, *The Time of Your Life* (1939), produced by Eddie Dowling, was more elaborate and less purely lyrical. It remains, however, a paean to human goodness, virtue, kindliness, and gentleness as these qualities flourish in Nick's Pacific Street Saloon in San Francisco, "a good, low-down, honky-tonk American place that lets people alone." In this terrestrial paradise a wealthy dipsomaniac (Eddie Dowling) sits day and night sipping champagne and listening to the Missouri Waltz on the juke box; he sends his devoted follower Tom on whimsical errands for toys or a Rand McNally Atlas or chewing gum of all flavors; he befriends a dreamy prostitute (Julie Haydon) and encourages her self-respect and basic innocence. Despite his rough exterior, Nick, owner and barkeeper, has a soft heart: he employs a penniless dancer (Gene Kelly) who thinks he has discovered a new kind of comedy, and also takes in a starving Negro boy whose piano playing is superlative. To the saloon comes a parade of Saroyan characters: Willie, the marble-game maniac who is always pitting his wit against the Machine; Dudley R. Bostwick, a young man in love whose natural and valuable ignorance has been spoiled by education; a policeman and his longshoreman friend who find themselves on different sides in the waterfront strike; Kit Carson, teller of tall stories that make Lightnin' look like an amateur; an Arab who keeps muttering in his beer, "No Foundation. All down the line." There are other lovable eccentrics, but someone always has to spoil things—Blick of the Vice Squad, lascivious and narrow-minded reformer who takes pleasure in hurting little people like the Negro boy and the prostitute, so that even the gentle Saroyan is forced to rise in his wrath and kill him off by the end of the play. *The Time of Your Life* has some resemblance to the vaudeville show with numerous separate acts, but all are blended together in the mellow mood of a mildly inebriated symphony which proclaims that people are wonderful and that the best ideal in life is to live and let live. In its own way, like *My Heart's in the Highlands,* the play emerges as a work of art. At the end of the season Saroyan was offered and promptly rejected the Pulitzer Prize because he felt that this particular piece was no better than his other dramatic work or different from it.

Many familiar elements appear in *Love's Old Sweet Song* (1940), presented jointly by Eddie Dowling and the Theatre Guild, but they were seasoned by impish satire. Here Saroyan is poking fun at the current sociological and leftist fad for writing about the Oakies, perhaps especially at Steinbeck's *Grapes of Wrath.* In Saroyan's fantasy the migrants from Oklahoma to California are Cabot Yearling, his pregnant wife Leona, and fourteen children—be believes he's the father of more than half of them—who camp en masse in Ann Hamilton's home and soon take possession of it. The Yearlings are perfectly happy and contented with their lot, but they are trailed wherever they go by a radical newspaperman who is collecting material for a novel of social significance and by a female photographer for *Life*—large, plain, bespectacled—a former Vassar girl. From the newspaperman Cabot has learned to his surprise that he has left Oklahoma to escape the dust, but he finally gets bored by the incessant talk and picture taking. At last the novelist and the photographer give up in despair and decide to get married; they will devote themselves henceforth to raising "the God-damnedest punks in the world." Ann's house is systematically wrecked and eventually burned down under the stress of the Yearling tenancy, but she wastes no time on worry, for she is desperately pursuing a vender of Dr. Greatheart's Five-Star Multi-Purpose Indian Remedy (Walter Huston), with whom she has fallen in love. As a matter of fact this love affair has been engineered by a comic Postal Telegraph messenger, who after the fire invites the entire group to the home of his father, Stylianos Americanos, an amiable Greek who practices fancy wrestling and possesses the reassuring philosophy, "Everything's going to be satisfactory"—as indeed it proves to be at the end of the play. This brief account does not do justice to many amusing lines and situations, but for all its excellence as a reading play *Love's Old Sweet Song* lasted but briefly on Broadway.

The minnesinger of tender family life delivered his most sentimental onslaught on the emotions in a play with "sadness in it," *The Beautiful People,* which he produced and directed himself in 1941. Owen, the hero, a preternaturally sensitive boy of fifteen, is grieving at the absence of his older brother, who has left the family circle and is now in New York, 3333 miles away. Owen prides himself on the fact that he has never done a day's work in his life; like his father, he is a loafer and a failure. True, he is an author, but as yet has written books of only one word each—"Trees," "Mouse." Verbs are pretty tricky and he's not ready to use them yet. His sister Agnes is on terms of intimate understanding with the mice in the house—the others call her St. Agnes of the Mice. These little creatures show their appreciation by praying for her when she is sick and by spelling her name on the floor with flowers—though it is Owen in reality who contrives these miracles. Agnes has been indifferent and even antipathetic to men, but now she falls in love with a stranger she meets on her way to the public library. The young man has aroused her deepest nature for the reason that his shoes don't fit, a description that induces her father to remark, "He's a good boy, Saint." Overwhelmed with pity and love, Agnes makes the discovery that all people are beautiful, and when she finds the boy again, her happiness is complete. Several quaint characters appear and there are temporary complications about a lost mouse and also about a monthly insurance check that the father has been cashing illegally for years, but the real climax comes at the end when a cornet solo is heard outside heralding the return of the absent brother. Owen is so moved by excess of emotion that he suddenly writes a book of two words—"My Brother"—and the family is happily united again under one roof. This gentle fantasy enables Saroyan to write touchingly about the sadness of love, the loveliness of people and of animals, the miracle of faith, the sweetness of family relations, the pleasures of idleness, the wonder of the universe. While the play was more an artistic than a commercial success, it managed to run 120 performances on Broadway and it won over many of the normally dour critics. It further showed Saroyan's uncanny skill in the unorthodox method of casting his plays by approaching strangers in bars, subways, garages, nightclubs, and other public places. By this unconventional method, which Belasco occasionally used, he selected Betsy Blair for the part of Agnes, an excellent choice. Young Owen was played by Eugene Loring, ballet dancer and choreographer of *Billy the Kid*.

A later Saroyan production on Broadway, *Get Away Old Man* (1943), proved to be an inferior and unsuccessful piece about an unsavory moving-picture producer who is shown in sharp contrast to the usual lovely characters in the play, apparently a reflection of the author's brief experience in Hollywood. His numerous other plays either were not produced or were put on by the nonprofessional theatre; the latter productions including *Across the Board on Tomorrow Morning* at the Pasadena Community Playhouse, another barroom fantasy, and *Sweeney in the Trees* at the Cape Theatre, Cape May, New Jersey, an involved play in which the hero is strangely bisected into two characters—Sweeney and Sweeney Himself. Saroyan's minor work is extravagantly labored and over-whimsical, with fatal reminiscences of his earlier plays. A popular but excessively tearful movie with Mickey Rooney as the inevitable telegraph boy was based on the novel *The Human Comedy*, which Clifton Fadiman had once called the Kiddies' Tolstoy, but in theatre or cinema Saroyan has so far never equaled the artistic achievement of *My Heart's in the Highlands* or *The Time of Your Life*.

It should be evident that the content of Saroyan's fantasy is simple and general. His ideas are understandable but limited. He sings the basic goodness of man, with the violent exception of a few individuals like Blick or the moving-picture magnate. The child and the poet are blessed with the highest spiritual values. The dipsomaniac Joe expresses a characteristic Saroyan sentiment when he says: "I believe in dreams sooner than statistics." Eager as Saroyan is to support the rights of little people, he dislikes both unionism and communism because of their infringements on individual freedom. Idleness and alcoholism are infinitely more commendable than the sordid practice of selling things for profit; the only reasonable motive for acquiring wealth is for the pleasure of giving it away. Formal education, particularly in college, spoils man's natural and charming ignorance. Romantic love is a beautiful and infinitely sad emotion. In family relationships, particularly between father and son and between brothers and sisters, is to be found the most tender expression of love, a motif in the plays amounting to a veritable cult of childhood. Without denying the validity of many items in the Saroyan credo we must admit that they are often infantile, repetitious, and unduly naïve, showing little contact with the real world. His theatrical devices also tend to wear thin—

the philosophical messenger boys, the benevolent alcoholics, the eccentric personages that pop in and out, the "cuteness" and sometimes infuriating whimsicality of dialogue and stage business, all presented with a certain sameness that gives the impression that Saroyan is imitating himself. And yet, once his many faults and limitations as a playwright have been catalogued, one must admit that by some obscure miracle his plays show more real originality than those of O'Neill, Green, and Anderson put together.

The sampling of imaginative plays offered in this chapter should serve to justify the insurgent movement of 1912–1917. In the past, in regionalism, in fantasy, in folk drama, in poetical tragedy the art theatre found its special fields of cultivation. If the crop of imaginative plays was not as ample as expected or as widely in demand as other types by the theatre public, the quality at its best was extremely high. Modern American drama would lose a large part of its lustre if plays like *Our Town, Green Pastures, My Heart's in the Highlands, Mary of Scotland,* or *Here Come the Clowns* were to be struck from the rolls—productions that would scarcely have reached the boards at all in the Frohman-Belasco era. Equally important, the drama of realism and social significance was modified and ennobled by the new stagecraft and the new imagination, so that poetic beauty and even fantasy might be pressed to the uses of propaganda.

Chapter 5

THE WORLD WE LIVE IN

*T*HE POETS, the mystics, the historical dramatists, and even the local colorists turned their backs deliberately on humdrum reality or else tried to delve behind it to
discover their special version of the inner truth. The majority
of American dramatists, however, were hard-bitten, literal-
minded individualists who preferred to examine the contemporary scene with accurate and often jaundiced eyes. In
their plays they might merely report what they saw, or thumb
their noses from the sidelines at the picture of human im-
becility, or take sides in the clash of contemporary issues.
Like the imaginative playwrights they looked at first to
Europe for models and inspiration—Shaw, Galsworthy, Tolstoy, Chekhov—and like them also they claimed O'Neill and
Anderson for their own, but for different reasons. What they
admired most in these American dramatists was realism of
dialogue, frankness about sex, concern about the Negro and
other underprivileged groups, interest in contemporary political and social issues. The new realists shared also with
their imaginative brethren the desire to reform commercial
Broadway and, as stressed earlier, they had no quarrel with
the art theatre. Many of them, indeed, might be called
imaginative-realists and are not too distinguishable from the
dramatists of the previous chapter.

Foreign models of realism were not new on Broadway.
Galsworthy's *Justice* with John Barrymore in 1916 has been
mentioned earlier, as well as the many productions of Shaw,
who after 1919 became duly enshrined in the Theatre Guild's
pantheon of dramatists. In 1918 Lionel Atwill and Alla Nazi-

mova appeared in the excellent Hopkins revivals of Ibsen. More spectacular were the same director's productions of Tolstoy's *Redemption* (1918) and Gorki's *Night Lodging* (1919), with John Barrymore in the former properly photogenic as a somber Russian ravaged by dissipation and unhappy passions. Early Guild offerings, too, leaned heavily on realism: Ervine's *John Ferguson* (1919) and *Jane Clegg* (1920), for example, or Tolstoy's *Power of Darkness* (1920). To these, the native plays were soon offering rivalry which included O'Neill's stark tragedy *Beyond the Horizon* and the Stallings-Anderson antiwar drama *What Price Glory?* Other playwrights were making realism more exclusively their field—among them were George Kelly, Elmer Rice, Sidney Howard, John Howard Lawson, and Robert Sherwood.

What topics and themes were proving attractive to these new realists and to the audiences that applauded them? How did their attitudes change in the twenty-five odd years after 1918? At the start the postwar playwrights shared the spirit of disillusioned questioning that pervaded the fiction and poetry of the "lost generation." The typical attitude was negative, critical, often cynical. In drama it generally took the form of debunking the pretensions and ideals of middle-class culture. All kinds of problems—social, ethical, psychological, religious, political—aroused dramatic comment. In manners and morals we have already noted the timid prewar discussion on the stage of topics like feminism, trial marriage, psychoanalysis, and Greenwich Village. The moral revolution, greatly accelerated by the First World War, was now reinforced by a systematic study of Freud, with the result that the ethical code of the Frohman-Belasco era was promptly relegated to the movies and producers plunged in where angels—heavenly and Broadway—had feared to tread. Not of course without the frenzied protests of censors, official and self-appointed, who objected to practically everything on the stage from O'Neill onward. In addition to liberalizing morals the dramatists delighted in attacking patriotism and hundredpercent Americanism, following the novelists in espousing pacifism. Yet the prevailing dramatic aversion to outright propaganda fostered the dramatists' naturally negative outlook and led to preachment by indirection. It was not until the thirties that Nazi aggression in Europe compelled the playwrights to adopt a positive stand in defending democracy, and even war. In the same period the business depression also converted many of them to the Soviet slogan that the theatre is a weapon. Thus the general trend was from disillusion to reform and from reform to propaganda. Without recourse to strict chronology or to unified discussion according to author it may be illuminating to trace the progress of the reformist movement as illustrated in the significant plays of the time.

No dramatic work better expresses the complete disillusionment of the postwar era than a later play by Robert Sherwood, *The Petrified Forest* (1935), in which the author portrays a hopeless intellectual suffering from inertia and a flock of neuroses in a world of outmoded ideas. This defunct world is symbolized by the petrified forest: "Platonism—patriotism—Christianity—Romance—the economics of Adam Smith—they're all so many dead stumps in the desert." The feeble hero (Leslie Howard) looks impotent and condemned; the futility of his life is expressed by his past: he wrote a New England novel, married his publisher's wife, and became separated from her after she had taken up with a Brazilian painter. Now a penniless hitchhiker, he reaches the Black Mesa Bar-B-Q in Arizona. The unconventional heroine, who waits on him in the lunchroom, offers him the opportunities for love and courageous living, but he lacks the vitality to accept and can find salvation only in death with the promise of burial in the petrified forest. The Bar-B-Q is temporarily occupied by a fleeing gangster (Humphrey Bogart), who later grants the hero his boon of extinction. But even the gangster belongs to the same graveyard, for he also is a relic of the past, "the last great apostle of rugged individualism."

The only hope for the world lies in the vitality of the young heroine, but it is clear that the hope is not a very high one. Sherwood's excellent concoction of philosophy and melodrama shows the playwright of the middle thirties fumbling desperately for conversion to something positive. In this respect the play shows some intellectual advance over the characteristic apathy of the earlier period, illustrated—let us say—in Gilbert Emery's *The Hero* (1921). Here the point is that for all his medals a war hero may be a rotter. Cautiously making his protagonist a veteran not of the United States Army but of the Foreign Legion, Emery shows him on his return to America making love to his brother's wife, seducing a Belgian refugee, and stealing money from a church fund. The play is interesting for its expression of disillusionment about heroism, but the issue is muddled by lack of positive comment and by the sudden sympathetic twist at the end whereby the villain is shown losing his life to save a child from fire.

To his itemization of dead stumps in the petrified forest Robert Sherwood might well have added Victorian morality, for the revolution in sex mores was manifested directly or indirectly in practically all the postwar plays, regardless of subject. The more comic variations will be reserved for the succeeding chapter; some traces have already been noted in the drama of imagination, including the plays of O'Neill. By 1924 the enthusiastic reception of Sidney Howard's *They Knew What They Wanted* showed clearly that, whether or not the conservatives approved, a freer and broader conception of individual morality had gained wide acceptance in America. This excellent play has to do with three main characters: Tony Patucci, Italian-American proprietor of a vineyard in California who has prospered under Prohibition; Amy, a waitress he saw in a San Francisco restaurant and to whom he has proposed by mail; and Joe, Wobbly and migratory worker, who is at the moment acting as Tony's foreman and correspondent. The basic desires in life of these persons are simple—Tony wants children, Amy wants a home, and Joe wants freedom from ties and responsibilities. But there are complications. Tony has impulsively enclosed Joe's picture with his proposal because he thought Amy would be more likely to accept a younger man, and Amy is naturally shocked when she discovers that Joe is not the bridegroom. In the excitement of the wedding day Tony has had an automobile accident; both his legs are broken and he will be an invalid for several months. Nevertheless Amy goes through the marriage ceremony because she loves the place, but, lonely and suffering an emotional rebound from her disappointment, spends her wedding night with Joe. When she later finds out she is pregnant, Joe offers to go away with her, but neither is happy at the prospect. While nursing Tony through convalescence Amy has grown to love him for his goodness, and now she bravely tells him the truth. At first he falls into a rage, but reflection shows him that convention is wrong and he insists that she remain with him: Joe is a natural wanderer and there will be no one to take care of her. Amy thus gets what she has wanted, a home; Joe is still free to move about with the I.W.W.; and Tony has a child, though not his own. All accept the situation with no concern about the moral code. The great success of the play, which received the Pulitzer Prize, was largely due—it must be added—to one of the memorable productions of the modern theatre, with Glenn Anders as Joe, Pauline Lord as Amy, and Richard Bennett as Tony. Their performance provided another example of inspired realism, which brought the play close to the drama of imagination. In the matter of moral freedom, of course, *They Knew What They Wanted* was far exceeded by later plays like *Strange Interlude* and *Design for Living*, where promiscuity becomes the normal thing.

An unsuccessful but interesting clinical study of the subject was offered by Maxwell Anderson in a realistic Greenwich Village tragedy. *Gypsy* (1929) is at once a study of Bohemian manners and a Freudian analysis of character. Ellen,

the heroine, is temperamentally and congenitally promiscu-
ous; her intentions are good but she just cannot remain true
to any one man—a weakness she attributes to childhood recollections of her mother's marital unfaithfulness—and she is
violently irked by the slightest suggestion of bondage in her
own marriage. Her husband is sympathetic and understanding, but she bitterly regrets having gone back on her principles
and having sworn away her freedom by accepting marriage.
She has an abortion rather than bear a child, insists on financial independence by working, leaves her husband (a second
time), parts from her favored lover, and is about to embark
on a new affair as the play ends. In production this conclusion
was altered and sentimentalized to permit the heroine to commit suicide, an ending more morally satisfying but not so
much in character. The play provides a good study of the
new woman, genus Greenwich Village, in her natural habitat,
but it was not sufficiently pointed and remained confusing in
purpose. While the portrait of Ellen is not a sympathetic one,
ten years earlier the mere fact of its frankness of treatment
would have kept it from the stage.

Numerous other playwrights raided Freud for themes and
ideas. In earlier drama the American worship of motherhood
had found embodiment in a plethora of saccharine stage
mothers—a good example was seen in *Turn to the Right*—or
in the even more cloying moving-picture version of the
species, the woman with white hair, spectacles, incredible
goodness, blind devotion to her son, and limited mentality.
While the central character was not meant to be typical, Sidney Howard's *The Silver Cord* (1926) nevertheless by contrast was refreshing in its debunking of motherhood of an
extreme type. In this play the mother has two sons—her "big
boys" she calls them—whom she holds and tyrannizes over
with fussing and affection. The elder has been in Europe,
away from her influence long enough to marry a biologist; the
younger brother is at the moment engaged. With deceptive
feminine wiles Mrs. Phelps breaks the younger son's engage-

ment and almost succeeds in separating the other one from his wife. But the biologist knows the facts and exposes the mother in her true light, bringing the boys to a realization of their Oedipus complexes. The younger son, doomed, is powerless to leave home, but the elder is able to break away from his maternal ties. Mrs. Phelps' abnormal devotion is shown as springing from an unhappy marriage which made her transfer her sexual emotion into incestuous love for her children. Convincingly played by Laura Hope Crews, Mrs. Phelps is perhaps oversimplified in characterization, but the play was a welcome relief from the usual sentimentality and it hit the popular taste.

Other types of psychological abnormalities made their appearance in drama. In 1926 Edouard Bourdet's *The Captive*, adapted from the French by Arthur Hornblow, Jr., aroused indignation and a violent storm of protest because of its theme, the abnormal love of one woman for another. The play won a *succès de scandale*, bringing crowded houses, but in spite of dignified and restrained treatment of the subject, it had to be withdrawn on threat of censorship. One of its humorous byproducts was to mark the inoffensive bouquet of violets as a symbol of Lesbianism, decreasing the popularity of this humble posy in the New York flower marts. The theme of *The Captive* in the milder form of schoolgirl crushes appeared again in Katharine Clugston's *These Days* (1928), in which young Katharine Hepburn attracted notice for her playing of a character bit, as well as in a German film of 1932, *Mäedchen in Uniform*. An unfounded accusation of Lesbianism formed the subject of Lillian Hellman's powerful play, *The Children's Hour*, in 1934. Homosexualism—that old standby of the burlesque show—became occasionally the subject of serious drama, but not with marked success, except perhaps in Mordaunt Shairp's *The Green Bay Tree* (1933), an English play. With or without sexual irregularities, insanity and subnormality were commonly represented on the stage. Steinbeck's *Of Mice and Men* made good dramatic material out of Lennie, the moron who loves anything soft and furry but accidentally kills the varied objects of his affection. Other controversial or formerly proscribed topics, such as miscegenation or abortion or incest, were receiving dramatic treatment, until by the thirties almost any subject—censorship notwithstanding—could be presented in the New York theatre.

Closely related to the new outlook on morality was a changed attitude toward religion. The ministry had formerly, as a rule, received deferential treatment on the stage; now the playwright began to apply his customary technique of debunking, exposing hypocrisy and charlatanism in the church and gleefully pointing out the subconscious relations between religion and sex. A daring example in 1922 was the popular *Rain*, a dramatization by John Colton and Clemence Randolf of a short story by Somerset Maugham. Among passengers debarking at Pago Pago in the South Seas are the Reverend and Mrs. Davidson, missionaries, and the vulgar but happy Sadie Thompson with her victrola and her retinue of sailors. Davidson forthwith decides to reform Sadie by the persistent application of exhortation and force. As a missionary he has had many battles with depravity; of the natives under his care he says, "We had to teach them what sin is. We had to make sins out of what they thought were only natural actions." Putting the pressure on Sadie, he finally works her up to religious hysteria until she is willing to save her soul by returning to San Francisco to serve a prison sentence. The good missionary's sexual repressions have been finding expression in dreams about the mountains of Nebraska, mammary symbols, and when he visits Sadie at night to clinch her soul his inhibitions break down completely. As a result, the disillusioned Sadie returns to her sinful ways and Davidson is found on the beach next day, his throat cut. The play is melodramatic and rather obvious in its psychoanalysis, but with the playing of Robert Kelly as Davidson and Jeanne Eagels as the hard-boiled Sadie it made good theatre.

Patrick Kearney's dramatization of Dreiser's *An American Tragedy* (1926) had something to say about the hero's repressions in a childhood dominated by religion and the Salvation Army. A more direct blow below the Bible belt line appeared the same year in William Hurlbut's *The Bride of the Lamb*, a good psychological study of sex and evangelism. In it Alice Brady gave a moving portrayal of an unhappy, frustrated woman, wife of a dentist in a small town, whose religious frenzy turns into passionate erotic attachment for the Reverend Albaugh, tent evangelist and "go-getter for the Lord." Her carnal affair with the evangelist ends with the poisoning of her husband and the discovery that Albaugh is already married; at this point she goes completely insane and the final curtain finds her introducing everyone to the bridegroom, Mr. Christ. Later plays—*Bless You, Sister* (1927) and *Salvation* (1928)—deal with female evangelists engaged in the business of religion in a period when Aimée Semple McPherson and her godly sisters were figuring prominently in the news. *Tobacco Road*, too, includes a comic example of a woman preacher with an eye to business and sex.

Nowhere was the technique of debunking applied with more force and vigor than in a concerted attack on war and patriotism. Maxwell Anderson fired the first big gun of the campaign in 1924 with *What Price Glory?*, written in collaboration with Laurence Stallings, a fellow newspaperman on the New York *World*. The play, produced by Arthur Hopkins, was widely publicized at the time as the first attempt in the theatre to give a realistic portrayal of war in contrast to the sentimental, patriotic, and musical-comedy versions of previous years. *What Price Glory?* deals with the United States Marines in France, either at the company headquarters back of the lines or at the front itself. Brave and capable fighters, they are a truculent, hard-boiled lot, especially in their moments of relaxation, which they devote wholeheartedly to profanity, gambling, drinking, and whoring. Toughest

and most picturesque of the lot is Captain Flagg—at least
until the arrival of a new top sergeant, Quirt, with whom
Flagg has had encounters before all over the world, usually
about women. The remainder of the play is mainly concerned
with the epic rivalry between the two men for the favors of a
French girl, Charmaine, who proves equally obliging to both.
War is represented at its most brutal and realistic in the second
act when the men are fighting in the trenches, and this portion
especially attempts to tarnish its glory. The final act returns to
more romantic matters, most notable being the heroic drinking bout between Flagg and Quirt, in which with elaborate
etiquette and barbed compliments the two men review their
past rivalries and play cards for possession of Charmaine.
Quirt is caught cheating and the Captain wins with the aid
of a pistol, only to learn that his outfit is immediately ordered
back to the front. Quirt is left with a clear field, but although
a wounded leg entitles him to remain hospitalized he rushes
heroically in his pajamas out of Cognac Pete's with the well-
known line, "Hey, Flagg, wait for baby!"

The play thus combines an indictment against the horror
and futility of war with a series of colorful episodes which
tend to make the two rivals, in spite and because of their very
toughness, grandiose and heroic. In performance the superb
playing of Louis Wolheim (Yank of *The Hairy Ape*) and William Boyd emphasized the romantic characterization with
correspondent weakening of the antiwar message. However,
the play brought crowded houses and was probably more
effective in driving home its point than an all-out propaganda
play would have been. The realistic second act was particularly successful in its satire, which hits both at the combatants
and the people back home—the "army majors back in Paris
who ain't going to let anybody do any seducing but themselves," the "thirty-day-wonder lieutenants" fresh out of college, the "band of Gideons from Headquarters bringing more
of that world safe for democracy slush," and the "Yankee
Doodles back in Hoboken." Lieutenant Moore, wounded and

hysterical, gives the title and expresses the point of the play: "What price glory now? Why in God's name can't we all go home? Who gives a damn for this lousy, stinking little town but the poor French devils who live here?" These lines will give a faint idea of the quality of the dialogue; in profanity and strong language the play followed the tradition established by O'Neill which led eventually to *Tobacco Road* and *Dead End*. The sensational success of *What Price Glory?* in the face of agonized protests from patriotic and conservative forces showed clearly that pacifism was in the air, and, like *They Knew What They Wanted* of the same year, the production indicated significant postwar trends. It is debatable whether Anderson, with or without collaboration, ever wrote a finer or more important play.

Other early broadsides against war include an English importation, R. C. Sherriff's *Journey's End* (1929), which revealed tragically the psychological effect of war on the men in the trenches. The attack was continued when war threatened again in the troubled thirties. In 1935 Sidney Howard wrote his grim but unsuccessful *Paths of Glory*. Only slightly more successful was Paul Green's *Johnny Johnson* (1936), an imaginative and ironical "biography of a common man" with multiple scenes and the aid of music by Kurt Weill. Johnny Johnson—a plain man from the sticks—takes literally the slogans of 1917 that "this is a war to end wars" and that he is fighting the German leaders, not the common people. In France he makes valiant attempts to end the war by getting the ordinary German and Allied soldiers together; he succeeds in administering laughing gas to the Allied High Command and temporarily halts the conflict, only to be adjudged insane and sent to a mental hospital. Green brings out effectively, of course, that Johnson is the only sane character in the play with the insight and courage to get at the heart of the matter. Irwin Shaw's *Bury the Dead* (1936), first brought out under radical auspices, is a forceful though somewhat hysterical fantasy about a handful of dead soldiers in a new war who refuse to be buried. The generals, the church, the state, their womenfolk, all plead with them to submit to quiet burial, but they are determined to enjoy the experiences they have been deprived of by poverty and war. They are joined by several living soldiers with a symbolism which suggests a world revolution by the downtrodden. In this play as in *Johnny Johnson* the methods of imaginative drama are employed for realistic propaganda purposes in support of pacifism.

Opposition to war, in less sermonizing form, was a favorite theme with Robert Sherwood, whose first play, *The Road to Rome* (1927), included some pointed satire on the subject. In 1936 his *Idiot's Delight* brilliantly united a diversity of themes and characters into a much stronger attack on war. A heterogeneous collection of guests find themselves in an Italian hotel near the Swiss and Austrian borders. Some are vacationing; most are merely held up, unable to cross the frontier because of the imminence of a new war. Among them are a German scientist about to discover a cure for cancer; an English couple on their honeymoon; a voluble French Communist; a munitions magnate with his exotic Russian mistress, Irene, superlative teller of tall tales; and a bevy of American chorus girls piloted on a Balkan tour by Harry Van, hoofer and supersalesman in any venture requiring sharp wits. When Italian planes bomb Paris and war actually comes, the Europeans—even the French Communist who has been preaching internationalism—become violently chauvinistic. The only true internationalist is the munitions maker, who sells his wares impartially to all sides. Irene stirs him to unpleasant self-reflection in a scene of sadistic irony. He goes on to Paris alone, leaving her without papers or passport. Van, who has been trying to place Irene in his memories of the past, suddenly decides she is a dancer with whom he spent the night in an Omaha hotel back in 1925. He sees his chorus girls safely on the train, but chooses to return to the hotel, where he and Irene order champagne and sing "Onward Christian Soldiers" as the bombs begin to fall.

In Van, salesman and sharper, the author has portrayed an optimist whose many deceptions of the human race have not made him contemptuous of it but rather have impressed him with the value of faith: "No matter how much the *meek* may be bulldozed or gypped, they *will* eventually inherit the earth." He has shown his chivalric spirit in returning to Irene, and she feels that he has a trustworthy heart. They—the decent little people—are the victims of a war designed just to kill them. To this injustice God remains casually indifferent. In a speech that gives the play its title Irene says:

We don't do half enough justice to Him. Poor, lonely old soul. Sitting up in heaven with nothing to do, but play solitaire. Poor dear God. Playing Idiot's Delight. The game that never means anything, and that never ends.

It should be evident from this résumé that Sherwood's play has numerous points to make about the universe, patriotism, munitions, faith. At the same time it includes a bizarre love affair between an engaging liar and a likable charlatan with roles made to order for Lynn Fontanne and Alfred Lunt, who played them with customary perfection. The pyrotechnic diversity of interests may minimize the impact of the antiwar and pro-faith message, but it undeniably adds to the naturalness and humor, and it avoids the propagandizing that makes plays like *Bury the Dead* seem unpleasantly obvious. In the same way *What Price Glory?* as an antiwar play gained rather than lost by the Flagg-Quirt rivalry over Charmaine. In the final analysis the question boils down to whether one likes to have a message presented obliquely or be hit over the head with it.

The rapid march of European history in the thirties left the realistic playwright gasping and confused. We may detect, however, the change from a negative to a positive attitude in a play like *Idiot's Delight* that envisions at least the possibility of faith in the midst of chaos and disillusionment. The dramatists of the previous decade had been distrustful of preachment, but their Olympian objectivity was disturbed successfully by the financial depression and the rapid expansion of totalitarianism in Europe. Faced with unmistakable signs of a crumbling social order and a new world war, the playwright now felt a desperate need of conversion to something or other. But years of puncturing ideals and of conditioning himself and his audience against war were placing him in an uncomfortable position. Then again, to what should he be converted? For some communism offered a faith, but the older established dramatists—while liberal or even radical—were individualists at heart and unwilling or unable to hew to any party line. The only solution, sometimes a painful one, was to espouse democracy, a political system whose defects they had long been pointing out, and to hug the once-abused middle classes to their bosoms. The leftist writers held out as long as possible for pacifism, since this was one of the cardinal tenets in their propaganda directed at American youth, but sooner or later events forced all dramatists to reverse their position on war.

Liberal and leftist could agree on attacking fascism and nazism. Plays like Elmer Rice's *Judgment Day* (1934) and Victor Wolfson's *Bitter Stream* (1936) dealt dramatic blows at European dictatorship. Sinclair Lewis' *It Can't Happen Here* (1936), dramatized with the aid of John C. Moffitt, pointed out the dangers of fascism in this country, while Maxwell Anderson's *Key Largo* (1939) blamed intellectualism and mechanistic science for its failure to provide moral ideals. This and other plays deplored the tragic defeat of Loyalist Spain by Franco's fascist cohorts. By the late thirties Anderson and other playwrights were writing in defense of democracy, though not without some mention of its defects. One good example was *The American Way* by George S. Kaufman and Moss Hart, with music by Oscar Levant, which opened in 1939 at the large Center Theatre. This was a panoramic spectacle—not unlike Noel Coward's *Cavalcade*—depicting the fortunes of German immigrants, Martin and Irma

Gunther, from their arrival at Ellis Island in 1896 to the rise
of the Nazi Brownshirt movement in the United States.
Among the high spots covered during three generations of
Gunthers are the election of McKinley, the outbreak of the
First World War with its tragic implications for German-
Americans, the Lindbergh flight to Paris in 1927, the election
of Roosevelt, the effects of the depression on the young
people, who are driven to false panaceas, and Martin's sacrifice of his life in denouncing the antidemocratic Brown-
shirts. The play's thesis that democracy has successfully met
crises before and will survive as long as men are willing to
die for freedom is offered as a ray of hope in a world gone
mad. With the able support of Fredric March and Florence
Eldridge as the German couple, *The American Way* provided
stirring patriotic propaganda devoid of the satirical cynicism
of the twenties concerning the American scene.

Two interesting plays of 1939 were calls to positive action.
Irwin Shaw's *The Gentle People,* labeled variously by the
author "a Brooklyn fable" and "a fairy tale with a moral,"
treated the Nazi problem symbolically in a story of two harmless old men who turn on their gangster tormentor. Jonah
Goodman (Sam Jaffe) and Philip Agnagnos (Roman Boh-
nen) find surcease from domestic and financial worries in
fishing from an old boat off a Coney Island pier. A petty
gangster (Franchot Tone) breaks into their peaceful life by
seducing Goodman's daughter (Sylvia Sidney) and demanding exorbitant sums of money for "protecting" their boat.
When they protest to the police they discover that the
gangster is working in cooperation with the courts and they
are finally driven to take the law into their own hands. They
plan the gangster's murder in a dramatic scene quaintly set
in the steam room of a Russian bath and later—in spite of
their distaste for violence—they succeed in their attempt. In
its simplicity and originality, without recourse to oratory,
this Group Theatre production proved one of the best of the
anti-Nazi plays. The other work, Robert Ardrey's *Thunder*

Rock, employed fantasy to drive home its message. The protagonist is a disillusioned newspaperman who has completely retired from the world and is now enjoying his lonesome job as keeper of Thunder Rock Lighthouse on Lake Michigan. He flatly refuses the invitation of an old college friend to fly planes in China against the Japanese. In the lighthouse his only companions are ghosts—the crew and passengers of a ship that sank at this very spot in 1849. From conversation with them he discovers that they too faced discouragement and disillusionment in their day, and he is eventually convinced that he can no longer stand by but must join the conflict, "not fighting for fighting's sake, but to make a new world of the old." Also presented by the Group Theatre, with Luther Adler in the lead, *Thunder Rock* was unsuccessful on Broadway but proved one of the great London hits during the war. Though not as well-knit or convincing as Shaw's play, it was unusual in its use of fantasy, and it shows the desire of the more radical writers to lure the disillusioned intellectuals down from their ivory towers.

By the late thirties Robert Sherwood had already heeded the call. The historical *Abe Lincoln in Illinois* had expressed his faith in the New Deal and *Idiot's Delight* had reasserted his faith in the common man. In 1939 the Russo-Finnish war offered an opportunity to champion a small democracy engaged in an unequal struggle. *There Shall Be No Night,* which opened with the Lunts early in 1940, traces the conversion of an eminent scientist—an internationalist to whom patriotism is "one of the most virulent manifestations of evil"—to the firm belief that while war is a dirty job it is one that must be performed. Although he and his wife are urged to take refuge in the United States, they choose to stay; eventually the scientist goes calmly and bravely to his death in battle. In his analysis of the world situation, the scientist feels that the most prevalent modern diseases are degenerative ones—insanity and cancer. Against these, man's only defenses lie in the mind—in men's desire to know themselves and in their will-

ingness to die in this quest, thus "conquering bestiality with
the power of light that is in our minds." Can we complete the
exploration of man himself, he asks, "before the process of
man's degeneration has been completed and he is again a witless ape, groping his way back into the jungle?" Sherwood
takes occasion to attack German theories of racial superiority
and to cast a few jibes at Americans for their easy living and
their indifference to European events. *There Shall Be No
Night* is notable for its simple, moving presentation of middle-
class life and ideas without the aid of theatrical tricks or fireworks. Before long it became dated, however, in one of the
intricate political turnabouts in Europe which saw Finland
fighting on the side of Nazi Germany. The play's general message still held true, as Sherwood pointed out, but the American
public began to wonder whether Russia might not have
had good reason for its Finnish policies. After 1939, for that
matter, even the radical playwrights had difficulty in keeping
abreast of historical events. The labor review *Pins and
Needles*, which had ridiculed Hitler and other political figures
in the sketch "Four Little Angels of Peace," was shocked by
the Soviet-Nazi Pact of 1939 into adding a fifth angel in its
revised version of the play—none other than Joseph Stalin.

With the outbreak of war in Europe the dramatists had
stepped up their efforts to denounce nazism abroad and at
home, including the related perils of complacency or isolationism in America. While the plays were competent and often
effective, few of them rose above the stage of black-and-white
propaganda nor were they able to compete with the dramatic
sweep of actual events. Among the better stage examples was
Elmer Rice's *Flight to the West* (1940), set entirely on the
Yankee Clipper during the flight from Lisbon to New York.
The passengers include a few refugees, an American business
man who advocates playing ball with the dictators, a confused liberal, a young American Jew with his Christian wife,
a Nazi diplomat, and a German secret agent. Rice employs
this assorted group to prove convincingly that European di-

visions and hatreds must necessarily find their way to America. The weakness of the Nazi way of life, according to the author, lies in its uncompromising rationality, which becomes insanity when carried out to its ruthless, logical extreme. Another play, Maxwell Anderson's *Candle in the Wind* (1941), found the Achilles heel of the Nazi system in its effects on the human spirit; even the Germans must eventually break under the strain of performing actions that revolt them. Concerned with the fall of Paris, Anderson's plot relates the campaign of an American girl (Helen Hayes) to release her French sweetheart from a concentration camp. John Steinbeck's *The Moon Is Down* (1942), an account of the Nazi occupation of Norway, praised the quiet, relentless resistance of free men but was attacked vigorously for representing the German officers in not too monstrous or fiendish a light. Shifting to the American scene, *Tomorrow the World* (1943) by James Gow and Armand d'Usseau showed the results of Nazi indoctrination of youth in the diminutive but vicious person of a twelve-year-old (Skippy Homeier), brought to the United States from Germany. Some of these plays were not without the element of wish fulfillment in their predictions of eventual Nazi defeat, but they wielded considerable influence over their audiences in solidifying opinion against all forms of fascism.

The high point of anti-Nazi or pro-democratic drama is to be seen in two widely popular plays, one written before our entry into the war, the other after. The first of these, Lillian Hellman's *Watch on the Rhine* (1941), gently chided Americans for their complacent feeling of security about the European situation. To the luxurious home of a prominent and elderly Washington matron comes for a visit—after a long absence—her daughter Sara with the latter's German husband Kurt and their three children. For years Kurt has been a leader of the resistance movement in Germany. Now at last the exiled family has found rest and refuge. But not for long. A guest at the house, a dissolute Rumanian count and hanger-on at the German embassy, recognizes Kurt and demands a huge bribe in return for silence. Realizing what he must do to save the cause and continue his work, Kurt kills the count, shocking the Americans into a realization that they are living in a new and different world. With Lucile Watson as the Washington hostess, Paul Lukas as Kurt, and Mady Christians as his wife, *Watch on the Rhine* was enthusiastically received and was later turned into a successful movie. In analyzing the play's popularity on the stage, Irwin Shaw shrewdly pointed out that no mention was made of communism, to which underground forces would almost necessarily adhere, that Kurt and his family are drawn with almost unbelievable nobility, and that the Americans are depicted as thoughtless and wayward innocents with no suggestion of responsibility or culpability for the rise of nazism in the world. In addition, of course, Miss Hellman had the advantage of a good melodramatic plot to dramatize her message.

Watch on the Rhine and its companion pieces helped to prepare the nation for war. After Pearl Harbor the moving pictures provided a more vigorous and suitable medium for patriotic dramatization of the conflict, but of the many stage plays on the subject one clearly stood out above the others for its force and sincerity. This was *The Eve of St. Mark* (1942) by the same dramatist who almost twenty years before had lambasted war in *What Price Glory?* Abandoning verse for realistic prose, Maxwell Anderson relates in broad, general terms the story of a young farm boy who enlists in the army, leaves his devoted family, parts from his fiancée, and in the final act finds himself one of a small force guarding an atoll in the Philippines. The situation of this group is hopeless, but they know they are aiding other American forces by delaying the Japanese invasion. When the officers are killed, the boy is next in line to take command and at this point faces complete freedom of choice between escaping or fighting on until death. He selects the latter, and his fiancée and family—despite their personal loss—feel that his choice has been good.

In the theme of dying for one's ideals Anderson was reiterating his message of *Key Largo* and other plays. *The Eve of St. Mark,* simple in treatment and unabashed in sentiment, made an excellent case for the American way of life; it also reveals how far the realistic dramatists had traveled from their erstwhile detachment and cynicism to a positive stand on war and patriotism.

While morals, sex, war, and democracy provided important themes for the realistic playwright, they by no means exhausted his range of interests. Unlike his escapist predecessors, he discarded rose-colored for horn-rimmed spectacles and turned sociologist, examining all phases of the American scene and often showing distaste for what he saw. The drama of social protest developed in time from his critical analyses of native phenomena. The course of social drama, therefore, ran somewhat parallel to that of the war plays, starting with negative questioning and ending with positive demands for belief and action. This trend may be seen, for example, in regional plays, wherein the new realists followed the local colorists in looking upon the byways of America, though their search was for something other than quaintness and folklore. Realistic regionalism appeared in the drama of O'Neill and Anderson, who occasionally turned their eyes to New England and castigated the natives for their parsimony, repressions, narrow-mindedness, and intolerance. These same traits—along with the bleak climate—were evident in *Icebound* (1923) by Owen Davis, a domestic drama about Maine, and *Ethan Frome* (1936), an excellent dramatization by the Davises, *père et fils,* of Edith Wharton's melodramatic novel. The Middlewest was sometimes pictured on the stage, as in Sidney Howard's *Alien Corn* (1933), revealing the plight of the artist in a college community—stodgy, conservative, lacking in real culture. A play of the West, John Steinbeck's *Of Mice and Men* (1937), showed conditions among migratory ranch workers in California but is more clearly a study in abnormal psychology than a social document. In addition to solving a moral problem, Howard's *They Knew What They Wanted* offered a good picture of the California vineyards during Prohibition. However, as in the drama of imagination, it was the South that provided the widest opportunities for regional treatment.

Numerous realistic plays dealt with some aspect or other of life below the Mason-Dixon Line, where an ancient and con- servative system was breaking down in the long aftermath of the Civil War. In *The House of Connelly*, as we have seen, the poetical realist Paul Green recorded the profound social changes manifested in the decay of the Connellys and the rise of their "poor white" tenant farmers. The clash between old and new attitudes had been given dramatic point in an earlier play, *Coquette* (1927), by George Abbott and Ann Preston Bridgers, in which Helen Hayes was starred as a coquettish Southern belle, brought up under an outmoded social code which does not permit her to marry the man she loves. The inherently tragic situation ends with the fatal shooting of the girl's lover by her father and is climaxed by her inability to defend the latter on the stand because of the loss of her chastity. The only solution is suicide. The play well represents the foolish persistence of an outmoded chivalric code.

Of the many representations of social decay in the South none proved more picturesque or lasting than *Tobacco Road*, which opened in 1933 and ran for 3,182 performances in New York alone, surpassing the previous record set by *Abie's Irish Rose*. With lusty speech and broad, salty humor this dramati- zation by Jack Kirkland of Erskine Caldwell's novel lays bare the existence of a group of Georgia crackers, formerly tenant farmers, now shiftless parasites on the untilled land. The scene is Jeeter Lester's tumbledown shack on a tobacco road near Augusta, where Jeeter and the remnants of his family live in poverty and degenerate squalor. Ellie May, a daughter, has a harelip; Dude, the youngest son, is crafty, cruel, unfeel- ing, with a passion for loud automobile horns. The rest of the

brood have left home, and Ada, the mother, cannot remember
their names. She complains bitterly of lack of snuff to calm her
stomach; her only hope in life is that she will have a stylish
dress to be buried in. While Jeeter still feels the urge to plant in
the spring, he is weak from malnutrition and temperamentally
shiftless; nor can he get money and credit. His main fear—
on which Dude cruelly plays—is that when he dies he will be
thrown in the corn crib like his father, half of whose face was
chewed off by rats. Another one of the children, Pearl, mated
at twelve to Lov on payment of eight dollars to Jeeter, runs
away from Lov and comes back home. Lov complains, with
some justice, that the girl will not even talk. The colorful
Sister Bessie Rice, itinerant woman preacher, enlivens the
action by selecting Dude—with the official approbation of
God—to become her next husband. The boy is unimpressed
until Bessie states her intention of buying a brand-new automobile with a loud horn. The car cannot stand up long under
Dude's careless disregard of natural obstacles, but it performs long enough by the final act to run over his mother, an
accident that elicits little regret or sympathy on his part.
Throughout the play the complete vacuum of human emotions
provides much of the humor, as when Jeeter casually receives
the announcement that he is not Pearl's father, or when
Grandma fails to show up one day—she presumably died in
the fields—and Jeeter remarks, "I'll go and look around one
of these days." From a sociological standpoint the play is
interesting in showing the older Lesters' inability to adjust
themselves to a changed economic order. Jeeter still idealizes
his share-cropping past and refuses to move to Augusta to
work in the mills. People born on the land, he argues, should
live on the land. He and his family are doomed by change
and degeneration, but behind the play's grotesque humor
there is genuine tragedy. The play's long run, however, was
scarcely due to its social implications but rather to the colorful
profanity, the realism of speech and stage business, the display of completely amoral behavior. With regard to the last

the enthusiastic response of audiences perhaps represents the revenge of the subconscious for lip service paid to family duty and conventional morality. In any event, the superiority of *Tobacco Road* to earlier long-distance champions—*Abie's Irish Rose, East Is West, Peg o' My Heart*—would seem to indicate some improvement in popular taste. Even more so if we compare it to that ancient portrayal of rustic character and scenery, *The Old Homestead!*

Tobacco Road and *The House of Connelly* had social implications, but the treatment was mainly descriptive. An interesting contrast in the playwright's attitude and purpose is revealed in a grimly unpleasant regional play of 1939, Lillian Hellman's *The Little Foxes*, concerned with the rise of industrialism in the South around 1900. The tradesmen and shopkeepers who rose from the ashes of the old South are shown as rapacious, ruthless, predatory—far worse than the dying aristocracy. The Hubbard family—"the little foxes that spoil the vines"—have persuaded a Chicago industrialist to open a cotton mill in a town of cheap labor and no strikes. Immediately they begin quarreling about profits. In a successful attempt to secure the largest share, Regina—sister of the Hubbard brothers and worst of the lot—is willing to sacrifice her daughter and coolly allows her husband to die from a heart attack without supplying the medicine that would save him. The play powerfully reveals the acquisitive instinct at its worst, with Tallulah Bankhead giving one of her best performances as the tigress Regina. In Birdie—played by Patricia Collinge—the Pollyanna of the Belasco era—the author offers by contrast a lady of the old South, brutally tortured and badgered by the Hubbards. Masquerading as a regional period piece with a melodramatic plot, Miss Hellman's play was in effect a strong attack on capitalism, sufficiently disguised to permit transference to moving-picture form, where it enjoyed equally great success.

With or without a social message an important concern of the realist playwrights during the entire period was with the American middle class in a world dominated by business, a subject made popular in the novel form by Sinclair Lewis and others. At first this extensive theme took the form of a realistic picture of bourgeois and white-collar life, which might be merely descriptive but was more often critical, so that here again the general movement was from objective naturalism to social protest. Dramatic treatment of capitalistic society would naturally lead to the cities rather than the hinterlands and would result in sordid pictures of urban life.

One of the great dramatists of bourgeois types was George Kelly, former vaudeville actor and author of a hilarious satire on amateur acting, *The Torch-Bearers*. His plays are in reality character sketches, fundamentally actors' plays, developed usually with a skillful combination of humor and seriousness. Best known is *The Show-Off* (1924), about a freight clerk, Aubrey Piper, who brashly bluffs his way through life, making many blunders but always succeeding in rationalizing them. He is jaunty, self-possessed, talkative, boastful, splendidly inaccurate. But Amy loves and marries him despite her family's dislike and she can never see him in a true light. He becomes a heavy burden for his in-laws until he is somewhat vindicated at the end when his bluffing, based as usual on misinformation, brings the family a small fortune. The interest is focused on the characterization of Aubrey, at once irritating and pitiful, yet able to compel grudging admiration for his refusal to be beaten by life and his own insignificance, even if he has to flaunt the world by wearing a toupee and a carnation. Amy's complete belief and devotion give the man a certain grandeur quite at variance with his real stature. Kelly's next play, *Craig's Wife*, was a character study of a completely selfish wife who dominates her husband, drives out his friends, and goads him at last to rebellion and escape. As one of the characters remarks, Mrs. Craig married a house, not a husband, and the close of the play finds her in it, completely alone. This effective portrayal of a disagreeable woman won the Pulitzer Prize for 1925. Of the several other

plays Kelly wrote before his desertion to Hollywood, only
Daisy Mayme (1926)—character sketch of a breezy woman
of lower middle-class background—had any success or significance.

No one would accuse George Kelly of concern with social
problems; his interest was exclusively in human relationships,
with considerable stress on domestic selfishness. With awareness of social changes a dismal view of the altered status of
the white-collar worker was offered in several early plays. In
1921 Arthur Richman's *Ambush* ponderously showed the
problem of underpaid suburbanites whose ideals are "ambushed" by the high cost of living and a drab environment.
Frank Reicher played the part of a conservative clerk whose
daughter, played by Florence Eldridge, is driven to promiscuity by depressing circumstances and who, when his savings
are lost, has to suffer the humiliation of accepting money and
a job from the girl's current married lover. In this and other
contemporary drama it appears that a six-cylinder car was
a symbol of sin, and an apartment on Riverside Drive the
height of social aspiration. Another play, Gilbert Emery's
Tarnish (1923), dealt with the plight of the girl of good social
background who is reduced to working in an office to support
her family and herself. She falls in love with a fellow clerk,
a man of lower social origin, but is completely disillusioned
when she discovers that her admirer as well as her no-good
father have had relations with a manicurist of shady reputation, the kind who wears a kimono when she receives men in
her apartment. "Oh, isn't there *anything* clean *anywhere?*"
demands Ann Harding as the distressed heroine: "Girls like
me, who try to live decently, to—to— Aren't there men who
try to live that way too?" While the play is mediocre, it holds
interest for its theme of the respectable young woman forced
by financial reverses to earn her living in business, where she
finds herself no longer sheltered from the realities of life.

Of the countless bourgeois portraits that appeared on the
Broadway stage, usually set against a background of social

change, some of the most striking were provided by Sidney Howard. Two of his plays employed the device of setting old and new American types in dramatic juxtaposition. His unsuccessful *Lucky Sam McCarver* (1925) was a biographical study of the rise of Sam McCarver from his boyhood job in a Hoboken Turkish bath to the respectability of Wall Street, with the corresponding decline of Carlotta Ashe, society woman of conservative background, to moral and physical disintegration. Halfway in his career, when he is proprietor of a night club during Prohibition, Lucky Sam marries Carlotta, thrice divorced, partly because he loves her, partly because she will help his rise in the world. Carlotta also loves Sam, but her different outlook on life—she's a "runner-away" not a "go-getter"—makes her unable to meet him halfway, and in their differences neither will give in to the other. The play ends with Sam's complete success but with the death of Carlotta in meager and tragic circumstances. In spite of a good idea and of earnest defense of the play by the author, *Lucky Sam McCarver* seems prolix and amateurish in comparison with Howard's usual work.

Ned McCobb's Daughter (1926)—a better play—again shows conflict between persons of different character and social background. Carrie Callaghan, an indomitable Maine down-Easter—honest, straightforward, capable—has never allowed life or misfortune to beat her down. Ned McCobb, her father, former sea captain, has been reduced to skippering a Kennebec ferry with the aid of Carrie's worthless husband, George, to collect the fares. The family is visited by Babe Callaghan, George's brother, a flashy New York East-Sider who has prospered as a bootlegger and is trying to get a shipment of liquor through to New York. George has had a devious past, but Carrie is now suddenly confronted with new evidence of his utter worthlessness—theft of money from the ferry, shameless borrowing from her father, a sordid affair with a waitress leading to abortion. Captain Ned McCobb dies of a stroke and Carrie is forced by circumstances to enter into partnership with the bootlegger Babe. George decamps and at the end Carrie—worried about the fate of her children—cleverly tricks Babe into leaving also. All the characters are excellently developed but they are clearly dominated by Carrie (Clare Eames) and Babe (Alfred Lunt)—both strong individuals, aware of each other's good points. The contrasting dialects of Maine and the East Side add delightful humor to the play's situations. The excellence of the Guild production is indicated by the selection of Margalo Gillmore, Morris Carnovsky, Earle Larimore, Edward G. Robinson, and Alfred Perry for the minor roles—practically an all-star cast—decidedly in line with Sidney Howard's belief that truth of characterization is the one essential of playwriting and that the actor, Gordon Craig notwithstanding, is the sole important element in the theatre.

The bourgeois portraits of the twenties were not necessarily or wholly unsympathetic in treatment. Kelly seems to have had some sneaking admiration for Aubrey Piper, and Howard undeniably liked his upstarts Sam McCarver and Babe Callaghan. By the thirties the playwrights' attitude toward their characters was generally more critical. The tendency may be observed even in the work of a popular dramatist like George S. Kaufman, writer of satirical farce-comedies, who turned for a time to sardonic pictures of middle-class life. His *Dinner at Eight* (1932), written in collaboration with Edna Ferber, took delight in presenting the sordid, undercover background of a fashionable dinner party to which are invited a remarkably unpleasant set of guests—a ruthless business man, his trollop of a wife, a society doctor with a bedside manner and a weakness for female patients, a matinée idol gone to seed, and so on. In *Merrily We Roll Along* (1934) Kaufman and Moss Hart started with a completely unsavory character, a jaded and disillusioned popular playwright, and tracing his career backward through the years, showed in a final scene the idealistic youth who had been valedictorian of his class at college. There is perhaps a little more sympathy in Elmer

Rice's *Counsellor-at-Law* (1931), retailing the inside story of a brilliantly successful criminal lawyer, a Jew from the East Side who has risen from obscurity. Simon, played by Paul Muni, blindly worships his snobbish society wife—a Christian divorcée—but remains wholly unaware of the love and devotion of his Jewish secretary. When he finds himself on the verge of disbarment, completely betrayed by his wife and her circle, he attempts suicide but is halted by the faithful secretary. A sensational murder case conveniently comes up for legal action, and the two set to work with a new camaraderie, back in the mumbo-jumbo of criminal law. The play's interest comes partly from Rice's expert exposé of a law office and the colorful or shabby types that haunt it, but his main thesis seems to be the contrast between Simon's material success and what this success has done to him. His true friends are the old associates from Second Avenue, not the blue bloods of his new milieu. If we are to take the word of an irate Communist in the play, Simon is a traitor to his class—"You're a cheap prostitute, that's what you are, you and your cars and your country estate and your kept parasite of a wife." But other points of view are given too, and the author merely reveals the many-sided character of Simon and lets the spectator judge for himself.

The theme of the Jew who rises to material success is treated more profoundly and with greater social significance in John Howard Lawson's *Success Story* (1932), a Group Theatre production. Here the dramatic portrait is less objective and serves as an indictment of American business and a deflating of the success myth. A Russian Jew from the East Side, spiritually tortured but ambitious, has been driven by the prevailing social setup to desert his early radical ideals for the frenzied acquisition of wealth and power. The financial crash gives him the opportunity to sell short and achieve spectacular success, but only at the sacrifice of his youthful ideals, his business associates, the Jewish girl who has always loved him, and even the glamorous woman of pleasure he has married because she represents for him the exotic and unattainable. His success story is in reality failure—both his and society's for its inability to employ his great talents—and can only conclude with violent death. In contrast the author presents the financial wizard Sonnenberg, type of cultured and refined Jew who has learned to relax and temper finance with cultural and sensual interests. "Gee, I like Jews," says the glamour girl; "they're all poets or sugar daddies—or both!" By setting the action in a flashy, streamlined advertising agency Lawson is able to expose convincingly the utter shallowness of the American religion of selling. Excellent in its characterization and social criticism, the play shows the bourgeois portrait, like the regional play, entering the lists against the capitalistic system.

In the same manner sordid pictures of city life might range from the purely photographic to careful slanting for a social message. The contrast is well illustrated in two plays of New York life—Elmer Rice's *Street Scene* (1929), a Pulitzer Prize winner, and Sidney Kingsley's *Dead End* (1935). The former—a masterpiece of objective realism—was the first play to record city noises and amplify them throughout the performance to add to the verisimilitude. The rising curtain reveals the outside of a brownstone walk-up apartment house in a decayed neighborhood. It is summer, and sitting on the stoop, leaning out of windows, or strolling in and out, the dwellers lead their undistinguished lives. We see the Italian singing master, the Jewish radical, the prying gossip, the lecherous shopgirl, the old woman who has sacrificed her life for her mother, the white-collar clerk whose wife is having a baby, and a dozen others—Rice has omitted no one. The humdrum flow of existence in this microcosm of city life is violently broken by a double murder when a brutal stagehand comes home unexpectedly to find his wife in the embraces of a collector for the milk company. The husband kills the lovers, escapes, and is later captured. But this is a mere interlude in the busy life of the city, which goes inexorably on. In the play the Jewish radical makes scattered comments about capitalism and the stagehand's wife wonders why people can't live in amity without perpetually trying to hurt one another, but the author remains in the background and ventures no explicit thesis or propaganda. Not so with *Dead End*, written in the height of the depression, which marshals its realism for an attack against slums and the social order. Viewed from the river, the scene shows in dramatic juxtaposition the rear entrance of East End Terrace—a fashionable apartment house—and a slummy dead-end street, where crime and gangsterism are born and where they flourish. The tenements lining the street are filthy and run down; because there is no upkeep, the owners are making large profits. The tough city kids meet at the river, build fires to bake potatoes they have stolen, jump naked into the grimy water, organize street battles with other gangs. They learn cruelty, stealing, extortion, and other vices; when they are caught and sent to reform school, their criminal education is complete. For the ambitious boy, the natural leader, material success can come only through crime. In the character Baby-Face Martin we have the full-fledged gangster and in the street kid Tommy the potential one. Of the girls, some sink to prostitution, others rise to the opulence of kept womanhood. The one person who has had the stamina and character to rise above his environment cannot secure employment and is, ironically, on relief. The picture of general degradation is enlivened by ribald street talk and the melodramatic killing of Baby-Face, but the real villains of the piece are poverty and the slums. While *Street Scene* merely depicts and the tragedy is mainly a personal one, *Dead End*—less perfect and convincing as a play—has greater direction as a social indictment.

Sidney Kingsley proved partial to the formula of combining realistic city settings, melodramatic action, and a social message. His *Men in White* (1933), set realistically in a hospital, shows the problem of the young intern engaged to a wealthy girl, whose money and influence are not entirely a boon to his medical career. The melodramatic punch comes when the fiancée, invited to watch an operation, discovers from the delirious patient—a nurse suffering complications from an abortion —that the latter has had an affair with the intern. A later play, *The World We Make* (1939), dramatized from Millen Brand's *The Outward Room,* relates the story of a mental patient who escapes from a sanitarium and finds release from her psychological difficulties by working in a steam laundry and cohabitating with one of the workmen in his cold-water tenement flat. This is a kind of *Dead End* in reverse where the heroine finds refuge and happiness in the slums among common men and women, the play's thesis being that only through faith in people and their good instincts can we have strength to go on in a troubled world.

The various playwrights considered from Kelly to Kingsley were struggling toward social reforms and were laying the foundations for leftist drama. An interesting group of early plays that are somewhat apart from the main currents of American drama went considerably further in this direction, first satirizing American business and ideology and then strongly attacking them. These plays borrowed the expressionist technique from Eugene O'Neill or from his German models, thus departing from the photographic realism of the twenties. In spite of their imaginative treatment, they must be considered essentially realistic in purpose and effect. Two of them appeared in March, 1923, Elmer Rice's *The Adding Machine* and John Howard Lawson's *Roger Bloomer.* Rice's play tells the inglorious story of Mr. Zero, accounting clerk for twenty-five years in a department store, browbeaten by a nagging wife to whom he never speaks, lascivious yet morally conventional, quarrelsome with his fellow-clerk Daisy—secretly in love with him, servile to the Boss who doesn't even know his name but who fires him when the firm installs an adding machine, rendering Zero's services unnecessary. "I'm sorry—" says the Boss; "no other alternative—greatly regret— old   employee—efficiency—economy—business—*business*—

BUSINESS—" In a rage Zero kills the Boss and is later tried
and found guilty. After his death the play shifts sharply to
fantasy. In a graveyard scene he meets Shrdlu, a religious maniac who has cut his sainted mother's throat instead of the leg
of lamb he was supposed to carve. In lieu of the punishment
they expect, the two find themselves in the most favored section of the Elysian Fields, reserved for murderers and other
nonconformists. Here Zero meets Daisy, who has committed
suicide and is now free to love him for eternity. But Zero's
stuffy, conventional soul is shocked and infuriated by heaven's
unconcern for the moral law and he insists on leaving. We next
see him getting his soul refurbished in a celestial repair and
service station before his next appearance on earth, where he
will operate "a superb, super-hyper-adding machine." The at-
tendants consider him a slave and a failure from the start, a
"poor, spineless, brainless boob," and tell him that he is inevitably destined for slums and wars, inclined by nature toward
jingoism and demagoguery.

Elmer Rice is less at home in the fantasy than in the earlier,
more realistic scenes—Mr. Zero lying silent on the bed during
Mrs. Zero's long, whining tirade; the office scene where Daisy
and Zero call out figures for entry into the ledgers and end
by speaking their separate inner reveries; the visit to the Zeros
of the Ones, the Twos, the Threes, the Fours, the Fives, and
the Sixes, all of them doing and saying precisely the same
thing; the expressionistic trial of Zero. The conversation of the
numerical nonentities is restricted to weather, clothes, ail-
ments, gossip—except for occasional outbursts in unison
against foreigners, Catholics, Jews, and Negroes. This merci-
less satire of the white-collar drudge, slave to his job and victim of the very system he champions, did not prove unduly
successful in the excellent Guild production, but it aroused
wide critical interest for its thesis and technique.

Satire of the middle classes was combined with a study of
baffled adolescence in *Roger Bloomer*, produced by the Equity
Players shortly before the opening of Rice's play. Roger

Bloomer runs away from Excelsior, Iowa, where his father owns a department store run on the principle of bigger profits and lower wages. In New York the boy suffers from poverty and maladjustment. With Louise, another youngster of rebellious tendencies, he has a hectic but platonic love affair. The girl tries to find him a job at her office in Wall Street, but the boss recognizes that Roger is too unorthodox—he lacks the "money-making manner." He tries with his usual ineffectuality to poison himself; later Louise—also baffled—has more success in a similar attempt and dies, still a virgin. The play ends with Roger, in prison, having a nightmare of pursuit in which eroticism and death are strongly recurrent motifs. In the dream, however, Louise inspires him with the strength to go on.

Like the *Adding Machine*, Lawson's play was more an artistic than a popular success. The expressionist technique proved a worthy handmaiden of satire in representing the dull Bloomer family at dinner, where they repeat the same banal lines and eat with clock-like regularity, or in the excellent Wall Street scene showing five separate offices across the stage with identical equipment and with five business men at the five desks working in exact unison. There is effective satire, too, of the conventional college student in the person of Eugene Poppin, football player at Yale, whose only aims are to meet the right people and do the right things and whose advice is to keep away from "Jews, highbrows, and guys that eat with their knives." Eugene's father has sent him to Yale, where he can be a "real American"—there are too many socialists in the state college. Besides satire the play has a certain picaresque humor, as when Roger's fat and suddenly amorous landlady in New York bids him sit on her lap and kiss her, and Roger replies, "I'd sooner kiss a horse." It should be evident that *Roger Bloomer* makes a good reading play, regardless of any limitations it may have on the stage, and that it offers biting ridicule of bourgeois mores and ideals.

In attempting to discover a new medium for dramatizing

the American scene John Howard Lawson turned in his next play to vaudeville with its painted curtains and comic types. *Processional* (1925), produced by the Guild with ingenious curtains and sets by Mordecai Gorelik, caused quite a critical stir and ran for almost a hundred performances. The scene is a large West Virginia town under martial law during a coal strike. The plot, almost nonexistent, is concerned with Dynamite Jim (George Abbott), who escapes from jail in a coffin, rapes Sadie Cohen (June Walker) in a coal mine, and later satisfies the moral scruples of the Ku-Klux-Klan by marrying Sadie in a final jazz wedding. Lawson explains in a preface what types he has borrowed from vaudeville: the Jewish low comedian (Cohen), the Negro comedian (Rastus), the hard-boiled officer of the law (Sheriff), and the smart city feller (Phillpots). Especially interesting is the fact that *Processional* includes the same ingredients as the left-wing play—the strike, the capitalistic press, the conservative forces of law and order—but treats them with humor and satire ready to break out into song and dance, not as propaganda. The satire hits at such widely scattered items as American sentimentality toward motherhood and the forces of conventional respectability represented by the Ku-Klux-Klan (the King Kleagle announces that the entire Congress of the United States has just joined the Klan.) The play holds interest, on the one hand, for its attempt to combine expressionism with vaudeville and revue, and on the other, for its nose-thumbing at one hundred percent Americanism.

Brief mention might be made of an expressionist play by a Harvard graduate, John Dos Passos' *The Moon Is a Gong*, first given in 1925 by the Harvard Dramatic Club and tried out later in New York. Here again we find satirical treatment of the American scene—the conventional young men with "Arrow Collar Faces," the attempts by Washington to suppress parlor bolshevism, the Tammany Prosperity Parade, the treadmill of American business. The hero and heroine are individualists who yearn to lead their own lives, not lockstep in a conventional, humdrum order, but they are defeated by the universal garbage-man Death. The play was deservedly a failure, but it again shows the young intellectuals of the twenties like Dos Passos and Lawson striking hard at the prevailing standardization of business and culture, and feeling their way toward left-wing drama. Their efforts led to the formation of the New Playwrights' Company which for three seasons gave radical plays, usually expressionistic, until it gave up the ghost in 1929. The group, ironically, was patronized by the capitalist Otto Kahn. Its productions were given off Broadway, first on West Fifty-second Street and later in Greenwich Village; none of them was successful, although some praise was accorded to Paul Sifton's *The Belt*, an attack on Ford and the factory system, and to Upton Sinclair's *Singing Jailbirds*, an exposé of the fate of an I.W.W. in solitary confinement. By 1929 expressionism had become clearly passé, and when radical drama arose from the backwash of the depression it was in realistic propaganda form.

Since the early days of O'Neill and the Provincetown the realistic playwright, in his social and political credo, had stood in varying degrees to the left of center. Harding, Coolidge, and Hoover found no apologists on Broadway. In domestic matters the reformist urge was present from the beginning, but it was not until the crash of 1929 and the depression of the thirties that the writers became imbued with a new missionary fervor. The victorious artistic revolution was therefore replaced by a social revolution which found expression in plays of "social significance," protest, or outright propaganda. In this drama the message came first, with mere escapist entertainment branded as a sign of decadent bourgeois taste. The social and political opinions presented might range from warm support of the New Deal to complete adherence to Marxian ideology. Gradually a new theatre audience appeared, recruited from organized labor and the large urban populations that voted Franklin D. Roosevelt into office. Aesthetically uncritical, this audience demanded social themes and calls to action. The resulting plays, representing the radical movement in contemporary drama, have usually been called left-wing or leftist. In this loose usage, the designation is only relatively accurate. While the dramatists were unanimous in denouncing the evils of capitalism, their work was marked by wide divergence of views and ideas. In his *Fervent Years* the director Harold Clurman describes amusingly a meeting at the radical John Reed Club at which the Group Theatre—very conscious of its social progressiveness—was dubbed middle-of-the-road, with the Theatre Guild representing the right. Conversely the mildest of liberal plays might appear completely revolutionary to a Congressman. Leftism has so many gradations, in other words, that caution must be exercised in the use of labels.

A favorite technique of the drama of protest was to apply insistent pressure on various tender spots in our social and political system. This method was evident in several plays already mentioned—*Dead End*, for example, with its exposure of the evils of slums. Another reformist play, Maxwell Anderson's *Both Your Houses* (1933), launched a bitter satirical attack on extravagance, hypocrisy, and corruption in the two houses of Congress. Using terse, incisive prose dialogue, it presents a young idealistic Congressman, newly elected and eager to expose and beat the Washington political setup. With the expert help of a hard-boiled girl secretary he tries to win out by playing Congress' own game, organizing a group to back the most wildly extravagant financial bill ever proposed. His expectation is that the measure will tumble to defeat from its own weight, but to his surprise it passes without public protest and his reform scheme is defeated. Much incidental satire is directed at the politicians' hypocrisy and cynicism regarding Prohibition, not yet repealed. In prisons and the courts the reforming playwrights found another sore spot which deserved attention. Considerable protest about the American legal system appeared in Martin Flavin's *The Criminal Code* (1929), which shows a man unjustly given a long term in prison because the criminal code forces the district attorney to secure a conviction; later when he is about to be released on parole, he is an unwilling witness to a prison murder, and the criminal code—from the inmate's point of view—compels him not to reveal the murderer, at the cost of his own disaster. The play has effective denunciation of legal processes, sentimental juries, and the yellow press. Of the last, the prison warden asserts, "They'd put Christ on the Cross again to get an extra on the street." Even stronger demand for reform of prison life was offered in John Wexley's *The Last Mile*, dealing with an attempted jail break by the death-cell occupants in an Oklahoma prison, with Spencer Tracy—not yet in the movies—as the lead. Several radical *causes célèbres* also found their way on the stage. *Gods of the Lightning* (1928) by Anderson and Harold Hickerson, ahead of its time as a journalistic propaganda play, protested against the injustices of the Sacco-Vanzetti execution. In 1934 John Wexley's *They Shall Not Die* passionately denounced the trial of nine Negro youths in the notorious Scottsboro case, picturing the trial as a complete frame-up motivated by race prejudice. Worthy as the cause may have been, for a general audience Wexley probably weakened his case by overstatement—the usual defect of outright propaganda.

Racial injustice offered fertile ground for reform, and we find the drama of protest strongly affected and reinforced by the rapid emergence of the Negro in the American theatre. As an actor the Negro reached Broadway via the back door, through vaudeville comedians like Bert Williams, through dancers and singers like Bill Robinson, Josephine Baker, Florence Mills, and Ethel Waters. Until the twenties serious colored roles were habitually taken by white actors. As late as 1930 Daniel Reed's *Scarlet Sister Mary* was played by a white cast in blackface, headed by none other than Ethel Barrymore. Eugene O'Neill was a pioneer not only in the writing of plays about Negroes but in the employment of such excellent actors as Charles Gilpin and Paul Robeson. Later plays like *Green*

Pastures and *Porgy* gave the Negro a firmer foothold in serious drama, but his real opportunity came with the depression.
The Federal Theatre organized numerous Negro units, which
showed their versatility in productions like the Harlem *Macbeth*, the Chicago *Swing Mikado*, and the melodramatic *Haiti*.
As a symbol of racial equality workmen's theatres and leftist
plays made it a point to include Negro actors in their casts.
Katherine Dunham, dance director of Labor Stage, soon became an outstanding Broadway dancer with a company of
her own which appeared in many productions. By the forties
the Negro had become firmly established in the professional
theatre in both musical and serious drama. In 1940 the Negro
Playwrights Company became a Broadway producing organization. Three years later, for the first time, *Othello* was presented with Paul Robeson, a Negro, as the dusky Moor.

Along with his rise in the acting profession, largely due to
liberal and radical endeavor, the Negro as a stage character
appeared in a different light. Formerly he had been portrayed
as a quaint or comic simpleton, given to malapropisms and
shuffling gait. After 1918 the playwrights drew him with
greater realism either in folkplays or—despite the usual conservative outcries—in relation to the unjust social conditions
under which he lived. In *All God's Chillun Got Wings* O'Neill
boldly handled the problem of miscegenation, here and elsewhere depicting the Negro with sympathy and dignity. Paul
Green proved himself an earnest champion of the Negro in
Roll, Sweet Chariot, In Abraham's Bosom, and other plays.
Negro dramatists, too, were securing a hearing on Broadway
—Hall Johnson in the folk play *Run, Little Chillun*, Langston
Hughes in *Mulatto* (1935), Theodore Ward in *Big White Fog*
(1940), the last a revision of an earlier production by the Fed-
eral Theatre. An interesting collaboration of Paul Green and
Richard Wright was responsible for the dramatization of *Na-
tive Son* (1941), a melodramatic but powerful play in which
Canada Lee played a Negro on trial for the murder of a white
girl. The character is undeniably if unintentionally guilty, but

the authors bring out clearly that he is the product of poverty, injustice, and discrimination; that even in the North he is victim of a cancerous growth in the social organism. While not as propagandist as the more leftist plays, *Native Son* is nevertheless effective as drama of protest.

Negro plays tended to veer to the left, but for the real war on capitalism one must turn to proletarian drama, a type which emanated from the movement for workers' theatres that started shortly after the First World War but did not reach maturity until the thirties. Inspired by the Soviet theatre and defended by a vigorous Marxist critique in publications like *New Theatre,* this "agit-prop" drama (as it was named from a combination of "agitation" and "propaganda") took the form of vigorous attacks on all phases of bourgeois society. Eschewing all personal and escapist topics, it dealt exclusively with labor agitation, war, fascism, strikes, social injustice. In place of personal heroes it sometimes had abstract protagonists, such as "mass pressure." As we have seen, it enlisted the support of the Negro in the class war. Its embattled playwrights mercilessly burlesqued the industrialist and his confreres of church and state. They developed the concepts of the noble worker and the noble labor organizer. At their best the propaganda plays did not scorn convincing realism of plot and characterization; at their worst they were mere caricatures, more crudely put together than the melodramas of a past era. Judgment of their work depends mainly on the ideology of the observer, but no one would deny them force and emotional sweep in stating their points.

The one-act play, which had virtually disappeared with the decline of the little theatre movement, was now revived. It proved particularly adapted for performance in halls or off-Broadway stages by amateur or semiprofessional groups. Among many producing organizations that were active in the thirties were the Workers' Laboratory Theatre, the Theatre of Action, the Theatre Collective, the New Theatre League (originally the League of Workers Theatres), and Labor Stage,

Inc. The best proletarian one-acters—like *Bury the Dead*—usually moved uptown to Broadway and became widely known. Paul Green's *Hymn to the Rising Sun,* produced first by labor groups and subsequently by Federal Theatre, depicts with terrifying effect the plight of chain-gang convicts hired out to work on the railroad. The sadism of the captain and guards, the lashing of a white boy, the killing of the Negro "Runt" in a sweatbox, pile up to an almost unbearable climax in one of the best of the social propaganda plays. Well-known, also, is Clifford Odets' *Waiting for Lefty,* written in three days in 1935 for competition in a New Theatre League contest. First presented on Fourteenth Street, the play was later put on by the Group Theatre with Odets himself playing one of the roles. The author cleverly adopts the technique of the old-fashioned minstrel show in representing on the stage a committee of taxicab drivers who call for a strike in opposition to the wishes of Harry Fatt, their oily union leader, and his gangster henchmen. Fatt in reality represents the capitalistic system—an identification made evident by the fact that he smokes a cigar during the whole performance. The several members of the committee rise in turn from their seats and come downstage to enact the crises that have led to their presence on the platform. Hard times have prevented one driver from marrying his girl and are about to drive another one's wife into adultery. A laboratory assistant has indignantly refused to help manufacture poison gas and to spy on his superior. He is now driving a taxi, as is a doctor who has been forced out of his profession by nepotism and anti-Semitism. Another episode shows the dramatic exposure of a labor spy. Finally news comes that Lefty—the man for whom the meeting has been waiting—has been found murdered, and the union members (the audience) are asked to voice their demands for a strike—which of course they do with thunderous gusto. Throughout the episodes Harry Fatt and the committee are visible in the background as a chorus, improvising comments as in the minstrel show. Occasional music further helps to stir up the emotions. The play lacks subtlety, a quality consciously avoided by proletarian drama, but it has excellent dramatic conflict on a rather elementary level. As a vehement call to action against employers and crooked union leaders it has few rivals.

Labor plays, of which only a few have been mentioned, were not necessarily one-acters. In the full-length genus the themes were essentially the same. For the production of this drama a nonprofit organization, Theatre Union, was formed late in 1932 to play in the old Civic Repertory Theatre on Fourteenth Street. In four seasons until it disbanded in 1937 Theatre Union offered a program of vigorous proletarian plays, starting with the antiwar *Peace on Earth* (1933) by George Sklar and Albert Maltz. Also antiwar in theme was the excellent *Sailors of Catarro* from the German of Friedrich Wolf. The play was based upon a mutiny in Austria during the First World War. Other productions were concerned primarily with strikes—Albert Maltz's *Black Pit* (1935), Albert Bein's *Let Freedom Ring* (1935), John Howard Lawson's *Marching Song* (1937)—with the corollary topics of organizing, blacklisting, and eviction because of labor agitation. Best, perhaps, of the American plays was *Stevedore* (1934) by Paul Peters and George Sklar, both a protest against racial discrimination in the South and a plea for closer cooperation between white and black workers. A false charge of rape—at the start of the play—leads to a wholesale roundup of Negroes, including Lonnie, a stevedore with a rebellious temper. Later his labor activities bring on a second arrest on the same charge, but he escapes not only the police but also a gang of white hoodlums in the pay of the stevedore company. When the gang threatens to attack and burn down the houses in the Negro quarter, Lonnie persuades his companions to defend themselves. Reinforced at the last minute by a white organizer and some of his union men, the Negroes win the pitched battle that ensues, though Lonnie himself is killed. All this action proceeds swiftly and directly to its melodramatic climax with suspense

and emotional punch, though the arrival of the white workers
is decidedly reminiscent of the last-minute rescue in the early
Western films. *Stevedore* makes its racial points incisively.
Particular stress is laid upon the need for unity among workers, regardless of color, in order to overcome the reluctance of
both blacks and whites to form mixed unions. Although the
play's action and characterization are on the level of melodrama, its very simplicity and obviousness help to make it
effective as propaganda.

Leftist drama, not normally seasoned with humor, was enlivened in the 1937–1938 season by the success of two musical
plays—Marc Blitzstein's *The Cradle Will Rock* and the labor
Pins and Needles. The former, written for production by the
Federal Theatre but deemed dangerously controversial by
Washington, was put on by John Houseman and Orson Welles
as the first offering of the Mercury Theatre, which later produced the anti-Fascist *Julius Caesar* and the vivacious *Shoe-
maker's Holiday*. More satirical than humorous, *The Cradle
Will Rock* is set in Steeltown, U.S.A., during a union drive.
On the bare stage that proved so popular that season the entire
cast sat or stood during the performance, doing their respective numbers or pantomime down front. The music was played
by the author, Marc Blitzstein, who introduced the characters
to the audience and interpolated stage directions or relevant
comments. The main action takes place in night court, where
a streetwalker has been run in. Also, by mistake, the police
have arrested the entire Liberty Committee appointed by Mr.
Mister, the town industrialist, to combat all forms of radicalism, particularly unionism. In separate scenes the respectable
Committee members—Reverend Salvation, Editor Daily, Dr.
Specialist, President Trixie, and others—are shown to be far
more contemptible prostitutes than the girl because they are
willing to sell even their souls for money. Mr. Mister, who is
caricatured with his clubwoman wife and moronic children,
practically owns the town through his control of church, university, newspapers, and real estate. There is particularly

rough satire of Yasha and Dauber, effete musician and painter, who act as mere lap dogs to the idle rich. They sing a hilarious song about Art for Art's sake. By contrast Larry Foreman, the noble organizer, refuses an immense bribe from Mr. Mister. Just as Larry threatens that the cradle will rock and fall when the wind blows, shouts and music outside announce that complete unionism has been effected. Unduly simple and naïve in its caricature, the satire has enough bite nevertheless to cause discomfort to the bourgeois-minded. The informality of the piece and its somber music in minor key helped it to run for over a hundred performances.

Even more popular was the revue *Pins and Needles*, produced by Labor Stage, Inc., acting organization of the International Ladies' Garment Workers' Union (I.L.G.W.U.), with music and lyrics by Harold J. Rome and sketches by Marc Blitzstein and Arthur Arent, among others. A social slant appeared even in the songs—"Sunday in the Park," "One Big Union for Two," and "Sing Me a Song with Social Significance." Many topics received satirical or burlesque treatment in the sketches: Mussolini's prizes for prolific motherhood, the four (later five) little angels of peace, and even so domestic an institution as the Vassar daisy chain. After a long and successful run the show was succeeded in November, 1939, by a *New Pins and Needles* with only three of the original sketches and new vicious jabs at Father Coughlin, Fritz Kuhn ("Flat-Foot Fuehrer with the Floy-Floy"), and Senator Reynolds. Labor's ability to laugh at itself and its own dissensions was seen in "Papa Lewis, Mama Green," and in banter directed at the dramatist Clifford Odets. *Pins and Needles* proved that a revue could be outspoken and literate, yet hold as much entertainment as the typical Broadway girl-show with its vulgar comic sketches.

With this whirl of proletarian dramatic activity, off and on Broadway, it is not surprising to find a militant radicalism stirring even the established theatre into demanding not only specific reforms but also a change in the entire system. *The*

Little Foxes, mentioned earlier, was a thinly disguised attack on capitalism. George O'Neil's *American Dream* (1933) produced by the Theatre Guild, illustrated in a trilogy the sordid progress of a New England family (the Pingrees) from the acquisitive Puritanism of its founder in 1650 to the decadent parlor communism of its latest representative. The American dream of utopia—a fiction from the very start—has gone particularly sour in modern times, and the last of the Pingrees concludes both his life and the play by firing a bullet through his head. In a final speech addressed to a true, not a dilettante, Communist he utters a plea to hurry up with the revolution, a call that seems to have remained unheeded by the respectable Guild audiences. A much more effective and convincing appeal was provided by Elmer Rice in *We, The People* (1933), a play in twenty scenes showing the tragic and unjust effects of the depression on the family of a respectable and conservative foreman in a factory. His daughter, a school teacher, has not been paid for several months; his son is about to enter the state university. Decrease in pay and finally unemployment cause the family to lose their home. The savings bank closes its doors. The girl cannot marry her fiancé because she is afraid of losing her job; she is forced against her principles into premarital relations with him. The foreman is killed by factory guards during a peaceful march of the unemployed. The son cannot remain at college; he eventually speaks at a pacifist rally and is arrested and convicted on trumped-up charges of murder. By contrast, during the play, Rice has presented the ruling class of the town: the wealthy banker who cuts wages and dismisses employees rather than skip a dividend; the pompous university president, who is drafted into politics because he is "safe"; the unctuous Senator, who makes promises he never intends to keep. In this rarefied circle there is much talk about suppressing agitators, pacifists, Reds. The final scene represents the platform of a mass meeting, at which various liberals or radicals protest the unjust conviction of the son. The last of several stir-

ring speeches is made by a former instructor, who has re-
signed from the university because of its lack of freedom of
speech. The only thing people want—he asserts to conclude
the play—is the right to live: "And no social system that
denies them that right has a claim to a continuance of existence." Vividly recalling in simple human terms the newspaper headlines of the early thirties, the play is a stirring
indictment against the ills of a free enterprise gone wrong,
and it is interesting in showing Rice departing from the objectivity of plays like *Street Scene*. This venture into social
propaganda by an accepted Broadway playwright, a liberal
rather than a radical, was hailed with enthusiasm by *New
Theatre* as a significant development in the theatre.

Liberalism and social drama were fostered by several developments of the middle thirties. One was the formation of
the sprawling W.P.A. Federal Theatre, a vast project which
revealed the tremendous possibilities of a low-priced national theatre. Heading this enterprise was Hallie Flanagan,
former student of George Pierce Baker and for ten years
director of the Vassar Experimental Theatre. After taking
the oath of office on August 27, 1935, she proceeded to organize five great regional theatres, securing the cooperation—
advisory or official—of capable theatre people. Among them
were Elmer Rice, Sidney Howard, Paul Green, Frederick
Koch, Harry Minturn, John Houseman, Orson Welles, Lee
Shubert, Susan Glaspell, and D. W. Griffith. In New York
five separate units were formed, each with its own playhouse:
the Living Newspaper; the popular price theatre (for original
plays by new authors); the experimental theatre; the Negro
theatre; and the tryout theatre. Similar units, modified by
local conditions and requirements, were established throughout the country. The purpose of Federal Theatre was not to
provide direct relief but to employ theatre professionals from
the relief rolls, giving them an opportunity to exercise their
skills and if possible to return to private employment. In this
task the project had to steer a difficult course to avoid op-

position from theatre unions, the commercial theatre, and federal or local politicians. Promised freedom from interference, Federal Theatre ran nevertheless into censorship, occasionally from Washington, much more from local authorities which prevented the showing, among others, of Paul Green's *Hymn to the Rising Sun,* Meyer Levin's *Model Tenement* (about a rent strike), and even Elmer Rice's venerable *Adding Machine.* Disregarding all obstacles, Federal Theatre in four years put on thousands of productions—classics, new plays, old plays in experimental form, dance dramas, children's plays, religious plays, vaudeville and variety, even a theatre of the air. It created and perfected the Living Newspaper. It showed the feasibility of multiple production of the same play when in 1936 *It Can't Happen Here* opened simultaneously in over a score of theatres throughout the country. It enlisted the support of George Bernard Shaw and Eugene O'Neill, who for nominal royalties agreed to nation-wide production of their plays. Until funds for the purpose were withheld, it published a *Federal Theatre Magazine,* and organized excellent research and service bureaus. Most important of all, perhaps, it brought the theatre to a vast new audience, some of whom had never seen a play before.

The most original and socially significant contribution of Federal Theatre was the Living Newspaper, a form suggested by Miss Flanagan and derived from widely scattered sources—among them the *commedia dell'arte,* Mei Lanfang, Aristophanes, and the movies. Under the sponsorship of the Newspaper Guild, the Living Newspaper unit was organized on the plan of a city newspaper with editors, reporters, copyreaders, and so on, who would be responsible for research, facts, and writing. The resulting dramatic form, which had no plot in the usual sense, was intended to dramatize a current problem, tracing its historical origin and development and taking a positive stand on its solution. Great ingenuity was displayed in devising new technical methods or devices—employment of a loud-speaker for the voice of the Living Newspaper or of an old tenement house; frequent use of scrim, projection, and moving pictures; action on different levels or ramps with imaginative use of spotlight and blackout; playing of scenes in silhouette; clever stage business and properties to illustrate abstract points. The current problems considered in the plays were not designed to ease the minds of rugged individualists and ultraconservatives. *Ethiopia*, first Living Newspaper, never reached the boards because of political complications. *Triple-A Plowed Under* (1936) and *Injunction Granted* (1936) gave the liberal point of view on controversial topics. Arthur Arent's *Power* (1937) made a strong plea for TVA and public ownership of utilities, denouncing monopolistic private concerns for their flexible rate base, intricate holding companies, subsidized college professors, and undercover political activities. *Spirochete* (1938) by Arnold Sundgaard outlined the long fight against syphilis and ended by urging all states to require premarital blood tests. Best and most spectacular of the Living Newspapers was Arthur Arent's *One Third of a Nation*, which opened in New York in January, 1938, and was soon produced throughout the country. Borrowing its title from President Roosevelt's second Inaugural Address, the play begins with a fire in an "old-law tenement," explains the helplessness of city authorities in remedying fire hazards and insanitary conditions, then proceeds to trace the history of land speculation in New York City from the early days of Trinity Church to the present with its malodorous story of criminally neglected tenements. Ascribing the still-existent evils to the profit motive and to public inertia, *One Third of a Nation* not only supports rent strikes but forcefully argues for cheap government housing. The play dramatically ends, as it started, with a tenement fire. A properly frightening set was designed by Howard Bay for the New York production—an entire house in the slums with rooms exposed to view whenever the action required. Objective lessons in insanitary toilets were further strengthened by moving pictures in a nightmarish exposure of filthy living conditions. The older playgoer might feel the theatre had traveled a long way from the days of *Pollyanna* and *Peg o' My Heart*, but he would nevertheless have to admit that *One Third of a Nation* put on a good show.

Living Newspapers proved to be only too successful in calling attention to current evils and in arousing public opinion. Other productions, too, like *Turpentine*, provoked the ire of private industry, and by 1938–1939 strong opposition to Federal Theatre made itself felt in Congress. In her book *Arena* Hallie Flanagan has told simply and without rancor the lurid story of the political battles that ended Federal Theatre on June 30, 1939—a story of malice and misinformation, of trailing the red herring of communism across the path, of trying a case behind closed doors with no adequate presentation of the evidence. Two Congressional committees, headed by Martin Dies and Clifton A. Woodrum respectively, were most instrumental in defeating the project. Not even a great rally by all forces in the American theatre and a temporary victory in the Senate could save the Federal Theatre. The highlight in this Congressional farce-tragedy came with the question by Representative Starnes as to whether "this Marlowe"—author of *Dr. Faustus*—was a Communist. Sinister political implications were also seen in Conkle's *Prologue to Glory*, about Lincoln's early years, and in *The Revolt of the Beavers*, a play for children. The former seems unduly to have wounded the delicate sensibilities of Washington politicians. The latter, by Oscar Halpern and Lou Lantz, is concerned with the overthrow of a tyrannical beaver king and his gang by a group of beavers who have been deprived of bark. The barkless beavers start their revolution by organizing a strike. In its theme and lines (a little girl in the play wishes first that she had a big piece of chocolate and second that her father might get a job) *The Revolt of the Beavers* had undeniable leftist coloring, but it is doubtful that its influence could have proved too nefarious. In any case, the entire history of Federal Theatre, as Miss Flanagan points out, shows that the most violent criticism came from persons who had never attended its productions. No one would claim that the project offered a true model for a permanent national theatre, or that its performance equaled the best on the commercial stage, but its achievements in experimental drama, in the Negro theatre, in unusual productions like *Murder in the Cathedral* and *Dr. Faustus,* in the development of the Living Newspaper and other drama of social significance, give it an important place in the history of the period—quite apart from its primary function of aiding the unemployed actor.

Another important development of the thirties was the formation of the Group Theatre, which had the distinction of developing the most capable dramatist of the leftist movement—Clifford Odets, author of the militant *Waiting for Lefty* and of half a dozen long plays which brought him recognition as the most brilliant new playwright of the thirties. Odets was member and product of the Group, as they decided to call themselves, organized in 1931 by Harold Clurman, Lee Strasberg, and Cheryl Crawford, who had been associated with the Theatre Guild. Their primary aims were to establish new and more vital relations between actor and author, between actor and actor, and above all, between the actors and the society in which they lived. They were not committed to social and political radicalism, especially at the start, but were in search of serious, nonescapist scripts, preferably with social implications. Only by living, rehearsing, discussing, working, and thinking together—they felt—could they realize the full possibilities of a permanent acting company and as a result achieve in their productions greater unity and more significant social connotations. After a summer spent in the country with Lee Strasberg developing novel acting techniques based on the Stanislavsky system, the Group—with the financial aid of the Guild—put on *The House of Connelly* in the fall of 1931. In the next ten years, often bumpy ones and scarcely marked by the desired community of feeling, the Group emerged as the outstanding producing organization on Broadway. Some of its memorable presentations have been mentioned—Lawson's *Success Story*, Kingsley's *Men in White*, Shaw's *The Gentle People*, and Green's *Johnny Johnson*. They produced practically all of Odets' work and the first play by Saroyan, *My Heart's in the Highlands*. Even their failures were honorable ones: Paul and Claire Sifton's *1931*, Anderson's *Night over Taos*, Lawson's *Gentlewoman*, and Ardrey's *Casey Jones*. The Group continued the pleasant practice of rusticating en masse during the summer. Occasionally actors deserted—notably Franchot Tone—but most remained for many seasons, among them Morris Carnovsky, J. E. Bromberg, Art Smith, Stella Adler and her brother Luther Adler, all original members. Among later acquisitions were Elia Kazan, Alexander Kirkland, Frances Farmer, Jane Wyatt—to name a few. Their skillful acting in diversified roles showed the advantage of a permanent company and gained for the Group a regular and growing audience. The company was never officially disbanded but internal strife and the failure of two productions in 1940 halted its operation. Its disintegration Clurman blames primarily on the inevitable conflict between its ideals—artistic and social—and the necessity of surviving on commercial Broadway. Without a fair number of hits it could not keep going financially; yet the scripts it most wanted to produce offered little promise of large box-office returns. In surviving ten years the Group achieved almost the impossible.

One of the original members of the Group, Odets acted minor roles and attempted writing on the side. The second act of his *I've Got the Blues*, which did not impress Clurman unduly, was tried out with fair success at an adult camp where the company was performing one summer. Revised and renamed *Awake and Sing*, it was presented by the Group on Broadway in 1935, some six weeks after the first performance of *Waiting for Lefty*. While it has a Marxian slant, *Awake and Sing* is mainly a realistic portrayal of lower-middle-class life in the Bronx. To the Berger family, weighed down by drudgery, petty poverty, and bourgeois convention, life seems pretty hopeless. The real head of the family is Bessie Berger, the mother, who has had to assume responsibility in lieu of her ineffectual, unsuccessful husband. Ralph, the son, is trapped by the business depression and a hopeless love affair. When the daughter, Hennie, is discovered to be pregnant— and her lover conspicuously absent—the practical, self-reliant Bessie gets her married off in haste to an unsuspecting suitor, Sam Feinschreiber. A boarder in the household, Jacob, an elderly unemployed barber, divides his time between playing victrola records and reading Marxian literature. "If this life leads to a revolution," he tells Ralph, "it's a good life. Otherwise it's for nothing." Later Jacob advises the boy to forget the girl for more important matters; the world needs remaking and at no time have opportunities been as favorable as now. Only after the old man has committed suicide does Ralph emerge from the doldrums and follow his advice to awake and sing—read radical books, act, get together with his fellow workers. Hennie, too, unhappy in the marriage forced upon her, experiences a conversion to action. Discarding the shackles of usage and sentimentality, she runs away from her baby and husband to live with the man she has always loved. She feels liberated and awakens to a new life. The play stresses the meanness arising from poverty and Jacob makes occasional radical speeches about war and capitalism, but along with its effective social significance *Awake and Sing* has the advantage of superb and convincing characterization—a feature usually lacking in proletarian drama. The play's spirit of rebellion leading at last to optimism and direct action offers an illuminating contrast to the early *Ambush,* where characters in somewhat similar circumstances become merely depressed and disillusioned.

Waiting for Lefty and *Awake and Sing* made Odets immediately famous. In comparison, his next two plays—*Till the Day I Die,* a melodramatic anti-Nazi one-acter, and *Paradise Lost,* an account of the disintegration of the middle-classes—were both disappointing. Harold Clurman has written eloquently in defense of *Paradise Lost* and Odets has called it his favorite play (compare O'Neill's preference for *Lazarus Laughed*). It was unsuccessful in the theatre, however, and careful reading of the script reveals few merits. The fall of the middle-class Gordons is confusing dramatically and the characters never come to life. They are credible neither as human beings nor as symbols—which Clurman argues they are. The play, however, gave Odets the excellent record of having four Broadway productions within one year, after which he departed for Hollywood. There, among other activities, he married Luise Rainer and was author of a moving picture on a Chinese subject—*The General Dies at Dawn*.

Odets' later plays were leftist more by implication than direct statement; they dealt with personal situations and continued to stress character. *Golden Boy*, financially most profitable of all Group productions, opened in November, 1937. It bears some slight resemblance to Lawson's *Success Story* in its account of a man whose success in the wrong direction and in a world of commercial enterprise brings on his own destruction. Joe Bonaparte, son of an Italian peddler, introverted by hurt feelings and a keen sense of his own insignificance, has a tremendous driving ambition to become somebody, to win fame and fortune. At great sacrifice his father, who believes in the possibility of a good life through the arts, has made a musician of Joe and for his twenty-first birthday has brought him an expensive violin. Joe has learned boxing, however, and discovers in prize fighting the career that will bring him wealth and recognition. But he retains an inner yearning for music and tends to save his hands by pulling his punches. Soon he discovers that he no longer belongs to himself, that the managers, gamblers, and gunmen who own "a piece of him" have taken over his life. They are able to turn him into a fighter, a killer. Glorying in the fistic cognomen of "the cockeyed wonder," he becomes arrogant, conceited, disagreeable. His bitterness has arisen in part from an unhappy love affair with his manager's mistress. An important prize fight ends tragically when with a furious punch Joe kills his opponent, an accident that brings him to a realization of what he has done to himself and his own life. With the manager's girl he drives out furiously in his new expensive car until the two are killed in a crash. Joe's tragic dichotomy is contrasted to the complete psychological integration of his older brother, an organizer for the C.I.O., who fights not for fame and luxury but for his principles and is therefore "at harmony with millions of others." It is obvious that the story of a musician who becomes a prize fighter holds far wider application than its immediate theme and refers to the problem of the individual in modern society, who desires and demands recognition but in order to secure it in a commercial world must sell his soul. Some have seen a parallel, also, between Joe Bonaparte's career and the author's desertion of Broadway for Hollywood.

Rocket to the Moon (1938) has more personal than social significance. Its chief figure is a henpecked, middle-aged dentist, plodding along in a drab, uneventful life, punctuated only by quarrels with his nagging wife. He falls in love with his secretary—a cheap and silly but highly emotional little girl who is trying to escape from a depressing home environment. Their ensuing love affair is doomed; the dentist cannot break off with his wife and as soon as the secretary realizes this she departs. But from the experience the girl has grown in confidence and maturity. She now knows what she wants from life: "a whole full world, with all the trimmings." The dentist, too, has profited; the affair has brought him exaltation and a sense of his own importance. "Take a rocket to the moon! Explode!" his father-in-law advised him earlier, and love for the first time has brought him a sharp, clear view of the real world.

This paean to love in a dental office was followed with two failures—*Night Music* (1940), a kind of tone poem with musical accompaniment, and *Clash by Night* (1941), first work of Odets not produced by the Group. Since then this best of leftist playwrights has remained silent, halting—temporarily perhaps—a dramatic career that seemed as brilliant and meteoric as O'Neill's two decades earlier. As we have seen, the proletarianism of *Waiting for Lefty* and (in part) of *Awake and Sing* became less explicit in his later work. For all his leftist ties and sympathies Odets was by no means a complete or consistent Marxian, but it is precisely because he is more artist than propagandist that his plays have greater vitality than, let us say, *Marching Song* or even *The Cradle Will Rock*. His virtues as a dramatist are great. No one has shown keener observation of the little people of the bourgeois world—the Berger family; the philosophical Mr. Carp; Siggie, the wisecracking taxi driver; Sam Feinschreiber, who runs to his mother-in-law for consolation after a marital dispute; Cleo Singer, dental secretary and eternal Eve. These and similar types are made to live on the stage with the aid of Odets' great gift for stage dialogue—crisp, dramatic, humorous. Odets' humor is rarely contrived or factitious but arises naturally out of character. The author's concern with love is unusual in proletarian drama. In his plays this passion is often shown as frustrated by social or personal restraints; only by the breaking of sentimental or conventional shackles does it find true fulfillment. This personal rebellion seems as prominent in Odets' work as his more Marxian protest against society. Be yourself, lead your own life—he seems to say—give in to love but don't allow it to interfere with your mission; protest against poverty and social evils, and unite with others in creating a better world. Through love, self-expression, and rebellion Odets' characters are driven to personal conversion—not unlike religious conversion in its intensity—which leads to full realization or to action. This is characteristic of the reforming movement of the thirties and rather than strict ideology accounts for much of the leftism in Odets' plays.

The many pages of this chapter have sought to explain and

illustrate the native playwright's changing view of American life during a period of some twenty-five years. There need be, in retrospect, no serious quarrel about the hazardous classification of plays as realistic or imaginative, especially when we learn that the Group interpreted *Awake and Sing*, seemingly the height of realism, as poetic drama. Many plays could appear with equal justness in either category. Regardless of their exact form or treatment the dramatic works herein considered attempted to reveal, dissect, ridicule, or modify the American scene. More often than not, imaginative drama lost itself in the picturesque unrealities of *Marco Millions* or the rhetoric of *Elizabeth the Queen* or the philosophical platitudes of *Here Come the Clowns*. Excellent as these three plays are in many ways, they are more of the theatre than of the outside world. Realistic drama provided a forum for the free discussion of current ideas in a difficult and troubled period. Right or wrong in their opinions, the playwrights wrote scathingly and earnestly on what they saw or felt. They maintained always a liberal or radical point of view. They showed sympathy for the downtrodden and the exploited. It is difficult to avoid the conclusion that their work has been the most significant drama of the period. In tracing their contribution we have seen that the insurgent art theatre, victorious in the twenties, was followed in the thirties by a narrower dramatic revolution in favor of social significance and propaganda. The realistic playwright's depiction of the world we live in thus ended in the quest for a brave new world, democratic or proletarian.

Chapter 6

COMEDY—AMERICAN PLAN

*W*HILE REALISM and propaganda were de-
lighting the social critics, comedy, after 1917 as before, continued to draw the cash customers. The kind of laughter it
provided, however, was not the same. Most of the earlier
comic types survived, but sentimental comedy fell into a con-
sumptive decline, as did the tailored farce-comedy dear to
William Collier and George M. Cohan. These forms, along
with the romantic and period pieces, were soon taken over by
the movies, which could handle them better for a less sophisticated audience. We find Mary Pickford and William
Collier, for example, starring in 1920 in a screen version of the
sentimental *Pollyanna*—already passé on Broadway—and in
its search for tear-jerkers Hollywood exhumed even the hoary
Way down East. Domestic comedy, whether tearful or humorous, held its popularity in the theatre but tended to rise
into high comedy and manners, as a comparison of *Abie's
Irish Rose* and *Life with Father* would indicate. The prewar
bedroom farces and the timid discussions of trial marriage or
feminism became more closely wedded to domestic drama and
developed into what may loosely be called "sex plays," concerned with such topics as marriage, divorce, and the Younger
Generation. They, too, tended to become elevated to a comedy of manners. As for high comedy, practically nonexistent
before 1917, it found worthy practitioners at last in Philip
Barry and S. N. Behrman. Perhaps the greatest change in the
twenties and thirties was to be found in the gaudy blossoming
of low comedy, which turned first to realism, then to satire
and the depiction of mores, discovering thereby the potential-

ities of a genuine comic spirit. To an earlier, more polite
audience the Kaufmans, the Harts, the Abbotts might seem
to have debauched the comic muse into a ribald trollop of
the horselaugh and Bronx cheer, but the impartial and less
sensitive observer must recognize her vast improvement in
the process. One of the older comic formulas was well expressed by George M. Cohan in 1920: "In my own plays
I have assumed that audiences wouldn't mind if the plays I
wrote made them laugh a bit, cry a bit, and go out whistling."
The 1930 or 1940 audience would have little cause to cry
and it would be more apt to go out leering than whistling.

Considering the period as a whole, one is struck not only
by the infinite variety of comic forms but also by the efforts,
largely successful, to develop a true native comedy with distinctly American characters and themes. Like the serious
playwrights the comic dramatists surveyed the American
scene and faithfully recorded their observations—even to the
smell of frying onions in a lunch wagon. In lieu of indignation
and propaganda, however, they preferred the traditional cor-
rectives of laughter and satire, and who will say that they
were not more successful in the long run than the Jeremiahs
of social significance? Prohibition's early rout on the Broadway stage must have had considerable effect on its eventual
repeal, and *Chicago, The Front Page*, and *Once in a Lifetime* were bound to leave a few scars on American politics,
journalism, and movies. All this is not to say that comedy had
become suddenly Aristophanic or Voltairian. Broadway
comedy was still mainly escapist, but it was gradually becoming topical, realistic, outspoken; and on occasion it was not
without its social comment. What comic types were prevalent
and popular from 1917 to the middle forties will be the concern of the present chapter; as heretofore the plays will be
loosely classified, with no rigid attention to chronology.
Comedies of fantasy and imagination have been discussed
earlier. Excellent as they are at their best, notably in the
work of Saroyan and Wilder, they are relatively few and stand

rather apart from the main line of American comic tradition. Except for occasional casual comment they will not be considered again here.

The evolution of public taste is necessarily gradual, and we find sentimental and romantic comedy—prewar favorites—still going strong after 1917. Among popular pieces of 1918 were Austin Strong's *Three Wise Fools*, a pleasant sentimental opus about a girl (Helen Menken) brought up by three middle-aged bachelors, and John L. Hobble's *Daddies*, a drippingly tender play in which a group of war orphans are adopted by no less than four bachelors. Rachel Crothers' highly sentimental *A Little Journey* attracted attention for its then unusual setting in a Pullman car and was enlivened by a train wreck. John Taintor Foote's *Toby's Bow* (1919), another sweet comedy, featured George Marion in the Negro role of Uncle Toby, dignified Southern servitor who develops an intense dislike for a visitor's Japanese valet, whom he insists on calling a "yallah niggah." *The Charm School* (1920) by Alice Duer Miller and Robert Milton tells the *Saturday Evening Postish* tale of an automobile salesman who inherits a girls' school, revolutionizes the curriculum, and falls in love with one of his students. Similarly escapist is a Belasco production of 1922, Hubert Osborne's *Shore Leave*, in which Frances Starr as a spinster dressmaker engages in a sentimental love chase ending in the capture of one Bilge Smith, a U.S. sailor. Another star, Jane Cowl, appeared in Allan Langdon Martin's *Smilin' Through* (1919), wherein ghosts of fifty years ago attempt to interfere with a present-day romance. Other romantic pieces include Robert Housum's *The Gipsy Trail* (1917) and Arthur Richman's *Not So Long Ago* (1920), a period comedy about New York in the 1870's with Eva Le Gallienne as the tender heroine. These plays were all competently written and popular, though they could scarcely be called distinguished.

Many sentimental or humorous potpourris took the form of

dramatic character sketches. Best known and longest lived
was *Lightnin'* (1918) by Winchell Smith and Frank Bacon,
in which the latter played an eccentric Rip Van Winkle character with a penchant for liquor and tall stories. His best yarn
about driving a swarm of bees across the plains in the dead of
winter was employed to humorous advantage in a courtroom
scene. One factor in the play's success was the colorful western
setting, including the Calivada Hotel, half in California and
half in Nevada, with its boundary complications and its
clientele of aspiring divorcées. Other popular ingredients include the machinations of rascally lawyers, an upright young
hero who foils the rascals at the price of temporary estrangement from the heroine, and a final sentimental reconciliation
between Lightnin' and his wife, after the latter had started a
divorce action. All this may not add up to a great play, but
it did add up to 1,291 performances on Broadway.

Cut on the same pattern, though far less successful, was
The Old Soak (1922) based upon Don Marquis' newspaper
character. In keeping with Broadway's strong antiprohibition
sentiment the hero was an alcoholic and the villain an abste-
mious deacon. Another comic personage—this time from F. P.
Adams' column—was transferred to the stage in *Dulcy* (1921)
by George S. Kaufman and Marc Connelly, with Lynn Fontanne giving a perfect performance as a blundering, bromidic
nitwit whose efforts to help her husband's business career
nearly bring about his ruin but unexpectedly turn out all right
in the end. Character plays made good star vehicles if nothing
else, and several young players were establishing their reputation in them. In 1919 Alfred Lunt gave comic life to the role
of Clarence in Booth Tarkington's play about a famous en-
tomologist recently discharged from the army who enters a
household and becomes confidant and peacemaker for the
entire family. In the same comedy Helen Hayes appeared as
a self-willed adolescent. A few years later Edna Ferber and
George S. Kaufman collaborated on *Minick* (1924), character
sketch of an old man who comes to live with his son and

daughter-in-law, to everybody's discomfort. Old Minick finally decides he has his own life to lead and happily sets out for the Old Men's Home and the more congenial companionship of his cronies. Among subsequent character comedies might be mentioned *Kibitzer* (1929) by Jo Swerling and Edward G. Robinson, a combination of humor and pathos about Mr. Lazarus, owner of a cigar store on Amsterdam Avenue in New York City, whose addiction to kibitzing very nearly brings about his ruin. With the excellent acting of Edward G. Robinson as the kibitzer, the play did much to popularize a term which was then still quite novel.

Except perhaps in emphasis there is little difference between the character play and domestic comedy. Comic drama between two world wars was predominantly bourgeois, with marriage and the family providing one of the main concerns of the popular dramatist. Whereas the sex plays were often satirical, the true domestic comedy tended to remain sentimental or humorous, with occasional lapses into farce. Negligible as it may be as drama, Anne Nichols' *Abie's Irish Rose* (1922) deserves mention here for its longevity record— 2,327 performances—not surpassed on Broadway until the over seven-year run of *Tobacco Road*. The Nichols farce, deservedly ridiculed by most of the critics, relies upon simple and obvious slapstick elements. The Jewish hero, Abie, has secretly married Rose Mary, a girl of Irish parentage, in a Methodist ceremony. His father is as rabidly anti-Irish as hers is anti-Semitic. Abie therefore introduces the girl to his father as Miss Murphyski and in the farcical complications that follow the couple are married again by a rabbi and once again by a Catholic priest. The embattled fathers are not reconciled until Rose becomes the mother of twins (the third act surprise), who are named respectively Patrick Joseph and Rebecca, thus buttering both racial sides of the family. From this feeble situation Anne Nichols derives an object lesson against race prejudice. In the words of Father Whelan, "Now if the Jews and the Irish would only stop fighting and get together,

they'd own a corner of the world." This little message helped
the play's success in the tolerant twenties, along with the
perennial Romeo-Juliet situation and the profusion of comic-
strip Jewish dialect ("esk," "nize," "texeskebs"). The play offers dismal enough reading, but it is undeniable that its broad
humor proved stageworthy.

Other domestic hits were somewhat wittier. Consider, for
example, Anthony McGuire's *Six Cylinder Love* (1921), a
play with a homely moral about the evils of extravagant living
in the suburbs. A newly married couple are getting along
nicely, with only the traditional burned biscuits to cloud their
felicity, until they are persuaded by a high-pressure salesman
(he introduces himself by crashing the car into their backyard fence!) to buy their neighbor's six-cylinder car. This
misstep leads the husband to mortgage the house, support
a flock of parasites, and eventually lose his job. He ends up in
a city apartment and gradually pays off his debts. This new
mode of life wins him a better job from his erstwhile boss, and
his happiness is complete when he sells the six-cylinder white
elephant to the janitor and learns his wife is going to have
a baby. Ernest Truex and June Walker were naïvely charming
as husband and wife. Another domestic comedy, which was
truly a family affair, appeared in 1922. *Kempy*, by J. C. Nugent, a vaudeville monologist, and his son Elliott, included
the two authors in its cast as well as Ruth Nugent, Elliott's
sister. Slight as the play is, the situation has considerable
humor. A young plumber coming to fix the pipes for a suburban family impulsively marries one of two unmarried
daughters only to discover—all this on the same day—that
he really loves the other one. That the latter reciprocates
his affection is made clear by an astonishing bit of stage business. She has polished Kempy's wrench in his absence and
lovingly wrapped it in cheesecloth; now as she goes upstairs
she hugs the wrench to her bosom.

At its best domestic comedy came far closer than *Kempy* to
the representation of actual life. Maxwell Anderson's *Satur-*

day's Children (1927), a successful production of the Actors' Theatre, was a veritable saga of white-collar marriage on forty dollars a week. Written with humor the play records the minutiae of lower middle-class life in New York. Rims O'Neill, the hero, has received the offer of a new job in South America, but Bobby, his girl friend, is persuaded by her older sister to hook him by time-worn but effective method. The result is that Rims remains in New York and Bobby gives up her job as secretary. But marriage on a limited income does not run too smoothly. The sister gives additional practical advice about having a baby or two to keep a husband, but Bobby is tired of playing the game and too honest to engage in further deception. She leaves Rims and goes back to her job; later, when Rims climbs up the fire-escape to her furnished room and the two are reunited, it is not as a married couple but as lovers. The raisonneur of the piece is Bobby's father, who feels that girls too are entitled to have their fling. "Fall in love—" he advises; "have your affair—and when it's over—get out!" Later he says significantly: "Marriage is no love affair. It's little old last year's love affair, my dear. It's a house and bills and dishpans and family quarrels. That's the way the system beats you." The reflection of postwar changes in manners and conditions makes *Saturday's Children* a social as well as a realistic comedy, but it proved to be an extremely engaging one with Ruth Gordon doing an excellent job of interpreting Bobby.

An earlier marital play, *The First Year* (1920) by Frank Craven, author of *Too Many Cooks*, offered a simple story of a small-town girl who after much hesitation accepts one of two suitors. A year later finds her husband Tommy (Frank Craven) struggling along on a small income. Just as Tommy engineers a business deal which may prove successful, the other suitor shows up and temporarily disrupts the deal. The ensuing domestic quarrel ends with the wife's departure for home and Tommy is left alone to drown his sorrows in a full shaker of cocktails. In an amusing scene of inebriation he advises the maid, if she must get married, not to get married until the *second* year. Needless to add, the business deal comes through, the couple are reunited, and the wife is going to have the inevitable baby. While *The First Year* lacked the intellectual implications of *Saturday's Children,* it offered an evening of pleasant and not irrational entertainment.

The play of family life, treated with humor or sentiment rather than satire, continued to find a place on the Broadway stage, the later examples often showing more maturity and higher literary quality. Paul Osborn's *Morning's at Seven* (1939) deserves brief notice for its quaint originality in representing a family of elderly New Jersey eccentrics. Homer, despite his forty-two years, is still Mamma's boy. He has never spent a night away from home and it is only with the greatest trepidation that he agrees to bring Myrtle, the girl with whom he has been keeping company for seven years, to visit the family. After a terrific struggle Homer is finally successful in breaking his home ties with the incredible announcement that Myrtle is pregnant. Equally amusing is Homer's father, a successful builder, who is seized with periodic spells during which he believes he is a failure because he took the wrong turning at the crossroads and did not become a dentist. In spite of its short run on Broadway the play is genuinely entertaining and as a matter of fact has proved highly successful in stock and on the amateur stage.

The changes in domestic drama may also be seen in a comparison of Rose Franken's *Claudia* (1941) with any of the marital plays of the twenties. Here we have a realistic study of a girl-wife who is prevented from completely growing up by the insistent pressure of a mother fixation. This emotional tie prevents full happiness in marriage and leads the girl to doubt her own sex appeal. It is only when an overheard phone conversation reveals to her that her mother will soon die of cancer that she is suddenly shocked into maturity and independence. Instead of the earlier comic minutiae of married life the author presents a realistic and psychological, though sympathetic, study of human relationships in a play that borders closely on tragedy. The popularity of *Claudia* with matinee audiences showed that its situation held considerable import for women. Frances Starr, once the hell-bent heroine of *The Easiest Way*, played the mother with humor and delicate understanding, with Donald Cook as the tolerant husband and Dorothy McGuire as the inhibited wife. The only circumstance Claudia had in common with her counterparts of the twenties was that she too became pregnant.

On occasion domestic comedy became reminiscent of earlier times when family life was more real, graceful, and dignified. *Ah, Wilderness!*, it will be remembered, gave a delightful picture of a middle-class American family of 1906 faced with the problems—among others—of the alcoholic uncle and the adolescent boy. Similarly Howard Lindsay and Russel Crouse in *Life with Father* (1939), their dramatization of the Clarence Day *New Yorker* sketches, drew a vivid portrait of a Victorian household. For all his brilliant plumage and explosive speech Father cannot cope with the wiles and tears of Vinnie, her romantic bookkeeping, her disregard of logic, her invitations to relatives, her insistence that he be baptized. He is inevitably beaten, but with topsails flying. Like the head of the family in *Ah, Wilderness!* he gives one of his sons timely advice about women but with a somewhat different slant: "A woman doesn't think at all! She gets stirred up! And she gets stirred up over the damnedest things!" The only hope for a man is to be firm. The play has little plot, outside of Vinnie's successful campaign to have Father baptized, but draws its humor from contemporary manners, the interplay of character, the long procession of maids, the visits of the rector, the sudden cordiality of Father when he discovers the guests are about to leave, the inability of the son Clarence—after he has had one of Father's suits cut down— to make the suit do anything Father wouldn't do: these are among the many touches or episodes one remembers. The co-author, Howard Lindsay, and Dorothy Stickney created the original roles of Father and Vinnie, but the couple were represented on tour by many other illustrious players.

American family life cannot be considered complete without children, and many domestic dramatists preferred to focus attention on them rather than on their elders. On the sentimental and quaintly humorous side was the depiction of youth in two plays of 1918 derived from Booth Tarkington— *Seventeen* and *Penrod.* Here we find small-town boys and girls with their growing pains, love affairs, embarrassments, escapades, and tragedies. *Seventeen,* dramatized by Hugh Stanislaus and Stannard Mears, tells of the tragicomic infatuation of William Baxter (Gregory Kelly) for the baby-talk girl who is visiting a neighbor, a part played to perfection by Ruth Gordon. Adapted by Edward E. Rose, *Penrod* has a simple little plot about the humorous activities of Penrod and his gang of "detectifs," ending with the unexpected capture of a criminal. The play is interesting for the appearance of Helen Hayes as Penrod's sister—one of her first roles— and of another child actress, Helen Chandler. Engaging children and adolescents—with no particular reference to social or moral problems—continued to appear on Broadway, but a score of years elapsed before dramatists fully capitalized upon the antics of youngsters in a number of hilarious farces. By then the stage adolescents have grown in sophistication, and despite their farcical elements the plays themselves become far less naïve than the Tarkington variety. Clifford Goldsmith's *What a Life* (1938), for example, with Ezra Stone as a high-school lad with an infinite capacity for getting into hot water, has a serious vein in its criticism of parents who expect their children to be bright and who insist on leading their lives for them. Poor Henry Aldrich is expected to go to Princeton but he is, alas, no scholar. When his mother insists on his getting the highest mark in a Roman history exam, the task proves hopeless from the start since he lost his history book three weeks before. Even his mother gives up hope finally, and it is decided that Henry will go to art school, for which at least he has some aptitude.

The preadolescent, 1941 model, received both recognition and glorification in *Junior Miss,* a dramatization by Jerome Chodorov and Joseph Fields of Sally Benson's *New Yorker* sketches. Thirteen-year-old Judy, youngest of the Graves family, and her inseparable confidante and accomplice Fuffy, live in a lurid world of their own—product in part of their devoted attendance at the movies. Judy's imaginative powers become evident in a highly romanticized autobiography she writes for school, in her mistaking her father's harmless affection for his secretary as the mark of an illicit affair, and in her assumption that Uncle Willis—back after some years' absence—has just been released from a jail term. Her effort to straighten things out leads to innumerable complications, which, however, are satisfactorily resolved. Patricia Peardon as Judy and Lenore Lonergan as Fuffy were convincingly comic and sometimes terrifying. The authors offered also an amusing picture of adolescence in the older sister Lois and her retinue of gauche admirers. While this was a far cry from the Tarkington era, even greater contrast appears in F. Hubert Herbert's *Kiss and Tell* (1943), amusing account of a family feud in which fifteen-year-old Corliss Archer—suspected of being pregnant—places the blame on perfectly innocuous Dexter next door. The misunderstanding is later cleared, but the play revels in *double entendre* and adolescent sophistication. "Ever since I had to wear brassieres," says Corliss, "my family has been watching me like a couple of hawks." And when Mrs. Archer objects to her husband's assertion that Corliss has "a streak of bitchery," he merely qualifies his statement: "Let's call it femininity, then." The moral climate is decidedly different from that of the world of William Baxter, the baby-talk girl, and the parents of 1918.

One important reason for this transformation in moral attitudes, affecting even domestic comedy about children in their teens, is to be found in the rise and popularity of "sex plays"—themselves product of the revolution in manners discussed in Chapter II, with Greenwich Village as its extreme manifestation. Although it occasionally appeared earlier, the sex play belongs mainly to the twenties. By then its predecessors on Broadway—the bedroom farce and the play with the punch—were dying out. *Up in Mabel's Room* (1919) and its hayloft variant, *Getting Gertie's Garter* (1921), just about marked the former's demise, both inexplicably revived twenty years later by the movies. The punch play was preserved in sensational melodrama on the order of John Colton's *The Shanghai Gesture*. The new sex play, as developed in farce and comedy, presented a variety of topics. It might deal with ladies of pleasure or with prostitution, as in *The Golddiggers* (1919) or *Ladies of the Evening* (1924). The latter, by Milton Herbert Gropper, argues that prostitutes are merely victims of circumstances and environment and can be regenerated. On a bet, an idealistic sculptor attempts to prove this thesis by separating one Kay from her professional activities and taking personal charge of her reformation. Learning that the hero's interest was motivated by a bet rather than by love Kay temporarily returns to her old life, but when the sculptor finds her in a restaurant respectably bustling about as a waitress, he confesses his own love and offers marriage. Produced by Belasco, the piece was no doubt designed to attract by its sensationalism rather than by a serious discussion of a social problem, but it indicates at least the direction of the theatrical winds.

Several plays of the twenties deal humorously with the theme of bastardy. Edward Childs Carpenter, writer of prewar sentimental pieces, developed with considerable humor in his *Bachelor Father* (1928) the idea of a gouty old Englishman—Sir Basil Winterton, V.C., K.C.B., K.C.G.M.—who gathers under his roof in Surrey all his available illegitimate offspring. Two of them show apparently incestuous affection for each other, but one turns out not to be Sir Basil's after all

and they are free to love. The old gentleman's favorite is
Tony a slangy gamin from New York's East Side, but she
too deserts her father for marriage. As she tells Sir Basil to
console him for losing her, "It'll be the first wedding in *this*
family!" Supposed illegitimacy motivates Clare Kummer's
Pomeroy's Past (1926) when everyone misunderstands a
young bachelor's desire to adopt a child, and the real thing
forms the basis of *The Little Accident* (1928) by Floyd Dell
and Thomas Mitchell. In this play the hero, on the verge of
marriage, learns that he has just become a father as the consequence of an affair with an art student in Boston. The
mother prefers her career to marriage and baby, but after
the hero has kidnaped the infant and the fiancée has withdrawn, she is finally persuaded to become an honest woman.
The theme of bastardy recurs in Laurence E. Johnson's *It's a
Wise Child* (1929), where a respectable girl succeeds in getting out of a distasteful engagement only by pretending she is
about to become a mother—a slight but excellently cast production by Belasco. This and the other comedies on the subject were written with verve and with evident delight at
making free with the conventions.

Most of the sex plays of the twenties were not concerned
with such potentially serious matters as illegitimacy and prostitution but rather with changes in manners and morals as they
affected the family. The Younger Generation, the new woman,
the gigolo, infidelity, divorce—these became the recurrent
motifs in a thousand permutations. Their interrelation of
theme and their variety make it impossible to discuss them
in any truly coherent order, but a few examples should suggest the interests of both audiences and dramatists. Few topics
were as absorbing to the twenties as the revolt of the Younger
Generation against conventions. The drama of the twenties is
replete with such assorted phenomena as flappers, jazz babies,
cake eaters, sex appeal, vamping, the shimmy, cocktails, lip-
stick, necking, roadsters, and flaming youth. The Greenwich
Village revolution had borne fruit, if not always of the kind

expected by the early intellectuals and feminists. The war had hastened the breakdown of barriers, and Prohibition with its hip flasks and speakeasies was offering a favorable climate for a radical change. To this change the playwrights might be personally sympathetic but for the sake of their bread and butter, depending primarily on the older generation, they tended to play safe. A common approach was to censure or ridicule the flapper and her male counterpart but at the same time to show that they had intrinsically good qualities and would come out all right in the end. Such was the burden, for example, of Lewis Beach's *The Goose Hangs High* (1924). The boy and girl of a family, both in college, are depicted as hard, selfish, unsentimental; but when their father loses his job, they show their true character and prove their worth and loyalty. The consternation of the parents, incidentally, had arisen from such relatively mild matters as the daughter's saying "damn" and the son's sophomoric attack on the institution of marriage. Pleasant and urbane, the play is valuable mainly for its picture of contemporary manners.

No one was more skillful at straddling the current moral issues than Rachel Crothers, a prolific writer of sentimental and problem comedies. A keen and sagacious playwright, Miss Crothers in her long and successful career showed an unerring gift for selecting a timely subject, treating it with apparent daring, properly diluted with sentimentality, and ending with the conventional—or at least the matinee audience—viewpoint. *Nice People* (1921) represents one of her typical contributions to the drama of flaming youth. Teddy Gloucester, daughter of a Park Avenue millionaire, practices all the vices of the younger set—smokes, drinks, wears revealing evening dresses, and talks about sex. All this is profoundly disturbing to Teddy's aunt (the girl's mother is dead), who deplores "the emptiness—the soullessness of it all." When Teddy's father forbids her to keep a midnight date with Scottie Wilbur, man-about-town and expert dancer, she goes off to meet him anyway. The two eventually reach the Gloucester summer

cottage on Long Island, with Scottie both bibulous and amorous and a big storm coming up. Teddy's reputation is saved,
after a fashion, by the arrival of Billy Wade, an upright young
stranger, who obligingly sleeps downstairs with Scottie while
Teddy retires upstairs. Next morning Billy Wade departs and
when Teddy's father and members of her fast set come in,
they assume the worst. In a few hours the scandal has incredibly spread all over New York and Teddy has refused to marry
Scottie, who is willing to do the right thing. Now honest Billy
Wade reappears; in an unexpected bucolic twist Rachel
Crothers has him and Teddy decide to turn the summer place
into a farm. In the third act the reformed Teddy has become
the ideal farm girl, devoted to her chickens and the mending
of Billy's socks, but it is only with the greatest effort that she
persuades the prim hero to marry her. He objects to her
money. Whatever its merits, this plea for reforming the wild
flapper by having her compromised and then turning farmer-
ette has some slight historical interest for the presence in the
cast of Tallulah Bankhead and Katharine Cornell as fast society girls. Francine Larrimore played the flaming Teddy.

In 1923 Rachel Crothers returned to the flapper in *Mary the
Third*, a considerably better play which shows the courtship
of three generations of Marys. The youngest Mary, frank and
modern, goes on an unchaperoned camping trip with another
girl and three young men—two of them her suitors. She wants
to find out what these boys are really like before rather than
after marriage. Evading the issue as usual, the author has
Mary suddenly feel her parents were right in forbidding the
trip; she therefore pretends an attack of appendicitis. On
the way home she accepts one of the suitors. Now unfortunately Mary and her brother overhear their parents quarreling
and are shocked at the apparent hate between them. The children insist on a divorce and call their mother a kept woman
because she is financially dependent on her husband. Mary
also decides she will live with her fiancé in sin rather than
wedlock, having discovered the horrors and hypocrisies of a

respectable union. The parents separate temporarily, but when Mary sees how much her opinionated father really loves his wife, though he won't admit it, she sends him back to her and accepts her own suitor in marriage. The final scene parallels the words of the proposals to Mary the first and Mary the second, her mother and her grandmother, which are given in the play's two introductory scenes. Thus each Mary gets her man, though the methods may be different, and each feels hers will be the only lasting marriage in the world. While Miss Crothers played safe in her treatment of the flapper and free love, the play was moderately daring for its time and had the advantage of many amusing lines.

What is the need of repeating these tales of the uninhibited Younger Generation? There were dozens of them—*Chains, Helena's Boys, The Best People*, etc.—most of them condemnatory. It is worth noting once more that the dramatists were treading cautiously, as neither Teddy nor Mary the Third in Miss Crothers' plays had any premarital relations with their boy friends. A more honest treatment of the situation was offered years later in a delightful play of 1937, Mark Reed's *Yes, My Darling Daughter*, where the daughter at least has the courage of her convictions. This play's wit arises from the fact that the girl's mother was a new woman and feminist of the twenties, in fact one of the Greenwich Village pioneers. How would such a woman feel and react when her own daughter goes off to spend a few days with the man she loves? The situation is cleverly contrived. After her free-love days in the Village, Ann has made a conventional marriage with Lewis Murray, a millionaire, charming but conservative. Ellen, the daughter, just out of college, is outspoken and straightforward. The depression makes it impossible for Douglas, whom she loves, to marry her without any means of support. He has given up his study of architecture to take a job in Belgium. It is Ellen's suggestion, which at first shocks the young man but to which he accedes, that they spend together at a summer camp the few remaining days before his sailing. When Ann discovers the plan and tries to prevent Ellen from going, Ellen calls her mother's moral stand both sentimental and hypocritical, not to mention inconsistent. It seems that at college Ellen had written a thesis on "The Contribution of Greenwich Village to the Cause of Freedom in American Art and Morals" and discovered in her research that Ann had had a celebrated love affair with a Village poet. Ann cannot endure to lose Ellen's respect and after seeing Douglas permits her to go. When the husband learns the facts, he furiously attacks Ann for her "perverted moral sense" and blunderingly provides a minister and a license to marry the couple when they return. This provides one of the big scenes of the play with Douglas indignant at discovering the family knew the whole story and insisting upon proposing to Ellen in public. "Darling, you're just having a moral spasm," protests the girl; "it'll pass." When she refuses marriage Douglas stalks out, but Ann solves her rebellious daughter's situation by her sympathetic wisdom: "I think when a man makes such a fuss over being seduced . . . a nice girl ought to marry him." The presence for a business visit of Ann's erstwhile Greenwich Village lover and Ellen's guessing of his identity give extra humor to this high comedy, whose unconventional attitude toward morality is evidently designed more for entertainment than for an argument in favor of illicit love.

To return to the twenties, we find that in the earlier plays the emphasis was sometimes placed on the parents rather than the children. In *Dancing Mothers* (1924) by Edgar Selwyn and Edmund Goulding a neglected wife is sorely distressed by her husband's affair with a young woman and by her daughter's infatuation with a dancing man-about-town. The daughter Kittens (Helen Hayes) is a typical flapper—hard-boiled, hard-drinking, cynical. Determined to save her, the mother visits the night club frequented by the man-about-town, and proceeds to vamp him. The two fall in love, however, and the mother discovers that life is not over at forty—"that it has just begun; and that a woman can still feel and thrill to the same

desires she had at twenty." In short, she becomes a dancing
mother. Her husband and daughter mend their ways and beg
her to return (Kittens makes her weaken by calling her "mum-
sey"), but she is not sure and goes to Europe for a year to find
her bearings. *Dancing Mothers* is a light and amusing piece
about the worm that turns, but usually the mother—especially
if she was a career woman—was not treated so sympathetically. *The Famous Mrs. Fair* (1919) by James Forbes, for
example, condemns the woman who is unable to settle down
to her domestic duties after an exciting wartime career over-
seas as ambulance driver and administrator. Back home Mrs.
Fair is not happy until she is able to run about the country on
a lecture tour, with the result that her husband finds solace
elsewhere, her son marries a secretary, and her daughter runs
away with a bounder. The girl is caught and brought back
but maintains her rebellious defiance until she learns that her
parents are going to live together again. Margalo Gillmore
drew enthusiastic notice as the neglected daughter who has
fallen in with a fast crowd that frequents the Drowsy Saint
and other freak places in the Village. Her parents were played
by the distinguished Blanche Bates and Henry Miller. *The
Famous Mrs. Fair* and *Dancing Mothers* are no great contributions to drama, but they indicate the interest in the housewife and career mother in a world of changing manners.

Similarly, the institutions of marriage and divorce proved
attractive to comic dramatists with special reference to the
new woman—her independence, her unconventionality, her
desire for a career. The resulting plays might range from farce
to near tragedy. Guy Bolton's *Chicken Feed* (1923), one of
the lighter pieces, shows a trio of wives who go on strike and
demand wages for their services. The sentimental and happy
ending indicates that the theme was not taken too seriously by
the dramatist. Another twist to the "rebellious wives" situation was offered in *Cradle Snatchers* (1925), a very successful
farce about three middle-aged housewives, determined to get
even with their philandering husbands, who hire three college

boys as gigolos (one of them was played by Humphrey Bogart). The matrons organize a cocktail and petting party which culminates in enthusiastic rumpling by the college boys and brings numerous complications. The play's reception was an indication of the changed moral outlook which argued that wives had the same rights and freedom as husbands.

New attitudes toward marriage are reflected also in Jesse Lynch Williams' *Why Not?* (1922) and in Lee Wilson Dodd's *The Changelings* (1923), though these authors hold opposite viewpoints. First hit of the newly formed Equity Players, *Why Not?* is a Shavian comedy of manners about two married couples who after fifteen years decide to exchange mates. The author criticizes the laws which compel these fundamentally respectable persons to commit adultery before divorce can be granted. There are difficulties about the children, so the two couples solve their problems in defiance of the decrees by all living in the same house together, to everybody's satisfaction. The more conventional attitude toward marriage and the family was expressed in Dodd's play about two couples who after a quarrel likewise decide to exchange partners but who eventually resume their former status after a rather solemn attack on feminism and the new freedom.

Marital infidelity was the subject of countless plays, whether treated as a problem or simply as a dramatic situation. Unsuccessful but amusing for its fantasy was Austin Strong's *A Play without a Name* (1928) concerning a bank clerk and his wife, both of them students in Extension classes at Columbia. Disappointed at not getting a desired job, the man is almost unfaithful to his wife. The titanic struggle is shown as it takes place in his brain, the stage representing a huge human skull from the inside with mysterious figures operating the nerve centers, the emotions, and the mental censor. Rachel Crothers, in more usual form, considered in several plays the problems of infidelity in a way which proved affecting and absorbing to her feminine audience. In *Let Us Be Gay* (1929) Kitty Brown has secured a divorce from her husband because of an affair which meant no more to him, he explains, than getting drunk. Hurt and disillusioned, Kitty has become emancipated—she earns her own living as a designer and has essayed a few love affairs of her own, which she has found shallow and unsatisfying. She unexpectedly meets her former husband again at a house party at the home of Mrs. Boucicault, an eccentric old woman who smokes cigars and talks with great frankness. Bob Brown is being pursued relentlessly by Deirdre, the hostess' granddaughter, "one of those gorgeous young things that are running around loose now. Lives alone—is alone—father one place—mother another—knows everything—everybody—done everything—and only twenty years old." Her ultramodernism is made graphic on the stage by her appearance in a one-piece bathing suit, orange and black. Eventually Bob discourages Deirdre and is able to persuade Kitty to marry him again. In spite of her arguments for independence, she is lonely. The double standard is further brought into the discussion when a young suitor of Deirdre expresses the usual male viewpoint that either a girl is decent or she isn't, whereupon Deirdre inquires where a girl will find the same standards in men. There is much talk of the new freedom for women, but Miss Crothers gives her eventual support to the old-fashioned marriage and presumably the double standard.

Another Crothers play, *As Husbands Go* (1931), came at a time when American matrons from the Middle West were making frequent pilgrimages to Europe. It takes occasion to contrast foreign men—attractive and romantic but frankly fortune-hunting—with the stodgy, dependable American husband, to the latter's glorification. With customary shrewdness the author makes the foreigners credible and not unsympathetic. Using the same formula of discussing a marital problem from a feminine angle with a seasoning of sentimentality, Miss Crothers in *When Ladies Meet* (1932) contrives a meeting between wife and mistress in which the two women have an opportunity to understand each other's point of view, to the natural discomfiture of the husband. These two plays were interesting and workmanlike, but it was not until 1937, after more than thirty years of Broadway playwriting, that Rachel Crothers produced her finest work to date—*Susan and God*. Here, in spite of her usual conventional and not too convincing ending, she has a sound situation and excellent satire. To her fast and fashionable set in the country Susan Trexel—chic, attractive, gushing—returns from a long stay in England where she has been converted to Lady Wiggam's movement (not unlike the Oxford movement). Lady Wiggam has found God, says Susan, in a new way. It isn't necessary to change one's faith. "You can keep right on being what you *are*—an Episcopalian—or Ethiopian—or Catholic or Jew—or colored —or *anything*. It's just love—love—*love*—for other people— *not* for yourself." You need only to be "God-conscious" and have the courage to confess your sins publicly. For all her religious fervor Susan has had no thought since her return for her unhappy, inebriated husband Barrie and even less for her fifteen-year-old daughter Blossom, who has had practically no home but school, and whose only desire is not to be sent away again to camp ("If I get any more healthy, I'll die!") but to spend at least one summer with both her parents. Susan's friends decide to cure her of her evangelical fad by having one of them pretend conversion and make a ridiculous public confession. The deception begins successfully, but as Susan warms up to her subject Barrie and Blossom wander in unexpectedly. The husband, somewhat drunk, takes Susan's words about reformation seriously, and trapped by her own eloquence Susan cannot back out. The result is that she agrees not to divorce Barrie, as planned, but to spend the entire summer with him and Blossom at their country home. If he touches liquor during this time he must grant her the divorce she wants, and she also makes it clear they will live together merely as friends. Blossom is overjoyed, but the prospects are dreary to Susan. "I wish I'd never *heard* of God," she complains. Barrie lives up to all conditions and Blossom is deliri-

ously happy, but by late August the husband finally realizes
Susan's complete selfishness and the fact that she is through
with him, drunk or sober. He then disappears on a two-day
drinking bout, allowing Susan time to think matters over. The
play ends—somewhat illogically in view of Susan's character
—with complete reconciliation. Susan was played by Gertrude Lawrence in one of the finest performances of her career—acting which helped to lift the play above the usual
marital and divorce piece into genuine high comedy. The
satirical slant was a welcome change from Miss Crothers' normal sentimentality, though the play obviously is not without
sentiment.

A similar development from domestic comedy and the
marital problem play to high comedy appears in the work of
Philip Barry from his Harvard prize play of 1923, *You and I*,
to *The Philadelphia Story* and later comedies. Barry ex-
perimented also, it will be remembered, in religious and philosophical fantasy. *You and I* deals with the frustrated
ambitions of Maitland White, who feels he has sold his soul in
business because of early marriage and family responsibilities. His wife persuades him to take a year off and paint to his
heart's content in the attic. An attractive housemaid will serve
as model, though not in the nude. After a year of painting and
financial reverses Maitland discovers that he has created not
a work of art but a pretty picture suitable only for advertising
a line of cosmetics. He abandons all thought of an artistic career and returns to business. Despite his failure the marriage
versus career thesis is well presented by Maitland, who argues
for complete independence for the artist. "After marriage
that's no longer possible. From then on 'it's you and I' always
—with the 'You' first every time." Except for occasional sentimentality the play is convincing, though one feels Maitland
would have had a better chance by himself in a Village studio
and with a professional model. In this early work we find
Barry's fatal attraction, never completely overcome, for "cute"
nicknames—Ronny, Rickey, Matey, and so on.

Barry's next play, *The Youngest*, was a mediocre account of a young man's revolt against a browbeating family. Here the author's cuteness becomes downright mawkish. "Martha" becomes "Muff," and the stage directions include the following: "She lifts her face to his, drowsy-eyed, smiling slightly, abloom for his kiss." Or consider the hero's: " 'N' all my books 'n' papers are there." *The Youngest* was obviously a juvenile effort. A far better and more mature play, *Paris Bound* (1927), offers a discussion of marriage, infidelity, and divorce. Jim and Mary, with an eye to Jim's parents, who have been divorced, agree to respect each other's individualities. Five years after their marriage, when they have two children, Mary is platonically playing patron to a young composer, who is staying at the house. Mary discovers quite accidentally that on one of his trips to Europe Jim lived several weeks with a former sweetheart. Without revealing her knowledge to Jim, who is again in France, Mary decides to get a divorce, despite the plea of Jim's father that sex is not the main part of marriage and that infidelity should not be a proper cause for divorce. In a scene with her musical protégé Mary finds herself almost yielding to his embraces but realizes the purely physical nature of her reaction. Chastened by this experience, she says nothing about it when Jim unexpectedly returns from Europe, nor does she mention his European affair; and even though it is four o'clock in the morning, they set out happily for the country to see their two children. *Paris Bound* develops the antidivorce theme in a pleasant, palatable way.

Since Hope Williams, a society girl, had made a hit in a minor role in *Paris Bound,* Barry decided to exploit her special capabilities in his next play, *Holiday* (1928). As Linda Seton she became the physical embodiment of one of the feminine ideals of the twenties—the slim, boyish, gauche, rather plain but witty and sophisticated young woman. In the play her sister has become engaged to a rather unconventional young man of ability who is opposed, however, to the money-mad business ideals of the time. After his first twenty thousand he plans to knock off for a while and enjoy life while he is still young. His point of view proves incomprehensible to his fiancée and her millionaire father. When Linda realizes her sister is no longer interested and the wedding is off, she rushes off to the boat on which the hero has engaged passage to Europe, presumably to share the cabin as his wife. *Holiday* somehow captures the spirit of boomtime days when a few individualists were rebelling against the feverish acquisition of money and when a millionaire's daughter like Linda could speak very casually of the tragedy of wealth.

Another play of marriage and potential divorce in the smart set was directly inspired by *Holiday*, in which a small part had been given to Donald Ogden Stewart, writer and humorist. Eager to employ Hope Williams' talents in another society play, Stewart wrote *Rebound* (1930), in which Hope as Sara (again the bored, slouching sophisticate) marries Bill Truesdale on the rebound. The man she loves has gone off to Europe and Bill has been jilted by a self-centered "vamp." In Paris the four meet again and Bill starts tagging after the "vamp." Dismissing her own former swain and accusing herself of lack of spirit, Sara starts a campaign of insult and ridicule which promptly wins back her husband. The play is clever—almost too clever to be convincing—but entertaining. Like Barry's plays it comes close to high comedy.

Tomorrow and Tomorrow (1931), the next Barry play, dealt again with marriage but without the author's usual lightness of touch. A childless wife in a small university town turns to a visiting psychiatrist for help, and from their clandestine union, unsuspected by the husband, a child is born. (Bad fellows, these stage psychologists, and preternaturally virile.) At the age of seven the boy falls seriously ill from a psychological ailment and the mother is forced to send for his real father. After curing the child, the psychiatrist urges that the boy and his mother go back with him, but she decides to remain with her unknowing husband. While the piece is interesting in

showing Barry's interest in Freud, which appears more prominently in his fantasy, it cannot be called a strong play.

In *The Animal Kingdom* (1932) Barry propounds the
unusual thesis that a mistress may have the true qualities of
a wife in camaraderie and idealism, whereas the wife may be
a meretricious and seductive Delilah playing upon her sex
appeal for the attainment of her personal, selfish aims. Tom
Collier, independent publisher of artistic integrity, has been
living for three years with a young magazine artist. In her
absence he suddenly marries Cecilia, who promptly alienates
him from his artistic friends, persuades him to publish popular
tripe, transforms his informal country house into "The House
in Good Taste" complete with dim lights and feminine furnish-
ings, and denies herself to him whenever he shows any resistance or rebellion. It is only in the final scene that Tom
recognizes the resemblance of his home to a high-class
bordello and decamps to rejoin the artist, his real wife. Barry
makes the situation credible and entertaining. It is not far from
high comedy, a type well represented by the author's popular
The Philadelphia Story (1939), again on his favorite subject
of marriage and divorce.

The Philadelphia Story gives with superb irony a dramatic
account of the wedding preparations in the Lord family, members of the old Philadelphia aristocracy, for the daughter
Tracy's second marital venture. Her first runaway marriage
to C. K. Dexter Havens, a man of her own social set, amateur
yachtsman and designer of class boats, ended in divorce.
Tracy is now about to marry the pompous and priggish George
Kittredge, a commoner up from the coal mines, who is already
being discussed as presidential timber. In order to suppress a
damaging gossip article about Tracy's father, Seth Lord, who
is at the moment separated from his wife, the family is induced
to allow two reporters from *Destiny*—Mike and Liz—to stay
at the house and cover the wedding. The family put on a
startling and hilarious show about their home life for the bene-

fit of these intruders. It does not take the Lords long, however, to return to more normal ways. In a rapid sequence of events, Dexter, the first husband, reappears; Tracy is upset by having him as well as her father accuse her of being a virgin goddess quite devoid of tolerance and human sympathy; she and the reporter Mike enjoy a grandiose champagne binge on her wedding eve which ends with their taking a swim *au naturel* in the pool; George assumes the worst about this escapade—which Tracy does not even remember the next morning—and acts with outraged conventionality; and the more sympathetic and broad-minded Dexter substitutes himself at the last minute as the bridegroom. In the stage presentation Katharine Hepburn was an ideal choice for the aristocratic Tracy—hard and unforgiving and yet thin-skinned, who has the misfortune of setting high standards for herself and others, beyond the capacity of most people. Dexter derides her as a moon goddess, a special class of American Female—the Married Maidens, type Philadelphiensis—and her father blames his moral irregularities on her inadequacy as a daughter: she is Justice with a shining sword and lacks an understanding heart. Only after her lapse with the reporter does she begin to acquire tolerance and feel like a human being. Mike too, snobbishly radical, derives tolerance from his sojourn with the Lords, having discovered that "someone from the bottom may be quite a heel and someone else, born to the purple, still may be quite a guy." The other persons are likewise brilliantly characterized—the tolerant Dexter, admirably played by Joseph Cotten; Tracy's precocious little sister, Dinah, interpreted by Lenore Lonergan; the old reprobate, Uncle Willie, who takes Liz in the garden to view "an ancient granite privy, of superb design—a dream of loveliness," and later pinches her *derrière*. Sharpest of the satire is directed at Sidney Kidd, editor of the widely read magazine *Destiny,* who does not appear on stage but who is so taken with a scandalous and libelous article about himself that he loves it and wants to publish it in *Destiny.*

Barry employed the talents of Katharine Hepburn in another comedy, *Without Love* (1942), in which she played opposite Elliott Nugent, and he returned to fantasy in *Liberty Jones* (1941) and *Foolish Notion* (1945). *The Philadelphia Story*, however, remains his best domestic high comedy. It shows clearly his predilection and sympathy for the leisure classes, or what might be called American aristocracy. He is their dramatist and lives in their milieu. In analyzing Tracy's faults, Dexter employs a yachting term when he accuses her of not being "yare." Yareness, we infer from Barry's work, is a quality most often found among the educated, the cultured, the rich, except where mere money-making is the ruling passion. His apparent conservatism in social matters, affected perhaps like his views on marriage by his Catholicism, does not preclude sympathy for the underdog, as may readily be seen in *Here Come the Clowns*, and he has all the traditional tolerance of the comic spirit.

Both domestic drama and the sex play have shown a gradual drift toward high comedy, where intellectual approach, irony or satire, and brilliance of style take the place of the broader comic devices on the one hand and sentimentality on the other. High comedy may be considered as almost synonymous with the comedy of manners except for its somewhat wider application, which would embrace not only social satire on the Restoration plan but plays of wit and fine characterization on the order of Shakespeare's *As You Like It*. Both types find their favorite milieu in high society among people of wealth, education, and intelligence. While the native playwrights showed little partiality to drawing-room comedy on the English style, they could occasionally modify it to reflect the manners of financial tycoons and their assorted females. Over satirical drama of this sort and over various other types of plays, the spirit of high comedy was likely to preside. We have beheld its gleam in the marital discussions of Jesse Lynch Williams, Rachel Crothers, and Philip Barry. It illuminates the dialogue at least of Clare Kummer's airy farces—*Rollo's Wild Oat* (1920) for example, or *Her Master's Voice* (1933). Even expressionism was not impervious to its influence if we consider *Beggar on Horseback* (1924), witty adaptation by George S. Kaufman and Marc Connelly of a German play, with new musical effects by Deems Taylor. Here Roland Young as a struggling young composer in New York becomes engaged to a wealthy girl from his home town, but in a terrifying nightmare of life with his *nouveaux riches* in-laws—a mad whirl of a life in which he sees twelve butlers, six dancing teachers, and slavery in the Consolidated Art Factory—he is glad to break off the match and return to his equally impecunious sweetheart, a fashion designer. The situation offers good opportunity for satire, with the expressionism more facile and streamlined—but also more successful—than in the serious plays. Kenneth Macgowan amusingly but very justly called it the *Roger Bloomer* of the Algonquin.

Costume or romantic drama, if witty enough, could likewise show the spirit of high comedy. An excellent example is Robert Sherwood's *Road to Rome* (1927), which attributes Hannibal's decision in 216 B.C. not to enter Rome merely to the sexual persuasiveness of Amytis (Jane Cowl), wife of Fabius Maximus, pompous senatorial prig and hundred percent Roman. *Reunion in Vienna* (1931) likewise combined romantic setting with a high-comedy situation which forces an eminent Viennese psychologist to try out his own theories on his wife when her former lover, the Archduke Rudolf Maximilian, returns for an *émigré* reunion. To cure her of her fixation the psychologist sends her to Rudolf but with pretty good assurance later that instead of effecting a cure he has become a cuckold. Brilliantly acted by the Lunts, Helen Westley, Henry Travers, and others, it was a spectacular success of the excellent 1931–1932 season. Some years later, in somewhat similar vein, Sherwood adapted *Tovarich* (1936), another high comedy about *émigrés*, from the French of Jacques Deval.

The names of Barry, Wilder, Crothers, Sherwood come

readily to mind in a discussion of high comedy, but only one American playwright, S. N. Behrman, devoted himself full-heartedly to its creation. For this task he was well qualified by his dispassionate wit and his sense of epigrammatic style. His initial Broadway production, *The Second Man* (1927) took eleven years to reach the stage. It wittily reveals the dual personality of a novelist (Alfred Lunt) who is amorously pursued by two women—beautiful young Monica (Margalo Gillmore) and the older but wealthy Mrs. Frayne (Lynn Fontanne). The novelist's dilemma is that he loves them both, or, to be more exact, his impulsive romantic self finds it easy to love Monica; but immediately the "second man" appears—his prudent, practical self—that requires luxury and fully understands that in the long run the older woman's largesse is preferable to penurious self-sacrifice with Monica. The young girl attempts to trap the novelist by the time-honored scheme of pretending to be pregnant, but eventually gives him up and leaves him free to resume financial and other relations with Mrs. Frayne. More European than American in tone, the play gives a treatment of love that is both unconventional and completely unsentimental. As artificial comedy it is delightful, with Behrman already showing himself a master of comic dialogue.

His next play, *Serena Blandish: or the Difficulty of Getting Married* (1929), was a dramatization of a current English novel. Its failure on Broadway Behrman attributed to the fact that "in the theatre, which is the bull market of the Arts, it is scarcely possible to achieve real success by an essay in defeatism." Serena, the heroine, lacks the instinct for success—she has too great detachment from life, views it and herself as a comedy. To the fault of being too honest she adds the weakness of too great docility, leading to a fatal inability to refuse. When she has the opportunity to move in high society under the tutelage of the worldly Countess Flor di Folio, she succeeds in attracting men by her beauty but lacks the knack of exacting a proposal, even though marriage is what she most

desires in the world. The end of the play does bring an unexpected proposal from an elderly and tremendously wealthy
Jew, but the security she has hoped for comes too late: she
has characteristically fallen in love with the illegitimate son
of the Countess' butler and will elope with him without marriage. She has not yet learned the great lesson—to ban sentiment, to become calculating and hard. Earlier in the play she
lost her chances of marriage with Lord Ivor Cream by being
unable to refuse "what to him who asks it appears such a real
desire," after which she remarks with customary candidness:
"Isn't it curious? . . . one can be at ease with a man . . .
really at ease . . . only upon the pillow." Different as it may
be in theme, *Serena Blandish* has much of the brilliant arti-
ficiality that marks the work of Wilde or Congreve; it is re-
grettable that its dramatic situation was not strong enough to
succeed on the stage.

In *Meteor* (1929) Behrman turned to character comedy of
more serious import. The play is a satire of business Napoleon-
ism in the booming twenties, a theme dramatized in the
megalomaniac career of Raphael Lord, which takes him from
maladjusted college student to rapacious multimillionaire
with his finger in all kinds of shady political intrigue in South
America. Fundamentally he is stupid and unable to envision
his own defeat; nor is he able to change himself in any way,
even when his wife ultimately leaves him. *Meteor* enjoyed
only mediocre success on Broadway, largely—as Behrman
explains—because audiences took Lord seriously at his own
valuation, including his supposed clairvoyance, not realizing
that his wife and another character, a friendly college professor, represented the forces of "sanity and ordinary humanity," being therefore the real heroes of the piece. This mistaken
attitude about Lord, typical of the times, blunted the edge of
Behrman's satire on business psychology and ethics.

Brief Moment (1931), concerned with the stormy marriage
of a millionaire playboy and a blues singer which shows the
hero a vacillating weakling and the girl a woman of strong

character, has some good lines but lacks Behrman's usual polish; it is notable mainly for the presence in the cast of Alexander Woollcott as a malicious busybody. "Oh, Sig, Sig," says the blues singer to him, "if you were a woman what a bitch you would have made." More in line with the author's capabilities in high comedy was the popular *Biography* (1932), with Ina Claire in the first of several leads she played for Behrman. The plot is slight. Marion Froude, artist, has traipsed over the globe doing portraits of famous men and enjoying a casual Bohemian life on the way, scattered with love affairs. Now in New York in reduced circumstances she receives a generous offer from a popular magazine to write her autobiography, the editor (Earle Larimore) hoping that it will include plenty of juicy scandal. Marion starts her memoirs airily, but finds herself in a mortal conflict between persons who wish to suppress her book and the radical editor who insists on publishing it, even at the expense of his job. Though her manuscript is in fact perfectly innocuous, she burns it and then she leaves for the West to escape the passionate love that has grown between her and the editor. The real struggle in the play is between the ideal of tolerance, personified in Marion Froude, and the forces of hate and fanaticism, represented by the Communist editor. Marion is the kind of person who insists on seeing the best in people, no matter how quaint or silly they may be. Her tolerance, like Serena Blandish's, comes from her detachment—everything is a spectacle to her and cause for amusement. When the editor sneers at her relaxed code, she says, "Code, nonsense! I gave up codes long ago. I'm a big laissez-faire girl." The editor, on the other hand, is an evangelist, a crusader, a professional rebel, who wants to extirpate the past. "Studying you," remarks Marion, "I can see why so many movements against injustice become such absolute—tyrannies." And while she really loves the editor, she realizes that his hate for tolerance means hate for her own essential quality. Among minor characters we find an amusing portrait of Orrin Kinnicott, pompous publisher of health magazines

and a man of superb chest development, who reduces all problems of life to roughage and metabolism. Everything makes
for a witty and entertaining play, with Marion Froude representing the feminine ideal of a playwright who has always
had his greatest success in the characterization of women.

Behrman's Voltairian interest in ideas took a grimly serious
turn in *Rain from Heaven* (1934), a play reflecting the sudden
rise of Hitler and the persecution of the Jews. Here again the
central character is a woman, Lady Lael Wyngate (Jane
Cowl)—liberal, tolerant, generous-minded. Her country
house in England becomes the meeting place for a miscel-
laneous company. Among the American visitors are a fascist-
minded capitalist who is trying to start an Anglo-American
Youth League to combat the subversive forces of communism;
his naïve and genial brother Rand, famous Antarctic explorer,
whose name and prestige the capitalist plans to exploit as front
for his movement; and the capitalist's empty-headed wife, described as an "adorable Kewpie." A recently arrived guest is
Hugo Willens, German music critic, only one-eighth Jewish
but placed in a concentration camp and later exiled for a satirical pamphlet. A Rhodes scholar, a long-exiled Russian aristo-
crat, and a young Russian-American musician are also present.
Lael and Rand, the explorer, are in love, though she doubts
the advisability of marrying him, but the new forces in the
world gradually place an insurmountable barrier between
them—especially after jealousy impels him to call Hugo "a
dirty Jew." This episode ironically reveals to Lael that it is
really Hugo she loves. Hugo loves her too, but feels a com-
pelling necessity to return to Germany to fight nazism, even
though it may mean death. All his life he has been a dilettante,
with illusions about mankind. "I see now that goodness is not
enough, that kindness is not enough, that liberalism is not
enough. I'm sick of evasions. They've done us in. Civilization,
charity, progress, tolerance—all the catchwords. I'm sick of
them. We'll have to redefine our terms."

Lael's most devastating barbs are directed at the capitalist.

"Hobart's an American and doesn't really understand democracy," she says, and of his Anglo-American project: "I hate Youth Movements. They all come to the same thing. Boy Scouts with bayonets." The end of the play finds Hobart weeping in his cups; he has sacrificed wife, daughter, everything to money and power. Now he thinks the rich are doomed and will lose all. Even Lael, different as her outlook is, has doubts about the future. "What security should I have, as a liberal person, if the world goes Communist? Or Fascist?" While in its dialogue and setting the play has superficial resemblance to drawing-room comedy, clearly it is anything but fluffy and frivolous—if indeed it can be called a comedy at all.

Less bitter, *End of Summer* (1936), Behrman's next play, also relies on the clash of ideas rather than on plot. In one of his customary luxurious settings—the Frothingham summer estate in Maine—the author throws into sharp contrast a wealthy oil dynasty and members of the depression Younger Generation. Other points of view are given, too, with refreshing variety and broad-mindedness. The main theme is expressed by the aged grandmother: "This money we've built our lives on—it used to symbolize security—but there's no security in it any more." Money has ruined the marriage of Leona Frothingham (Ina Claire); it threatens and postpones the marriage of her daughter Paula to a penniless young college graduate, though Paula herself has turned radical. Behrman's best portrait is that of Leona—ultra-feminine, helpless, decorative. Her only interest is love and her only career flirtation. Impulsive, childlike, generous, she is bewildered by the blunt directness of her daughter and the latter's wish to stand on her own feet. Her vast fortune, which has brought separation and later divorce from her husband, draws like flies a parade of parasites and fortune hunters. Boris, son of the famous Russian Count Mirsky and Leona's most recent favorite, is on his way out after a protracted stay during which he has ostensibly been writing his father's memoirs. Dr. Rice, a psychiatrist, who supplants him in Leona's love and patronage,

has hastened Boris' departure by exposing him as a victim of
"shadow neurosis": in reality Boris hates the Count his father
and has no intention of writing a book about him. Dr. Rice
(Osgood Perkins) is even more sinister than the usual stage
psychologist. He is completely ruthless, calculating, predatory; like the contemporary dictators he admires he has no
code whatever. While gaining Leona's trust and encouraging
her expectation of marriage he makes love to Paula, who—to
save her mother—cleverly forces him to show his hand and to
make an unwilling exit. Leona is left broken and lost. But a
newcomer makes a bid for patronage, a young radical who is
trying to start a revolutionary magazine. She promises to back
it, and thus ironically the money accumulated by industrial
depredation is to be used for the destruction of the system
that produced it. However, the editor assures her she will not
be entirely wiped out. "Don't worry about that—comes the
Revolution—you'll have a friend in high office."

[The confusion of the thirties, the bitterness and protest
about social conditions, the problem of technological unemployment, the alienation between the generations, these are all
reflected in *End of Summer*. The play is far from optimistic
but it has wit.] Its severest satire is directed at psychoanalysis
and the unscrupulous Dr. Rice, who has no sympathy for the
underdog and despises the herd, though he himself came from
the humblest beginnings. Early in his career he changed from
medical practice to psychiatry because he found the latter
more lucrative. "The poor have tonsils but only the rich have
souls," as he explains callously to Paula. On the bright side
of the picture is the delightful and decorative character of
Leona, who, useless and outmoded as she may be, has at least
an instinctive desire to do what she can to make those around
her happy. In no play has Behrman collected so brilliantly
convincing a set of characters and allowed them in good
Shavian style to speak for themselves.

Having annihilated the unscrupulous psychiatrist in *End of
Summer*, Behrman in *Wine of Choice* (1938) turned his atten-

tion to the equally unscrupulous Communist, the kind of man who is so certain of his ideology that he can entertain no doubt about it and is willing to sacrifice to it even the woman he loves. Denunciation of the Communist is entrusted to Ryder Gerrard, wealthy Easterner of independent views who has moved West to become Senator from New Mexico and who stands for democratic in opposition to totalitarian doctrine. Gerrard's prototype in real life was Bronson Cutting. The plot, thin as usual, is concerned with the efforts of Binkie Niebuhr (Alexander Woollcott playing himself), the New Mexico Senator, and a wealthy young Long Islander to effect the re-habilitation of a young girl, their protégée, who suffered in the past from a cruel and unhappy marriage. In order to prove what she can do on her own she now refuses to marry the Senator. Then, disregarding Binkie's advice about being hard and calculating, she falls ardently in love with the Communist, only to be dashed again to earth after he has enjoyed her person. Compared to *End of Summer*, the play seems forced and unnatural. It is not one of Behrman's best, despite its timely theme that dictators, actual or potential, are not mere charlatans but dangerous zealots.

In a lighter mood *No Time for Comedy* (1939) discusses the comic dramatist's dilemma in the tragic, chaotic world of the late thirties. Should the writer of light, sophisticated comedies stick to his frivolities, or should he indignantly turn his attention instead to serious issues, like the Franco revolution in Spain? This literary problem is dramatized in the stormy marriage of a comic playwright and his actress wife, for whom he has been writing plays. Now he is being encouraged to write serious drama by a purposeful young woman, a millionaire banker's wife, who is seeking to bring out his latent powers. The resulting triangle raises another question: which of two opposite types of women in the life of a writer is better for him—the builder-upper or the breaker-downer, "the critical faculty versus the clinging vine?" The ultimate answers are left to the audience, though the implications are clear that the writer will choose both his own wife, the "breaker-downer," and the comic muse. While the play is talky, the talk is lively, as in the actress' remarks to her antagonist: "Sleep with him if you like, but for pity's sake don't ruin his style." The critics made much of the appearance of Katharine Cornell in her first major comic role. Her performance did little to establish any marked excellence in sophisticated comedy; it was better, however, than the metallic and unconvincing performance given by Margalo Gillmore as her "builder-upper" rival. Whether the acting or the play was at fault, *No Time for Comedy* cannot be said to mark any advance in Behrman's dramatic work.

Since 1940, if anything, it has regressed. The *Talley Method* (1941), again starring Ina Claire, is an attack on intolerance and ruthlessness in the single person of Dr. Talley (Philip Merivale), a noted surgeon who is a failure outside of his work because he lacks all sense of the individual. The play has little humor except for the satirical portrait of a young Ph.D. candidate at Columbia who is attempting to prove in a dissertation that St. Thomas Aquinas was a Marxian. After this mediocre work Behrman forsook the drawing room for more romantic hunting grounds. *The Pirate* (1942) is an amusing costume play with Alfred Lunt as a traveling mountebank in the West Indies. Later scenes show him gaining entrance to a lady's boudoir by walking the tightrope and mesmerizing the lady herself (Lynn Fontanne). *Jacobowsky and the Colonel* (1944), also romantic, was based on an original play by Franz Werfel; it deals with the musical-comedy escape from Paris, at the time of the German invasion, of a Polish colonel and a practical-minded Jewish refugee. Their flight to southern France is complicated by the Colonel's insistence on first serenading his French mistress and then taking her, bag and baggage, with them in the car. Jacobowsky proves his worth to the skeptical Colonel, and at the last moment it is he and not the girl whom the Colonel takes to England with him. These last two plays have color, wit, and humor—there is no question that they have proved far more popular than Behrman's earlier work. But they lack the hard brilliancy of, let us say, *Serena Blandish* or *End of Summer*, and they depart from the satirical mood of high comedy. In some ways this is a pity, but regardless of what future directions his work may take, Behrman must be commended for having so consistently attempted intellectual comedy in a commercial theatre. His influence has been felt, even though high comedy can never hope to become as indigenous to the American stage as her low-life sister.

In any drama as varied and prolific as contemporary comedy there is great risk in selecting a single phase or development as having particular significance. Many fine and worthy plays, as we have seen, continue the tradition of sentimental drama, wrestle with moral problems, or provide for Broadway something akin to Viennese or English high comedy. Though excellent, these plays represent the old rather than the new. Other ones, beginning in the twenties, tend to cut loose from the past and from Europe, developing strictly American themes in a purely American way. Their starting point is realism, whether in local color or the exposition of American phenomena. They are commonly handled with broad humor, farce, and burlesque. They capitalize on the freedom won by the sex plays and are often rowdy, blatant, vulgar. Rarely do they preach except inferentially by rough-and-tumble satire. In the popular and extraordinarily vital drama which they provided one can see commercial Broadway at its best, as any constant theatregoer will attest. Eugene O'Neill and Maxwell Anderson may justly appear in the books as our greatest dramatists, but they can scarcely be called as typically American as, let us say, George S. Kaufman. A good case might even be made for considering Kaufman our leading playwright. What he and his fellows produced was entertainment, but entertainment with a point and a sting. For that matter even high-brow drama, to survive, needs a modicum of entertainment. Can anyone name a drearier play than *Lazarus Laughed?* Or one may inquire further as to what happens to a solemn tragedy like Anderson's *Masque of Kings* when a news story offers evidence that Maria Vetsera killed Rudolf by clouting him over the head with a champagne bottle? Without overstating the case, one may find great worth in low comedy when it offers the American virtues of clear vision, debunking of pretensions, and a sense of humor, even though it takes the form of a loud guffaw.

The representation of everyday America—its life, its pleasures, its occupations—with or without satirical point—became popular in the mid-twenties. One of its first manifestations was in sports, with special attention to argot and local color. Baseball was commemorated in a farce, *Solid Ivory* (1925) by Theodore Westman, Jr., in which the daughter of a club manager, temporarily in charge of the team, cures a dim-witted pitcher of conceit and draws his romantic attention to herself. The more polite sport of golf finds dramatic expression in Vincent Lawrence's *Spring Fever* (1925), about a shipping clerk who joins a fashionable golf club, and in Frank Craven's *The Nineteenth Hole* (1927), where an author becomes a golf addict, to the traditional neglect of his wife. *Buckaroo* (1929), a melodramatic comedy by A. W. and E. L. Barker and Charles Beahan, revealed the backstage life of a rodeo in Chicago. This was unsuccessful, but an earlier play with a background of pugilism—*Is Zat So?* (1925) by James Gleason and Richard Taber—had a long run. A prize fighter and his bullying manager are reduced by "skirts" and financial difficulties to enter a Fifth Avenue household as butler and footman, where their boxing skill turns eventually to advantage—a situation which offers amusing possibilities. The liberal use of ringside slang encouraged the writing of other realistic, low-life farces. The race track, among other themes of this kind, had a dramatic spokesman in Willard Mack, who in 1927 wrote a melodramatic comedy called *Weather Clear—Track Fast.*

Most of these sporting plays have little value, but another one, distantly related to racing, was widely acclaimed as a superior brand of hard-boiled farce-comedy—*Three Men on a Horse* (1935) by John Cecil Holm and George Abbott. An innocuous greeting-card poet, Erwin, after a quarrel with his wife in their standardized Ozone Heights (N.J.) home, drowns his sorrows in a New York bar, where he falls in with three racetrack gamblers and an ex-Follies girl, Mabel. For years Erwin has amused himself by "doping out" horses on his way to work by bus, acquiring an uncanny knack for selecting winners though he himself never bets. When the gamblers realize their gold mine they hold Erwin incommunicado, until they discover that his intuition works only on the Ozone Heights bus. There are numerous complications, but in the end Erwin, another stage worm that turns, finds himself with money, a better job, and a fully reconciled wife. The ribald race-track language and satirical tone make the piece considerably better than a brief discussion can indicate. Particularly amusing are Erwin's Mother's Day verses—his specialty—and the depiction of life in Ozone Heights, including its tabloid journalism. Then there are hilarious farcical scenes, like the one in the hotel room where Mabel starts to unbutton Erwin's pants before putting him to bed. An excellent cast included William Lynn and Joyce Arling as the couple, Shirley Booth as Mabel, and Sam Levene as her masterful lover. In addition the rapid pacing and staccato rhythm of the Abbott staging helped to turn this escapist farce, in actual production, into a minor work of art.

Like sports, the theatre in all its forms seemed to offer good comic material. More often than not the treatment was satirical. The dramatist particularly liked to give the inside story of some phase of theatre life, with the usual display of jargon and local color. Farcical attempts to ridicule amateur acting have already been mentioned—Kelly's *Torch Bearers*, for example, or Kummer's *Rollo's Wild Oat*. Satire of the tempestuous private life of actors—not a new theme—proved still popular. *Enter Madame* (1920) by Gilda Varesi and Dolly Byrne reveals the traditionally erratic prima donna who lives in a continual maelstrom of excitement and confusion. Her long-patient husband, craving a peaceful home life, is now divorcing her to make another marriage, but at the last minute he is again won over by the prima donna's glamor and elopes with her to South America, carrying the poodle as in the old days. With even more gusto *The Royal Family* (1927) by George S. Kaufman and Edna Ferber presents four generations of the Cavendish family, a theatrical dynasty modeled after the Barrymores. Try as they will, the daughter and granddaughter cannot escape the stage by either marriage or motherhood. The scapegrace Tony flees from Hollywood, pursued by a relentless Polish actress. He gets off to Europe, only to become entangled in various international complications. Good theatrical emotion was provided by Haidee Wright as Fanny Carr, the matriarch, whose sole desire is to go on the road once more but who dies before its fulfillment. The play well illustrates the glorious exploitation of a dramatic situation by shameless exaggeration, so characteristic of the work of George S. Kaufman. A later piece about a movie actress, Lawrence Riley's *Personal Appearance* (1934), indicated that the mad doings of a star continued to be good dramatic material, though a new twist might be required.

Plays about the theatre were by no means restricted to the vagaries of actors. Kaufman's *The Butter and Egg Man* (1925) has the amusing character of a yokel "angel" from Chillicothe, Ohio, who ventures twenty thousand dollars on a "turkey" but miraculously wins a fortune and a girl. Much is made of theatrical lingo and of what takes place behind the scenes in show business. Even the title—borrowed from one of Texas Guinan's stock remarks in her night club—has a true Broadway flavor. Some years later in collaboration with Edna Ferber (*The Royal Family* combination) Kaufman wrote *Stage Door* (1936), an unexpectedly tender play recording the progress of a typical young actress from the drabness of a cheap theatrical boardinghouse to final success on Broadway. Here the emphasis is on realism with all the humor and pathos one might expect from the particular setting. The heroine (Margaret Sullavan) refuses to be downed by hardships, disappointments, insecurity, sudden closings, and odd jobs between times. In spite of her financial straits she refuses a seven-year contract in Hollywood, for she realizes this would have a deleterious effect on her acting. When her real opportunity comes at last, she is both competent and deserving. There is some satire on the former Footlights Club girl who has become a movie star and particularly of the left-wing playwright who goes both Hollywood and high hat after his first play has become a hit. The two authors show clearly their knowledge of the theatre and deep affection for it. In 1938, with Moss Hart, Kaufman attempted the more difficult task of dramatizing the history of a playhouse, from its gay opening in the nineties to its decline into a cheap burlesque house. The Fabulous Invalid always manages to recover, however, and the play ends with the acquisition of the playhouse by an earnest group of young actors who will give it a new life. The play, while not up to par, argues well for the worth and indestructibility of the theatre.

The less respectable phases of theatrical life were not neglected by the playwrights in search of local color. Vaudeville formed the subject of John McGowan's *Excess Baggage* (1927) and—with bucolic variations—of James Gleason's *The Shannons of Broadway* (1927). Tin Pan Alley received farcical and satirical treatment in *June Moon* (1929) by Ring Lardner and George S. Kaufman. The two best plays in this group, both of 1927, were spectacular pieces with plenty of action and color. Kenyon Nicholson's *The Barker* is about a traveling tent show, whose ballyhoo man, Nifty (Walter Huston), is determined that his son will lead a more reputable life as a lawyer. The boy unexpectedly joins the show, where he soon falls easy prey to the lures of the snake charmer (Claudette Colbert). The youngsters discover that they are really in love,

however, and they marry, to the tragic despair of Nifty and
the shattering of his ambitions. He is so broken in spirit that
he is about to leave the show, but the call of the midway
proves too strong and he is persuaded to remain. The highly
popular *Burlesque* by George Manker Watters and Arthur
Hopkins has a similarly simple plot. Skid, burlesque comedian
in the Middle West, has real ability but a weakness for liquor
and women and a tendency to rely on old routines. When he
receives an unexpected call from Broadway his wife Bonnie,
also in the show, urges him to take it though she cannot go
along. In New York Skid's success goes to his head and his addiction to drink and dissipation induces Bonnie to start divorce
proceedings. At the last moment, however, she finds she cannot leave him. Trite as the plot is, it was given life by the excellent acting of Hal Skelly as Skid and Barbara Stanwyck
as Bonnie, the latter having been discovered the season before
by Willard Mack in an Atlantic City night club. A high spot in
the performance was Hal Skelly's dance burlesque of the wedding ceremony. In *Burlesque* as in *The Barker* the authors
capitalized freely on realistic argot and backstage atmosphere.
The plays are often more dramatic or sentimental than humorous, and the type, in fact, lent itself readily to melodramatic
use as in *Broadway* or in *Remote Control,* a murder play set
in a radio station.

Another variation of the theatre play saw the playwrights
dramatizing their own problems, as in Behrman's *No Time for
Comedy.* In 1934 Samson Raphaelson's *Accent on Youth* portrayed humorously a middle-aged dramatist who is completely
unable to divorce his life from his playwriting. In the tradition
of Cyrano he even composes a successful love scene which
wins for a young rival the hand of his attractive secretary. She
later returns to the playwright after discovering that existence
with an older man, pills notwithstanding, is preferable to an
exhausting life with a young athlete. The same author's *Jason*
(1942) pretended to reveal the problems of a newly married
dramatic critic, including just what critical slant to take to-

ward a Saroyanesque dramatist whom he has just found kiss-
ing his bride. These plays approach high comedy but they also
illustrate the desire to give the inside story of various pro-
fessions.

Broadway dramatists might handle themselves and even the
critics with kid gloves, but they spared no punches in attempting to humble Hollywood with epigram and wisecrack. The
silent films received glancing satirical reference in numerous
plays, including *Dulcy*. In 1918 *The Squab Farm* by Frederic
and Fanny Hatton dealt humorously with the subject. The
best of the early satire appeared in *Merton of the Movies*
(1922), adapted by Kaufman and Connelly from a Harry
Leon Wilson novel. Merton, movie fan and graduate of a cor-
respondence school of acting, goes to Hollywood on his savings as clerk in a general store. There, a complete failure because of his overacting, he becomes victim of a scheme by
which he thinks he is starring in a serious Western whereas
he is unwittingly burlesquing the type. Crushed at discovering the deception, he regains some of his composure when the
head of the motion picture industry and former Secretary of
Agriculture—a barbed hit, of course, at Will Hays—praises
him for raising the movies to a higher plane. Biting as it was,
the satire was mild in comparison with what Kaufman with
Moss Hart as collaborator did to the talkies in *Once in a Lifetime* (1930). Here the cumulative effect of wisecrack and burlesque becomes terrific. Three jobless vaudeville actors con-
ceive the idea of opening a school of elocution in Hollywood
for silent stars whose jobs are jeopardized by the success of the
new talkies. The undertaking is successful at first, with George
—literal-minded and addicted to cracking Indian nuts—becoming the eminent "Dr. Lewis." When the school fails—after
the voice tests—George is providentially placed by the great
Mr. Glogauer in charge of all productions. Everything about
George's first picture, *Gingham and Orchids,* goes askew and
he is promptly fired—until the newspapers bring out rave reviews about the splendid awkwardness of the heroine's acting,

the unusual lighting ("in the big scenes almost nothing was visible"), and the steady knocking during the film (George cracking his Indian nuts), which reminded the critics of the tom-tom in *The Emperor Jones*. Back in favor, George soon arouses Mr. Glogauer's anger by purchasing two thousand aeroplanes, but even this turns out all right: The other producers want to bring out flying pictures and now Mr. Glogauer has a corner on the plane market.

The satirical lines hit at almost every phase of Hollywood life—the gushy writer of a syndicated movie column, the dramatist (played by George S. Kaufman himself) who gets a nervous breakdown from underwork, the dumb little girl who breaks out into a recitation of "Boots" to catch Mr. Glogauer's attention, the twelve Schlepkin Brothers who scrap the superspectacle they have just finished for the silent films —*The Old Testament,* the entire paranoiac insanity of the film studios. The dialogue is more brilliant than polite. "I look eighteen under lights and I can talk like a virgin," protests a girl when she is told she is not the type for a certain part. Or consider the following conversation:

Coat Check Girl. Sure! There's a call for prostitutes Wednesday.
Cigarette Girl. Say, I'm going out there! Remember that prostitute I did for Paramount?
Coat Check Girl. Yah, but that was silent. This is for talking prostitutes.°

Then again, there's the bridesmaid in George's picture who has a date with an exhibitor and explains: "Well, I've got a chance to go out with an exhibitionist—" The speeches are delightfully double-edged: Mr. Glogauer's, "That's the way we do things out here—no time wasted on thinking," or the triumphant telegram from George, "The picture is colossal— it has put the movies back where they were ten years ago." *Once in a Lifetime* is a classic in impudent satire, and later

° The quotations in this paragraph are from *Once in a Lifetime* by Moss Hart and George S. Kaufman. Copyright, 1930, by George S. Kaufman and reprinted by permission of the authors.

efforts on the same subject seem feeble in comparison with it.
A few good words may be said in passing, however, for the
Spewacks' *Boy Meets Girl* (1935) with its classic cinematic
formula, "Boy meets girl—boy loses girl—boy gets girl," and
Clare Boothe's *Kiss the Boys Goodbye* (1938) with its satirical account of the search for someone to play Scarlett O'Hara
in the movie version of *Gone with the Wind.*

It is only a step from Broadway and Hollywood to café
society, and all three are well represented in *The Man Who
Came to Dinner* (1939), another Hart-Kaufman play, which
succeeds in raising the technique of insult to the level of a
fine art. Sheridan Whiteside (a friendly take-off of Alexander
Woollcott) is immobilized by an accident in the home of the
Stanleys in Mesalia, Ohio, where in the course of a lecture tour
he had been an unwilling guest at dinner. Here Whiteside
completely takes over the house, browbeating his hosts, ad-
vising the Stanley boy to run away on a tramp steamer and
the daughter to marry a labor organizer, monopolizing the
telephone, entertaining convicts, receiving such presents as
penguins and a community of cockroaches, breaking up a love
affair between his secretary Maggie and the local newspaperman, and insulting everyone indiscriminately. The antisocial
behavior of this bearded *enfant terrible* does not halt him on
Christmas eve from broadcasting his customary Yule program,
dripping with sentimentality, for Cream of Mush. Among
Whiteside's many distinguished visitors are "England's little
Rover Boy"—an English actor patterned after Noel Coward
—and Banjo, an eccentric practical joker from Hollywood.
The real interest of the play does not lie so much in action—
though there's plenty of that—as in dialogue, often vulgar
and low-life but unequaled in bite since Restoration comedy.
From Whiteside's entrance line as he maliciously surveys from
his wheelchair the good wives of Mesalia, "I may vomit," to
his second accident, which concludes the play, he speaks with
venomous wit. Miss Preen, his nurse, is chief butt of his in-
sults. "You have the touch of a sex-starved cobra," he tells her,

and again, "You remind me of last week's laundry." "My Lady
Nausea" (as he calls her in more tender moods) finally deserts
the nursing career for employment in a munitions factory. The
great man shows partiality to no one. Of Maggie's sudden love
affair he remarks, "Nonsense. This is merely delayed puberty."
Later, remembering Lord Bottomley's teeth, he says, "Every
time I order Roquefort cheese I think of those teeth." It should
not be imagined that he has been given a monopoly of good
lines, however; Maggie, Banjo, and the others are not too far
behind him. The play brings into sharp contrast the small-
town point of view and that of the urban literary and theatrical set, with obvious preference for the latter. Among other
things there is good satire of the current fad of memoirs by
country doctors when the local medico produces a bulky
manuscript, whose title Sheridan parodies as *Forty Years below the Navel*. Personal lampooning and genuine affection
are combined in the portrait of Woollcott with his wide-flung
acquaintance, his florid radio programs, his absorption in
criminal cases, his exultant egotism. In the New York production Monty Woolley "out-Woollcotted" his original, endowing
Sheridan Whiteside with a malice less petulant and more
demoniac. Woollcott himself took the part on the West coast.
Whatever its permanent value *The Man Who Came to Dinner*
is a supreme example of what Frederick Lonsdale called the
comedy of bad manners.

Sports, the theatre, movies, Woollcott were but a few of the
indigenous themes pounced upon by the comic playwright.
Prohibition and its attendant rackets served as background
for many plays, melodramatic or farcical. In 1925 George
Abbott and James Gleason brought out a realistic little comedy, *The Fall Guy*, about a naïve drugstore clerk who is induced by some racketeers, when he loses his job, to peddle
"snow," though he believes it is bootleg liquor. His domestic
quarrels in his Columbus Avenue flat, complete to dumbwaiter
and garbage cans, are presented with humorous realism; nor
is his situation made any easier by the presence in the house-

hold of his brother-in-law, who would rather learn to play a saxophone than look for a job. In another play, the speakeasy as an institution was given idyllic and romantic treatment. Preston Sturges' *Strictly Dishonorable* (1929) is truly a delightful comedy about a girl from Mississippi (Muriel Kirkland) who persuades her nagging fiancé, a New Jerseyite, to take her to an Italian speakeasy on West 49th Street. After a quarrel the fiancé is put out and the Southern girl, Isabelle, becomes friendly with a young opera singer, who has an apartment upstairs. This is the big romantic moment of her life and she eagerly accepts his invitation to share his apartment, even though he warns her that his intentions are strictly dishonorable. Her innocence, however, is too much for the singer, who leaves her in the apartment alone, though she is furious and shouts after him, "I'm not a baby! I'm not a baby!" Next morning the fiancé returns; he is apologetic, if suspicious; but eventually Isabelle's romance comes true when the singer proposes, having first cabled to Italy to secure his mother's permission to marry. The play combines charming naïveté with sophistication and very well suggests the atmosphere of the speakeasy at its best in all its friendly informality and casual relations with the law. Less delightful aspects of Prohibition, of course, are given in melodramas like *Broadway* and *The Racket,* though playwrights were never guilty of siding with the Anti-Saloon League.

As a center of racketeering and malodorous politics Chicago inspired a number of melodramatic comedies, not necessarily connected with Prohibition. One of the best was Maurine Watkins' *Chicago* (1926), a riproaring burlesque on the publicity mania of female murderers and on the ways of Chicago courts. Roxie Hart, played with commendable toughness by Francine Larrimore, shoots a lover to death as he is buttoning his pants. Then the fanfare begins—the reporters, the pictures, the dickering with criminal lawyers, the lawyer's directions about dress and make-up for the trial. Mad for more publicity, Roxie pretends to be pregnant, which also gives her lawyer a chance in the courtroom to orate about innocence and motherhood. After the jury gives the expected verdict of not guilty, Roxie's husband inquires about the baby. "What baby?" exclaims Roxie. "My God, do I look like an amachure!" Clearly the play is not dependent on subtlety or understatement, but the satire is excellent. In similar spirit a newspaper play, *The Front Page* (1928) by Ben Hecht and Charles MacArthur, made free with Chicago politics. Set in the pressroom of the Criminal Courts building, it romanticizes the life of the hard-boiled, profane newspaperman, showing the frenzied efforts of Hildy Johnson (Lee Tracy) to break away from journalism and marry, and the equally determined campaign of his managing editor (Osgood Perkins) to hold him. Earl Williams, an anarchist, is about to be executed for murder. When he escapes and surrenders to Hildy, the scoop is too much temptation for the latter. It is hours before he is able to make the midnight train with his irate bride-to-be and her mother, and then we know he'll be back the next day, victim of the managing editor's machinations. The political satire appears in the conversation of the sheriff and the mayor, the postponement of the Williams execution until just before election, the ballyhoo about his radicalism, the last-minute reprieve which the mayor interprets as a double cross by the governor and which he tries to conceal by bribery. As in *Chicago* the authors give the sordid inside story with the cynical debunking that delighted the skeptical twenties. While the play pretends to be toughly realistic, there is considerable romance and epic aggrandizement in the portrayal of the newsmen. In any case, if American politics and justice seem on a slightly higher plane than in the days of Mayor Thompson and Mayor Walker, the improvement may stem in part from rowdy comedies like the foregoing that served to expose and ridicule.

As we have already seen, New York, like Chicago, offered many themes for a sophisticated urban public. Some of the plays were purely realistic, such as *Love 'Em and Leave 'Em* (1926) by George Abbott and John V. A. Weaver, a comedy about the lives and loves of department store clerks in the city. With accurate detail and background the authors tell a homely story of two sisters in a boardinghouse—the selfish younger one's campaign to steal the other's beau, a clerk "in neckties"; the loss by gambling of the money collected for the store pageant; and the final victory of the older sister. No such commonplace realism marks a rollicking farce of 1940, *My Sister Eileen* by Joseph Fields and Jerome Chodorov, based on *New Yorker* sketches by Ruth McKenney. Two girls from Columbus, Ohio, sisters, come to New York to make their way in literature and the stage. By ill chance they land in a one-room basement studio in Greenwich Village. Their many misadventures with predatory males, including officers from a Brazilian training ship, provide much broad humor, as does the intermittent blasting for the new subway which violently shakes the walls of their troglodyte apartment. A month later, however, when their father tries to bring them back safely to Columbus respectability, they have become such ardent New Yorkers that they sign a six-month lease and stay. The exaggeration does not vitiate the fundamental truth of the ubiquitous small-town girl's experience in becoming adjusted to city life. An almost lyrical paean to Bagdad-on-the-Hudson had come earlier the same year in *Two on an Island* (1940) by Elmer Rice, who had already recorded less savory aspects of city life in *Street Scene* and set the fashion for a whole school of realistic local color. Here, with stylized and skeletonized scenery, Rice presents a city idyll about two eager youngsters—John from Iowa and Mary from New Hampshire—who arrive on the same day and start their painful education in the ways of New York. Though their paths cross several times, they do not actually meet until John, broke and discouraged, is about to go back home. Taking heart from each other's trials and experiences, they decide to stick it out—if New York doesn't kill you, it makes you tough—and the final act finds them living modestly but happily in sin until better fortune and pregnancy induce them to get married. The plot is

intentionally simple and Rice makes every effort to make it
sound typical.

Thus the main charm of *Two on an Island* arises from the
recognizable features of city life—the sightseeing bus, the
B.M.T. car, taxis, a Coffee Pot, the Metropolitan Museum, a
theatrical producer's offices. The characters, too, sound real,
from the high-brow taxidriver to the millionaire Communist
who is trying to unionize the Five and Ten girls. The most
mordant portrait is that of the producer, who has come to
Broadway from the St. Louis Community Theatre and who—
—in the critical words of his wife—has lost his heart and
head in the scramble for success. He has fine sardonic wit,
however, and moments of generosity, as when he brings the
youngsters a bottle of champagne in spite of personal disappointment in his love chase of Mary. Another delightful character is a wealthy socialite, who eventually chooses the millionaire Communist for her third marriage. "Yes, it sounds
simply fascinating," she says of her husband's patter. "Tell me
again what C.I.O. stands for, darling." In this New York vi-
gnette the young couple were played by John Craven and
Betty Field, the author's wife, with Luther Adler as the producer.

Elmer Rice's realistic studies of American life spanned the
Atlantic in 1931 to include expatriates in the Latin Quarter
of Paris. *The Left Bank* satirizes the small group of Americans
who can see no good in their own country and prefer to live
an amoral, aimless, hand to mouth existence in "the only civilized nation in the world." The hero brands America as "a
spiritual vacuum, a cultural desert," a place where no civilized
man can live decently, and he flatly refuses to return to the
States with his wife, whose love for Paris and long residence
in it do not prevent her from growing tired of this self-imposed
exile. They can never, she argues, become more than aliens in
a foreign civilization. The husband's violent rebellion against
America is shown as stemming from the domination in his

childhood of an older sister, who brought him up after the death of their parents. In contrast to him we have a sympathetic portrait of the American middle-class professional man, who remains gentlemanly and kind, even when his wife elects to remain in Paris with the expatriate hero. As usual Rice does no direct preaching, allowing his characters to speak convincingly for themselves, but there is no doubt his sympathies lie with the businessman and the hero's long-suffering wife, who has ceased believing that freedom is merely a matter of geography. The play was amusingly and for many playgoers reminiscently set in a third-rate Montparnasse hotel with its primitive *lavabos* and garish wallpaper. Despite its foreign locale *The Left Bank* remains a distinctive part of the American scene in the twenties and early thirties.

When the city dweller journeyed out of town in his own country, just what did he do? A large representation from the Bronx, for one, spent its vacations in adult camps like Camp Kare-Free, the locale amusingly described in Arthur Kober's *Having Wonderful Time* (1937). A little love affair that survives some emotional bumps is here related against a background of bungalow life, "college" waiters, "entertainments," and romantic assignations around the lake. The Jewish dialect, accurate and not of the vaudeville variety, provides much humor and the love affair has true human interest. *Having Wonderful Time* is a good example of the realistic local-color comedy. There is infinitely more exaggeration in *George Washington Slept Here* (1940) by Kaufman and Hart, a boisterous farce about the urbanite's mania for buying and renovating deserted country houses. By the time the Fullers have cleared the cows from the kitchen, installed plumbing, dug a dozen holes for a well, plugged leaks in the roof, worn themselves out entertaining friends and relatives, and gone practically bankrupt in the process, the once skeptical wife (Jean Dixon) has grown to love the place and fights to retain it just as fiercely as does her husband (Ernest Truex). Two

veteran players—Dudley Digges and Mabel Taliaferro—
helped to make real the broadly farcical scenes in what, again,
must be considered a typical American comedy.

Comic themes were infinite in their variety. College life,
which provoked so much shocked discussion in the twenties,
gave plenty of opportunity for humor or satire. *The Poor Nut*
(1925) by J. C. and Elliott Nugent showed an insignificant
and unstandardized student at Ohio State floundering about
in a rah-rah world of cheerleaders, athletes, "frat" brothers,
and coeds. The timid hero is pounced upon by a visiting "Miss
Wisconsin," whose mastery of Freudian psychology leads her
to delve into his sexual problems, to his great horror. A kiss
from another coed and a swig of grain alcohol make him temporarily forget his inferiority complex and he wins a relay race,
only to find himself unwillingly engaged to "Miss Wisconsin"
and destined for a career as bond salesman. Fortunately the
other girl extricates him from this fix, and he can look forward
to the double haven of marriage and an instructorship in the
biology department. Humor and satire are agreeably combined in this male Cinderella theme, which takes good-
natured pot shots at the typical undergraduate. Good lively
satire also gave spice to Howard Lindsay's *She Loves Me Not*
(1933), wherein a lightly clad night-club dancer takes refuge
—with unerring feminine insight—in a Princeton dormitory.
The best of the college plays, and one with a much stronger
theme, was *The Male Animal* (1940), with Elliott Nugent
as co-author and lead. His collaborator was the cartoonist
James Thurber, who had been a fellow student of Nugent
at Ohio State. The mainspring of the play is the casual announcement by Tommy Turner, young professor of English,
that he will read Vanzetti's last letter to his composition class
as a model of prose. The unexpected result is a flaming edi-
torial by the radical editor of the college magazine and a
tremendous furore among the timid faculty and ultraconserva-
tive trustees. "Why—they'll never ask us to the Rose Bowl
now!" wails one of the latter. The pleas of Tommy's wife and

the threatened loss of his job do not shake his determination
to read the letter. He had no intention of starting a crusade,
he explains, but he is now fighting for something bigger than
himself—the right of free thought and speech in a world
which has tried to suppress both. Tommy's situation is complicated by the return for a visit of Joe Ferguson, former football
hero and once a suitor of Tommy's wife, Ellen. Dancing to the
tune of "Who?", their favorite in the old days, Joe and Ellen
succumb to a reminiscent kiss. Tommy's jealousy brings on a
domestic quarrel, which assumes epic proportions when he
throws Ellen into Joe's arms and she shocks both Joe and the
trustees by announcing that she is going back with Joe as his
mistress. The big comic scene comes when Tommy and the
radical editor enjoy a terrific binge together, and Tommy
explains in his best professional manner that—except for man
—the male animal, even the penguin, will fight for his mate.
Its psychological understanding, its uproarious humor, its
satire of pusillanimous professors, flag-waving trustees, and
football players, and finally its anti-Fascist thesis, give *The
Male Animal* a high place among the best contemporary
comedies.

While a new attitude toward women—the natural consequence of feminism, Freud, and the First World War—was
not limited to this country, it took a specifically American form
in the lively comedies under discussion. "What angels women
are!" had exclaimed the hero of Robertson's *Caste* in 1867,
expressing superbly the Victorian attitude toward the female
sex, both in England and here. By contrast the contemporary
American dramatists have tried to demonstrate the very an-
tithesis of that noble sentiment, to subject woman to their
usual technique of debunking. The demoniac traits of women
were heavily underlined in innumerable stage portraits, but it
remained for a female playwright to utter the final word on
the subject of what has come to be called "bitchery." Clare
Boothe's *The Women* (1936), a play with no male characters,
takes the audience to such feminine purlieus as hairdressing

parlors, beauty salons, boudoirs, Reno hotels, powder rooms.
There is only one high-minded woman, and her marriage is
brought on the rocks largely by the malicious and insidious
gossip of her ostensible friends, until she too learns to sharpen
and use her claws. Numerous female types are displayed:
the pure feline; the sloppy overweight who is perpetually
having unwanted children ("Are you Catholic or just careless?" someone asks her); the tough kept woman; the antique
but wealthy "Countess," disciple of l'Amour, who is divorcing
her fourth husband and running around with a young cowboy.
"Gallop, gallop, gallop, madly over the sagebrush! But now,
Miriam, I'm having an emotional relapse. In two weeks I'll be
free, free as a bird from that little French bastard, oh, whither
shall I fly?" It's time she returned to marrying Americans,
she thinks, but of course the cowboy turns out as unsuccessfully as the others. Clare Boothe has a knack for pungent characterization and trenchant dialogue. One of her simplest yet
most effective scenes presents the maid and cook enjoying
a midnight collation in the pantry and talking over their employers' marital relations. Maggie, the cook, concludes very
practically that "the first man who can think up a good ex-
planation how he can be in love with his wife *and* another
woman, is going to win that prize they're always giving out in
Sweden!"

No other play deals as exclusively or as maliciously with
womankind, but several others—scarcely more flattering—
have a strongly feminine slant in characters and action. *First
Lady* (1935) by Katharine Dayton and George S. Kaufman
burlesques the social and political feud between two Washington matrons, respective wives of the Secretary of State and
a Supreme Court justice. The political ballyhoo, the behind-
the-scenes manipulations, the petty jealousies and intrigues
involved in selecting a presidential candidate are all satirically
presented, including the part played by Mrs. Louella May
Creevey, President of the Women's Peace, Purity, and Patriotism League, "every inch a clubwoman—all bust and

flowers and blue and gold sash." She is all the more formidable
when one considers that six million women stand behind her.
Jane Cowl played the wife of the Secretary of State, one of the
rival ladies, popularly identified with Alice Roosevelt Long-
worth. Another Washington play about women, Joseph
Fields' *The Doughgirls* (1942), was a broad and bawdy farce
about the wartime capital with its hotel shortages, its ex-Wall
Street generals, and its unmarried wives. The piece is entirely
lacking in subtlety and often turns into horseplay, but no one
can deny the overpowering humor of the situations and characters. There is, for example, the Russian female guerilla,
slayer of 397 Nazis, who fires her rifle into the court three times
according to Soviet custom when she learns her mother has
given birth to another baby. For exercise she takes a brisk walk
to Baltimore and back, but is disgusted when the dog she has
chosen for a companion becomes exhausted and has to be carried halfway home. Besides the "doughgirls" and their tangled
sex lives, Judge Honoria Blake, organizer of the War Wives'
Relief Corps, comes in for a share of derisive laughter. The
play, in short, is a rough but entertaining account of the less
heroic deeds of women in wartime.

From these numerous examples some idea may be garnered
of the boisterous, realistic, completely unromantic spirit of
typical Broadway comedy. Whatever its failings, it kept its
humor and its sanity at a time when civilization seemed to be
going to smash under the impacts of depression and war. Its
impudent escapism is admirably expressed in the Pulitzer-
Prize *You Can't Take It with You* (1936) by Moss Hart and
George S. Kaufman. In the seclusion of their Claremont
Avenue home near Columbia University, Martin Vanderhof
(Henry Travers) and his family consecrate their lives to
tolerant self-expression. The fact that they are not particularly
gifted in their endeavors does not disturb them. Essie, one
granddaughter, has been taking ballet lessons for years from
the hirsute Russian Kolenkhov—with no perceptible progress.
She also likes to make candy. Her husband delights in playing

the xylophone and in printing. The revolutionary messages
that he prints and encloses in Essie's candy boxes are no signs
of communistic belief—he merely likes to print and happens
to be using excerpts from a book by Trotsky. Penny, Essie's
mother, started writing plays just because a typewriter was
delivered at her door by mistake. Paul Sycamore, her husband, presumably head of the family, has a dual career: he
plays with an Erector Set and manufactures fireworks in the
cellar. His faithful assistant, Mr. De Pinna, came to deliver
ice one day and just stayed on—he has now been with the
family eight years. Martin Vanderhof, Grandpa, also has his
hobbies and diversions—hunting snakes, playing darts, listening to the funny Commencement speeches every year at
Columbia. His retirement from the world took place over a
score of years before when one morning he took the elevator
up to his office and came right down again. Why expend life
and energy in the acquisition of wealth you do not need? You
can't take it with you. When an Internal Revenue agent comes
to inquire why Grandpa has never paid an income tax, Martin
blandly explains that he doesn't approve: "It's just that the
whole thing is silly." Why pay for useless luxuries like battle-
ships, Congress, the President, or the Supreme Court? This
philosophic isolationism is accompanied in the play by many
farcical scenes, particularly the unexpected visit of the Kirbys
when the entire family are busily occupied at their respective
pursuits. Almost every playgoer or movie enthusiast will remember the resulting mad confusion, the wrestling match,
Penny's free association game, the arrest of the household by
the FBI, and Mr. Kirby's partial conversion the next day to
Grandpa's views, not to mention the blintzes cooked by the
Grand Duchess Olga Katrina, currently a waitress in Childs.
Of course, *You Can't Take It with You* must not be taken too
seriously, nor is it probably the best play in which Kaufman
had a hand, but it is characteristic of its time and genre in its
brazen nose-thumbing at the world. Here we find perhaps the

true significance of hard-boiled low comedy with all its exaggeration, flippancy, and lack of inhibitions—the dramatization of native themes illumined at best by that unique corrosive in the world, an American sense of humor.

Chapter 7

BROADWAY

JN THE YEARS of American drama's coming of age Broadway led anything but a placid existence. The famous actors' strike of 1919 ended in victory for the Actors' Equity Association over the managers and the rival Actors' Fidelity League, formed by E. H. Sothern and George M. Cohan. Complete organization of the theatre industry rapidly followed. A manager before he could ring up a curtain on opening night had to have agreements with a dozen or more separate unions. Organization was healthy and beneficial for the theatre, correcting most of the evils of the past but introducing some of its own and skyrocketing the costs of production. Except for the lean season of 1921–1922, professional Broadway prospered until late in 1927, when two depression years presaged the Wall Street debacle of 1929. In the boom days of the twenties playhouses mushroomed in the Times Square district; by 1926 there were no fewer than eighty first-class legitimate theatres. Annual productions averaged in number between 260 and 270 (the high mark was 302 in 1927–1928), with of course the usual percentage of flops. After the crash Broadway staggered on, but the financial ruin of many producers (Sam H. Harris is said to have lost three million dollars), the demise of *Theatre Magazine,* the deaths of Belasco in 1931 and of Ziegfeld the next year, seemed to mark the end of an era. About 1929 the popularity of the "talkies" threatened far greater competition than the already colossal rivalry of the silent films. The theatre, Kaufman's Fabulous Invalid, miraculously survived these blows, not to mention the ever-present dangers of censorship—the Reverend John Roach Stratton,

District Attorney Banton, the play juries, the Wales Padlock
Law, the Catholic White List. Some of the moral complaints
were no doubt justifiable, and no one worried about the closing of Mae West's *The Pleasure Man,* dealing with revenge
by castration, or of *The Drag,* a worthless play about homo-
sexuals. But, as always, the self-appointed censors showed a
fine lack of discrimination between mere salaciousness and
worthy drama, and sought to copy the emasculated orthodoxy
of the Hays office. In 1936, for example, the Catholic White
List designated *Porgy and Bess, Winterset, Parnell, Paradise
Lost, At Home Abroad,* and *First Lady* as objectionable in
part and condemned *Dead End, The Children's Hour, Tobacco Road,* and *Boy Meets Girl* as completely pernicious. In
the face of such attempts at control, official or unofficial,
Broadway—to its great credit—maintained substantially its
freedom of expression. During the quagmire of financial depression a promise of better things came with the NRA theatre
code of 1933 and its efforts, largely successful, to rebuild the
road. A few years later, under the direction of Hallie Flanagan,
Federal Theatre began its career, brief as it was turbulent. By
1937 the Fabulous Invalid was on the way to enjoying a
healthy convalescence. Even rival Hollywood gave assistance
by paying tremendous sums for the film rights of Broadway
plays and by financing promising productions. Among minor
improvements, about 1940, came the regular presentation
of Sunday shows.

The term Broadway, while it includes in its wider sense all
plays given in the Times Square district, has usually been
considered synonymous with the commercial theatre—the
show business—which, as we have noted, monopolized dramatic activity before the reforming impact of the art theatre.
O'Neill and Anderson notwithstanding, Broadway retained
its inveterate escapism, always with the main eye on box office and the real estate market. For all its commercialism and
artistic lapses it cannot be ruled out of a dramatic history of
the period; in fact, in the low comedies and farces of the pre-

ceding chapter it was seen to be responsible for a significant
development in native drama. On its own level Broadway was
supreme, for it had the money and the initiative, and it could
command the best talent. Once convinced, it was not slow
to recruit the new scene designers, and it was ever sensitive
to changes in popular taste. Not crusading or high-brow, it
devoted itself wholeheartedly to the plebeian task of turning
entertainment into a fine (and profitable) art. Besides the
farce-comedies already discussed, staples in this great business of entertainment were melodrama and the musical show.
Both were handled with professional expertness and as time
went by both showed advances in treatment and maturity.
The improvements in appearance and efficiency were not unlike what could be observed in automobiles or clothes or aeroplanes during the same period.

In its efforts to combine theatrical thrills and chills with
a happy ending, melodrama—in 1917 and after—continued
to deal with the traditional themes of spies, murder, and crime.
Perhaps the best of the war melodramas, *Three Faces East*
(1918) by Anthony Paul Kelly, had the usual complicated plot
of espionage and counter-espionage, centering in the home
of an English cabinet minister, with Violet Heming as a German fraülein and Emmett Corrigan as a mysterious butler.
The play's title entered into the plot as a cryptic password. The
old-fashioned crime play was well represented in Max Marcin's *Silence* (1924), in which H. B. Warner played an innocent man whose silence in attempting to save his daughter
almost brings him to the electric chair, and—with a sex angle
—in Martin Brown's *The Lady* (1923), about an elderly female cabaret owner (Mary Nash) who identifies a man killed
in the bar as her long-separated son. *Crime* (1927) by Samuel Shipman and John B. Hymer was similarly conventional
in depicting the misfortunes of an elevator operator and a department store clerk (Douglass Montgomery and Sylvia Sidney) who become seriously involved with a "master mind"

of crime and his gang. In the same year appeared one of the
most popular of modern melodramas, Bayard Veiller's *The
Trial of Mary Dugan,* starring Ann Harding as a young woman
who has been living in sin to send her unsuspecting brother
through law school. In a dramatic court scene the brother—
of course it's his first law case—exonerates his sister of the
charge of murdering her "sugar daddy" by proving dramatically that the crime was committed by a left-handed person.
While the situation was one of extreme theatricalism, the
courtroom scene itself was treated with minute realism. Ayn
Rand's *The Night of January 16* (1935) went one step further
in this direction by selecting a jury from the audience at each
performance and paying them at legal rates. In a search for
realistic setting and novelty Eva Kay Flint and Martha Madison in *Subway Express* (1929) contrived a murder melodrama in the New York subway.

Prohibition and gang warfare proved a windfall for pur-
veyors of melodrama, offering numerous new angles and situations. *Twelve Miles Out* (1926) by William Anthony Mc-
Guire was concerned with bootlegging and hijacking at sea
with a dash of love rivalry thrown in, and a gangster play, *Four
Walls* (1927) by Dana Burnet and George Abbott gave Muni
Weisenfreund (Paul Muni) his first important Broadway part
after he had played some three hundred roles in the Yiddish
Theatre. *Gang War* (1928) by the veteran Willard Mack,
author of some sixty-five plays, launched an all-out attack
on the spectators' nerves by his terrifying version of a Chicago
beer-running feud, complete with gunmen, machine guns,
bombs from the air, and the suffocating odor of gunpowder.
Of all the gangster plays none had more zest and color than
the famous *Broadway* (1926) by Philip Dunning and George
Abbott, set backstage in the Paradise Night Club and combining a gang murder with the lives and loves of a pony
ballet. Lee Tracy as a night-club hoofer in love with one of the
chorus girls shocked the more staid critics and audiences by
removing his pants on the stage and proposing in his under-

drawers. The play offered a masterly concoction of the three principal forms of Broadway entertainment—low comedy, hoofing, and melodrama.

Like the hard-boiled comedies of the twenties the melodramas were not without their social comment. Bartlett Cormack's *The Racket* (1927) drew a scathing picture of the interrelation of crime and politics that had come with Prohibition. The bootlegger Scarsi is working hand and glove with the Chicago politicians. An honest policeman, transferred to the sticks for his efforts to enforce the law, manages to arrest Scarsi's brother and then Scarsi himself, to the consternation of the authorities. Later the political boss decides to pretend to let Scarsi escape and then to shoot him dead, thus preventing damaging revelations at the trial. As one of the cops remarks cynically, this doublecross was contrived "so that gover'ment o' the professionals, by the professionals, and for the professionals shall not perish from the earth." The sinister Scarsi was played by Edward G. Robinson, one of his many gangster roles. The same cynical view of contemporary life and manners was expressed in other melodramatic plays, including *Five Star Final* (1930) by Louis Weitzenkorn, a strong attack on tabloid journalism.

A more venerable and romantic variety of melodrama depended on remote or exotic settings. Salisbury Field's *Zander the Great* (1923), set on the Mexican border, was an old-fashioned melodrama which yielded sufficiently to modernism to turn the old-time bandits into bootleggers. The cast included Alice Brady as the heroine and George Abbott, not yet a producer, in the character role of Texas. Mexico itself provided the locale and atmosphere for Willard Mack's *The Dove* (1925), a colorful melodrama about a cabaret singer (Judith Anderson) in love with an American employee in a gambling house (William Harrigan). The girl is vigorously pursued, however, by a rich Mexican oil man (Holbrook Blinn), who does not relent in favor of the lovers until the final curtain. Blinn had earlier played with equal *éclat* a Mexican bandit in

Porter Emerson Browne's *The Bad Man* (1920), a satirical
piece in which he summarily solves the problems of a group
of Americans with more logic than legality, for example setting the heroine free from her brutal husband by the simple
device of shooting him. Turning to an opposite region the in-
satiable Willard Mack in 1928 starred in his own *The Scarlet
Fox*, in which the Canadian Mounted eventually get their
man after a chase leading as far afield as a bordello and the
cellar of a Chinese laundry. Superficially these plays may resemble the popular regional plays, but the emphasis, of course,
was on violent and sensational action. They were expertly
handled and at their best theatrically satisfying.

For weird and mysterious sensationalism nothing could
surpass the Orient, which figures in several melodramas of
the twenties. *The Son-Daughter* (1919) by George Scarborough and David Belasco set its violent action among the
rival political groups in the redlight district of Chinatown.
To help finance the revolution in China a father has to sacrifice
his daughter (Lenore Ulric) in marriage, but when he is murdered she gains a justifiable revenge by strangling her husband
on the marriage bed. Earl Carroll's *The Lady of the Lamp*
(1920) mingled fantasy with melodrama in showing an opium
dream in which an American hero becomes in imagination
a Chinese emperor. His Chinese *inamorata* in the dream is
deplorably murdered but on waking up he finds her again in
the home of his Chinese host in New York. Most extreme both
in orientalism and sensationalism was John Colton's *The
Shanghai Gesture* (1926), in which Mother Goddam, sinister
keeper of a Shanghai brothel, revenges herself on an Englishman who had deserted her twenty years before. Ingeniously
she contrives to force him to witness the public sale of his
daughter for immoral purposes, the big scene showing the
unfortunate girl, in abbreviated costume, dangling in a gilded
cage while Chinese junkmen bid for her possession. When
Mother Goddam's own daughter is seduced by a Japanese,
the mother kills her without compunction. Fantastic and un-

convincing as it is, the story makes for good escape theatre, Florence Reed receiving much praise for her performance as the dynamic Mother Goddam.

In melodrama as in other dramatic forms Negro life provided themes as well as an entrée for the Negro actor. One of the early examples—after O'Neill's plays—was *Lulu Belle* (1926) by Edward Sheldon and Charles MacArthur, a Belasco production with one hundred Negroes and fifteen whites—the leads played by Lenore Ulric and Henry Hull. This vehicle told the lurid story of a Harlem tart who seduces a barber. She soon deserts him and eventually reaches Paris, becoming the mistress of a French count. Here both her sins and the barber catch up with her, and she is strangled to death. Just about as sensational was *Harlem* (1929) by William Jourdan Rapp and Wallace Thurman, the latter a Negro. There was only one white actor in the cast. The play shows the degradation of a respectable black family after it moves from Virginia to Harlem with its "rent parties," "belly-hug" dancing, and general promiscuity. The daughter, played by Isabell Washington, spurns her fiancé and runs away, first with a gangster, and after he is murdered, with a song plugger. The same mood and ingredients were present in the more recent *Anna Lucasta* (1944) by Philip Yordan, with its combination of vice and respectability. Negro melodrama, of course, shades very readily into folk or social drama, as in *Savage Rhythm* (1931) by Harry Hamilton and Norman Foster, about the Mississippi swamplands, or in *Never No More* (1932) by James Knox Millen, a play about rape, murder, and lynching. The same is true of the better Negro plays such as *In Abraham's Bosom* and *Native Son*. One might therefore say that violent melodramatic action was inherent in the Negro play, regardless of its classification. Refreshing for its old-fashioned straightforwardness with little stress on social implications was William DuBois' *Haiti* (1938), a Federal Theatre production about the successful

Negro revolution in Haiti led by Jean Christophe (Rex Ingram) and Toussaint l'Ouverture.

Supernatural, fantastic, and psychological horror offered vast opportunities for melodrama. *The Unknown Purple* (1918), for example, relates a weird and thoroughly incredible tale of a scientist who is "railroaded" to jail by his wife so that she can marry her lover. The scientist later discovers a way of making himself invisible—except for a strange purple light—and by virtue of this power secures a satisfactory revenge. Richard Bennett played the lead in this Monte Cristo yarn. Like the earlier *The Thirteenth Chair*, Crane Wilbur's *The Ouija Board* (1920) dabbled in crime and the occult, showing how a bogus medium is trapped by unsuspected supernatural forces. The same author in 1922 contrived a veritable chamber of horrors in *The Monster*, story of Dr. Ziska, a maniacal surgeon who revels in fantastic operations. He is waited upon and assisted by an amorphous giant who crawls about without legs. Then again, there was the dramatization in 1927 of Bram Stoker's *Dracula* by Hamilton Deane and John Balderston, dealing with the ancient legend of Count Dracula, the werewolf, who sucks his victims' blood until they too become vampires. The role of Dracula was played by a Hungarian actor, Bela Lugosi. Though entertaining, all these plays are pretty infantile. It was rather in mental and psychological terror that melodrama found the key to greater realism and maturity. On an elementary level John Willard's *The Cat and the Canary* (1922) showed the persistent attempts to break down a girl's sanity by a series of terrifying tricks. With far greater realism Edward Chodorov's *Kind Lady* (1935), based on a Hugh Walpole story, emphasized the mental torture of a kind-hearted elderly woman—played by Grace George—whose home in completely taken over by a gang of sadistic scoundrels who hold her incommunicado. There is not only realism but clinical interest in the superb melodrama by

James Warwick, *Blind Alley* (1935), about a gangster who takes refuge in the summer home of a professor of psychology and is brought to self-destruction by the latter's relentless psychological probing. By the middle thirties melodrama, like farce, was growing up.

Since terror and laughter are closely allied emotionally, it is not surprising to find Broadway playwrights exaggerating the melodramatic and the macabre for humorous purposes. An extremely complicated "whodunit" by Mary Roberts Rinehart and Avery Hopwood, *The Bat* (1920), in which the supposed detective turns out to be the criminal, became popular largely because of the farcical characterization and acting of the terrified maid (Mary Vokes). Cora Dick Gantt's *The Tavern* (1920), a George M. Cohan production with the elderly Arnold Daly in one of his last roles, was meant to be serious but was produced as a delightful take-off on old-fashioned romantic melodrama. The mystery play itself was neatly burlesqued in Ralph Spence's *The Gorilla* (1925) with all the conventional trappings and machinery of the formula—from the secret doors to the trick lights. At one point a huge gorilla—the criminal in disguise—hops over the footlights and wanders amid the audience, to the accompaniment of shrieks and laughter. In Damon Runyon's and Howard Lindsay's *A Slight Case of Murder* (1935) a humorous twist was given to the gangster play. Naturalness and comic characterization give a distinctive flavor to *Mr. and Mrs. North* (1941) written by the dramatic critic Richard Lockridge and his wife, where the murders are solved by a featherheaded Village housewife who almost succeeds unwittingly in sending her husband to jail for the crimes but at the last moment identifies the murderer by means of a cooking recipe. The height of the comico-macabre was not reached until Joseph Kesselring's *Arsenic and Old Lace* (1941), in which two elderly and pious spinsters (played by Josephine Hull and Jean Adair), agreeably demented, are responsible for a dozen murders, thus equaling the record of their violently maniacal brother (Boris Karloff). Few spectators will forget the mad Brooklyn household, the farcical stage business with the corpses, the comic antics of a second brother, who identifies himself with Theodore Roosevelt and, taking the stairs for San Juan hill, dashes up with a stirring cry of "Charge!" The play well indicates the growing inability or unwillingness of Broadway to take its melodrama very seriously, and along with the psychological pieces, marks the most significant advance of the thirties and forties in this ancient form—a startling advance if we consider by contrast Boucicault's *After Dark,* delightfully revived by Christopher Morley in 1928–1929 in his Hoboken theatrical venture.

Fewer melodramas reached the stage after 1930, the type tending to merge with more serious drama. Mention should be made of the keen competition from England from *Bulldog Drummond* in 1921 to *Ladies in Retirement, Angel Street,* and *Night Must Fall* of more recent date. A more devastating rivalry came from the movies, silent and vocal, which were ideally suited for the dispensation of thrills and action. Several Hollywood players made a specialty of melodramatic movie roles, including Theda Bara, Lon Chaney, Bela Lugosi, and Boris Karloff, though they ventured occasionally on the legitimate stage. Theda Bara, the deadly female vampire of the early movies, made one try at girlish sentimentality in the silent films as Kathleen Mavourneen and then took a disastrous plunge on Broadway in a melodrama called *The Blue Flame* (1920), notable only for her immortal remark to the villain, "I'll shake you like I shake my shimmy." Boris Karloff, as we have seen, appeared on the stage in *Arsenic and Old Lace.* But the true reputation of these actors was won and remained in the movies, which gradually took over the gangster plays, the fantastic pieces like *Frankenstein* and *Dracula,* the romantic melodramas, and more recently—as in *Shadow of a Doubt* and *Spellbound*—the psychological plays, discovering Freud a quarter of a century later than Broadway. With capable directors like Alfred Hitchcock the movies were able to develop a technique of thrills and pursuit quite beyond the physical capabilities of the stage play. Thus melodrama, like old-fashioned farce, moved over to Hollywood—to Broadway's eventual gain.

Hollywood could take over melodrama, but in spite of frequent and frantic efforts it could not capture from commercial Broadway its most individual and glittering dramatic creation, the musical show. For the theatre was able to produce the real thing, free from crippling censorship, free from the limitations of the camera, free from the pretentious ornateness of the movies, with the full audience response that the form at its best provokes and demands. The genesis of the modern musical play was seen earlier in the attempts of men like Irving Berlin and Jerome Kern to bring ragtime and jazz into the Victor Herbert type of operetta. Through the efforts of later composers—Cole Porter, George Gershwin, Richard Rodgers—as well as the orchestra direction of Paul Whiteman and his colleagues, jazz became exciting, varied, widely accepted as the native musical idiom. In the words of Chotzinoff, Gershwin made an honest woman out of jazz. The contribution of Negro rhythms must not be overlooked, nor must the varied influences of Balieff's *Chauve-Souris,* the *Grand Street Follies,* American folk song, or European music—as in the scores of Kurt Weill. At the same time Ziegfeld and his compeers were glorifying the American girl, requiring of the chorus and principals far higher standards of beauty, refinement, and skill than in the past. The Tiller girls and the Hoffman girls brought new ideals of precision and ensemble work. By the later twenties Albertina Rasch was introducing ballet into musical comedy, paving the way for choreographers like Robert Alton, George Balanchine, and Agnes de Mille, who devised more complicated dance routines and sought to integrate dance, music, action, and mood. With the great clowns and comics, most of them

graduates of vaudeville or burlesque, the formula often became—as succinctly expressed by George Beiswanger of
Theatre Arts—"low comedy, high dance." Stage dancing was
influenced by ballroom steps, folk dances, and ballet, but in
form and substance it was based on tap. Specialty numbers,
of course, were affected by current fads and fashions—the
shimmy, the Charleston, the Black Bottom, Bottoms Up, the
South American dances. Whatever may be said for or against
stage music and dancing, they did not remain static, and the
changes were usually for the better. At the same time the old
creaky plot of the operetta either disappeared or became
more sensible and better integrated with the rest of the performance. Even the lyrics turned witty and sophisticated in
the hands of writers like Ira Gershwin, George S. Kaufman,
Howard Dietz, Harold Rome, Moss Hart, and Lorenz Hart.
It is no exaggeration to say that between 1917 and the present
the Broadway musical play became streamlined and adult,
increasingly expressive of the American temper, worthy sister to the other dramatic types.

The stars that revolved in the musical firmament during
this transformation are practically household names. Older
comics like Al Jolson of the blackface makeup and mammy
songs or Ed Wynn of the ill-assorted hats and coats, inventor
of the corn-eating machine modeled after a typewriter, drifted
to radio and the movies, though they occasionally returned
to Broadway. A low-comedy technique was developed by
Leon Errol with his trick knee. Among the standbys of the
old *Follies* were Bert Williams, famed for his bell-hop act;
Will Rogers, homespun philosopher and lariat expert; and two
gentlemen who became instantly famous for one song: "Absolutely, Mister Gallagher; Positively, Mister Shean." Bobby
Clark, W. C. Fields, Fred Allen, Jimmy Savo, the Marx
brothers, Charles Butterworth, Jimmy Durante all came to
prominence in the twenties. A drawling personification of
naïveté and defeatism brought fame to Victor Moore in the
thirties and a raucous burlesque manner did the same for

Bert Lahr. As a rule the distaff side depended more on singing than on comedy. Fanny Brice could combine farcical
action with sentimental "gutter" ditties like "My Man."
Helen Morgan and Libby Holman specialized in blues singing—the latter's "Moanin' Low" stopped the *Little Show* of
1929. Ethel Merman's vigorous delivery of bawdy songs or
sentimental ballads shook many a theatre rafter, but she
was also an accomplished comedienne. Two English girls—
Beatrice Lillie and Gertrude Lawrence—brought a fresh and
engaging comic technique to the Broadway musical.

Better known as dancers, though they might have other
accomplishments as well, was a whole parade of nimble or
eccentric steppers: George M. Cohan, Ann Pennington of
the *Follies* and *Scandals,* Mary Eaton, Marilyn Miller, Fred
and Adele Astaire, Dorothy Stone, Ginger Rogers, Jack Don-
ahue, Ray Bolger, Gene Kelly. Clifton Webb's dancing career
long preceded his straight comedy acting, one high spot
being his imaginative "Body and Soul" number with Tamara
Geva in *Three's a Crowd.* Negroes were well represented,
from Bill (Bojangles) Robinson, "the Chocolate Nijinsky"
with a passion for stairs, to Katherine Dunham, student and
exponent of exotic West Indian rhythms. In her early days
Mae West—tough girl in *Some Time*—attracted notice as a
practitioner of the shimmy, an art whose high priestess became Gilda Gray of the *Follies*—inexplicably portrayed in
advertisements of the time as a testimonial for Madame X
Girdles. Years later, Carmen Miranda brought her voluble
speech and tropical steps to the Broadway revue. The influence of interpretive dancing was seen in Ray Bolger's
dance story, "Slaughter on Tenth Avenue," or Paul Haakon's
"Death in the Afternoon," a tragic narrative dance about a
bull fighter. These and other performers brought real distinction to American musical comedy.

The musical show was one of the first forms to capitalize
on the relaxation in manners and morals that overtook postwar drama, although one type—the operetta—remained suf-

ficiently staid and proper for the family trade. In vain did the Reverend John Roach Stratton hurl his moral thunderbolts against the evils of nudity and the shimmy. The bald-headed rows at the Winter Garden continued to relish the popular runway. Costumes became abbreviated to the vanishing point. Hassard Short's *Ritz Revue* (1924) displayed bare breasts in the Minsky tradition and one of the early *Follies* offered a glimpse of a girl stepping out of a bathtub. The Shuberts' *The Great Temptations* (1926) went Ziegfeld one better by having both a nude man (except for a few beads) and woman. Suggestive sketches and stage business gave spice to most of the revues, sometimes vulgar and in poor taste, sometimes witty. In 1930 Jimmy Savo was arrested for appearing in a sketch in Earl Carroll's *Vanities* as a neophyte window-dresser, assigned to remove articles of clothing from models—they turn out to be real girls, not dummies—in a shop window. The same show and the same police station were graced by the presence of Faith Bacon, a fan dancer. The best of the later musicals depended less on vulgarity and nudity, but they scarcely provided the austere moral tone of a girl-scout pageant or a church social. Both sketches and lyrics aimed at pungent wit and sophistication, as in Ethel Merman's plaintive ditty in the Irving Berlin show, *Annie Get Your Gun*, the stanzas of which terminate with the sagacious observation:

> And you can't shoot a male in the tail like a quail,
> Oh, you can't get a man with a gun.

With no intention of giving an exhaustive list it may be illuminating to name a few of the dozens of musical plays that have danced and laughed their way to success from 1917 to the present. The romantic operetta of an earlier day managed to survive on a jazz-mad Broadway. Near the start of the period there was *Apple Blossoms* (1919) with music by Fritz Kreisler and Victor Jacobs and dancing by the Astaires. A far superior piece was the celebrated *Rose-Marie*

(1924) by Otto Harbach and Oscar Hammerstein 2d, the music by Rudolph Friml and Herbert Stothart, a bright, sweet, and melodic operetta on a Canadian subject. The same year saw the production of *The Student Prince,* Dorothy Donnelly's musical version of *Old Heidelberg,* with music by Sigmund Romberg. This had a sentimental and fairly elaborate plot about a prince attending Heidelberg incognito as a student; he falls in love with an attractive waitress but is reluctantly forced to leave to inherit his kingdom and become affianced to a princess. Howard Marsh and Ilse Marvenga played the romantic couple. A successful pseudohistorical operetta, *The Vagabond King* (1925) by Brian Hooker and W. H. Post, with music by Rudolph Friml, was an adaptation of J. H. McCarthy's famous *If I Were King,* Dennis King taking the role of the scapegrace Villon. Several pieces dealt romantically with the lives of composers, borrowing freely from their music. Such was *The Love Song* (1925), a Second Empire play about Offenbach's love affair with the Princess Eugénie. An earlier operetta, *Blossom Time* (1921) by Dorothy Donnelly, gave the life and music of Schubert, and a much later one, *The Song of Norway,* paid the same compliment to Grieg. *The Nightingale* (1927) ingeniously adapted the career of Jenny Lind to musical purposes with Thomas Wise enacting the role of P. T. Barnum. Guy Bolton, P. J. Wodehouse, Armand Vecsay all had a hand in this piece, which like most operettas was produced by the Shuberts. Adventure and love motivated two musical plays with lavish and romantic settings—*The Song of the Flame* (1925) and *The Desert Song* (1926). The former, a collaboration of Harbach, Hammerstein 2d, Stothart, and Gershwin, dramatizes the dilemma of the Flame, a Russian revolutionist who falls in love with one of the aristocrats she has been seeking to overthrow; the latter, a Harbach-Hammerstein-Mandel play with excellent music by Romberg, relates the fortunes of a romantic spy in the Riff war. Noel Coward in *Bitter Sweet* (1929) gave Broadway a few pointers on how to develop a sweet, sentimental, and successful operetta from a very simple theme. Of foreign origin also were two versions of Strauss' *Die Fledermaus: Champagne, Sec* (1933) and *Rosalinda* (1942). It is evident that during the entire period operettas, though far outnumbered by other musical forms, at least found a faithful public.

The story of revue and musical comedy is far more elaborate; for convenience it may be divided chronologically into two parts—before 1932 and after. Selection of that date, marking the death of Ziegfeld, is quite arbitrary, but some differences may be noted in the two periods. The first covers the boom, Prohibition, the Jazz Age, until the start of the depression. It is essentially the period of the big lavish show, built around a star, loaded down with expensive costumes, statuesque show girls, extraordinary stage effects. Such were, of course, the huge yearly revues, glorified vaudeville, with topical references galore but no pretense of plot—the *Ziegfeld Follies, Passing Shows,* George White's *Scandals,* the *Vogues,* the *Artists and Models,* John Murray Anderson's *Greenwich Village Follies.* With no thought of permanence, they concentrated on relaxation and entertainment, relying upon dance, music, low comedy, and spectacle. With the depression their day was virtually over. Not unlike them but with perhaps a semblance of plot were the big extravaganzas and musical shows, normally revolving about a star. *Sinbad* (1918) and *Big Boy* (1925) with Al Jolson, *The Perfect Fool* (1921) with Ed Wynn, *Louie the 14th* (1925) with Leon Errol, *The Cocoanuts* (1925) with the Marx brothers, might be offered as scattered examples. There were dozens of others—*Monte Cristo Jr., Bombo, Kid Boots, Sunny*—but perhaps the spectacular *Sally* (1920) will best serve to illustrate the type. Written by Guy Bolton with lyrics by Clifford Grey, sets by Joseph Urban, and music by Jerome Kern, this musical piece broke box-office records at the large New Amsterdam Theatre, grossing $38,985 in one week. The plot, with bows to Cinderella, was agreeably simple. Marilyn Miller and Leon Errol are ignobly employed in a New York lobster palace—he as a waiter, she as dishwasher. But he is in reality a down-at-the-heels nobleman with memories of better things. By the second act they manage to crash a society garden party, Leon impersonating the Duke of Czechogovinia and Marilyn a Russian danseuse. Naturally they make an instantaneous hit. The piece ends with a triple marriage at the Little Church around the Corner, with Marilyn capturing a handsome and pecunious young man. Her sister brides were played by the statuesque Dolores and Mary Hay. Needless to say this slender success story was made the framework for many spectacular effects, including a butterfly dance in which the chorus ladies were chromatically costumed as butterflies with folding wings. Leon Errol's quips and collapsible knee provided most of the humor, and Marilyn Miller's graceful singing and dancing well justified her first billing as a star. Here was the very antithesis of O'Neill's soul-probing *Beyond the Horizon* of the same year, but at least it offered an evening of gay entertainment.

The big musical show was particularly well equipped to recapture the romantic past, usually with more than a touch of sentimentality and transient melancholy. These qualities are prominent in the Jerome Kern-Oscar Hammerstein 2d *Show Boat* (1927), considered by many the greatest of musical comedies, a pleasantly reminiscent play of the Mississippi River based on the Edna Ferber novel. Covering a long span of years from the eighties via the Chicago World's Fair to the middle twenties, the plot tells a simple dramatic tale of love and gambling, embellished with costume, dance, and music—including such classic tunes as "Why Do I Love You?", "Can't Help Lovin' Dat Man," and "Ol' Man River," the last superbly rendered by the Negro singer Jules Bledsoe. Charles Winninger, Norma Terris, and the torch singer Helen Morgan headed the rest of a capable cast. The play was successfully revived in 1946. The same Kern-Hammerstein combination was responsible in 1929 for *Sweet Adeline,* another sumptuous reminiscent show in which Helen Morgan, perched upon her customary piano, moaned the melancholy ditties "Here Am I" and "Why Was I Born?" Others in the cast were Irene Franklin, saved from the mediocrities of vaudeville, and Charles Butterworth, a wry, dead-pan comedian, whose skill at pantomime was in itself enough to raise a laugh, as when—back to the audience—he surveyed a set of rococo nudes adorning the walls of a Gay Nineties bar.

With equal facility, of course, the musical show could handle distance in space as well as in time. Such was the exotic *Rio Rita* (1927), a Ziegfeld production about the Mexican border with a melodramatic plot about a cabaret girl, a Mexican bandit, and a Texas Ranger. The piece was interesting in initiating a strong Latin-American influence on Broadway musical comedy and in being one of the early shows to feature the Albertina Rasch Dancers.

Other musical comedies on a less grand scale delighted the playgoers of the Jazz Age, becoming increasingly efficient vehicles for interrelated story, song, and dance. The sentimental sweetness of Romberg's *Maytime* (1917) soon gave way to rapid tempo and sophisticated gaiety. Among the dozens of pieces that clamored loudly for attention were George Gershwin's *La, La, Lucille* (1919), and *Poor Little Ritz Girl* (1920) with music by Richard Rodgers and Sigmund Romberg, lyrics by Lorenz Hart and Alex Gerber. The latter musical was a backstage affair about a little girl from North Carolina who joins the chorus, preserves her innocence, and finds happiness in marriage. *Irene,* a Cinderella piece that supported the scarcely novel thesis that clothes make the woman, brought James Montgomery a fortune in 1919. In 1923 Fred Stone's daughter Dorothy made a successful debut as co-star with her father in *Stepping Stones.* *Lady, Be Good* (1924), with a Gershwin score, featured the Astaires in a flimsy brother-sister plot in which Adele saves Fred from an unhappy marriage by impersonating a Mexican

widow. Musical shows often turned out to be old stage successes with their faces lifted—*Hit the Deck* (1927), in which
Stella Mayhew sang the popular "Hallelujah," was derived
from *Shore Leave,* and *Whoopee* (1928), a vehicle enabling
Eddie Cantor to play a hypochondriac, was merely a poor
version of *The Nervous Wreck.* Mark Twain's story inspired
two musical adaptations of *A Connecticut Yankee* by the
Fields-Rodgers-Hart combination, in 1927 and 1943 respectively, with such familiar song hits as "Thou Swell" and "My
Heart Stood Still." The musicals, like the farces, turned to
sports for inspiration, *Good News* (1927) and *You Said It*
(1931) being concerned with football, and *Follow Thru*
(1929) with golf. *Funny Face* (1927), a George and Ira
Gershwin show with the agile Astaires, had Victor Moore
as a tender-hearted bandit whose ruling passion is to take
photographs of eclipses. Rapid pace and smart sophistication
characterized Herbert Fields' *Fifty Million Frenchmen*
(1929), music by Cole Porter, a hilarious picture of American
tourists in Paris. A set of first-class performers, some of them
new, appeared in Gershwin's *Girl Crazy* (1930)—Ethel Merman, Ginger Rogers, Willie Howard, Willie Kent—about a
young Eastern barfly who travels to Arizona by taxicab, picking up eccentric characters on the way and ending up on a
dude ranch. *The Band Wagon* (1931) by George S. Kaufman
and Howard Dietz, with music by Arthur Schwartz, was another lively show with dancing by the Astaires. There were
many more, but even this fragmentary and kaleidoscopic
survey should indicate that musical comedy was very much
alive and prospering, increasingly aware of its own potential-
ities.

Several specific developments of the early period deserve
special mention. One was the appearance of the intimate
revue—in direct contrast to the big elaborate shows—with
emphasis on freshness, originality, wit, and satire. An early
example was Irving Berlin's *Music Box Revue* (1921) presented in a small new playhouse. A strong influence came

from England with the importation of *Charlot's Revue of
1924*, an ingratiatingly witty musical by Noel Coward which
had the distinction of introducing Beatrice Lillie and Gertrude Lawrence to the American stage. The latter's big number was the immensely popular "Limehouse Blues." The same
year saw the start at the Neighborhood Playhouse of the
Grand Street Follies, an intimate yearly revue on a high intellectual plane, the purpose of which was mainly to satirize
the contemporary theatre. With the aid of two excellent mim-
ics—Albert Carroll and Dorothy Sands—it mercilessly parodied scenes and individual performances of the current
Broadway plays. There was an amusing take-off, for example,
of the John Barrymore *Hamlet* with its multitudinous steps.
In the 1925 edition Albert Carroll cleverly parodied Pavlova's
Swan Dance. *They Knew What They Wanted under the Elms*
killed two dramatic birds with one burlesque. A blow at
censorship was delivered in a bowdlerized version of *What
Price Glory?* with two effeminate antagonists, one in white
yachting attire and one in periwinkle satin pajamas, engaging
in a daredevil drinking bout on straight cream soda. Charmaine of the original play became purified as the hostess of
the Morning Glory Tea Room. *L'Irlanda Rosa dell'Abie*, an
operatic take-off on *Abie's Irish Rose*, was even funnier with
its diminutive Abie in Romeo costume resembling the opera
tenor Gigli and a large majestic Rose in long robes and flowers
in her hair looking like a somewhat decayed Mme. Jeritza.
A memorable performance in a later Grand Street show was
that of Dorothy Sands as Mother Goshdarn. Another intimate
revue, emphasizing music and dance rather than satire, appeared in 1925—the *Garrick Gaieties*—performed by the
Theatre Guild juniors. Tuneful music by Richard Rodgers
included some appealing songs like "The Butcher, the Baker,
and Candlestick Maker." The leading roles were taken with
much vivacity and freshness by newcomers to the musical
stage—June Cochrane, Sterling Holloway, and Edith Meiser.
Among the dances was an amusing tour de force by Eleanor

Shaler showing the gradual metamorphosis of a classic nymph in Greek costume into a goddess of modern syncopation. *The Garrick Gaieties* of the next year, a Rodgers-Hart collaboration, had the same enthusiastic amateur spirit; it included one excellent satirical sketch, a burlesque of American musical comedy entitled *My Rose of Arizona*.

The impulse to satire, thus encouraged and developed outside the strictly commercial theatre, found its way more and more into the Broadway musicals, raising the I.Q. of the "musigirl" comedy. There was, for one, the J. P. McEvoy revue *Americana* (1926) with Charles Butterworth giving a devastating satire of a Rotarian after-dinner speech; all but one of his six listeners on stage were wax figures in slumbering postures. McEvoy's second *Americana,* appearing in 1932 after a lapse of six years, had the mordant depression song, "Brother, Can Ya Spare a Dime?" Satire was soon adopted by the regular musical comedy as in *Strike Up the Band* (1930), an antiwar musical by Morrie Ryskind, George S. Kaufman, and the two Gershwins. The same distinguished collaboration was responsible for *Of Thee I Sing* (1931), a political satire about the campaigning and ballyhoo for the United States presidency, first musical to receive the Pulitzer Prize. The treatment is biting—yet gay and whimsical at the same time—as the candidate, John P. Wintergreen, bases his entire campaign on love, giving occasion for the electioneering song, "Of Thee I Sing, Baby." There is appropriate ridicule of the typical Senators from the South and West, the Madison Square speeches, the presidential backers who fear they may have gone too far in selling Rhode Island but who nevertheless find a haven in the Cabinet. The plot is complicated by the rivalry of two women for the hand of the President, a rivalry which almost wrecks Wintergreen's chances until Mary Turner shifts the balance by announcing her impending motherhood, thereby hitting America in its national soft spot. The best comedy was supplied by Victor Moore, characteristically timid and insignificant, as Alexander Throttlebottom, the completely forgotten nominee for Vice-President who is shocked to learn that his duties include presiding over the Senate. Moore became the central comic figure also in the musical sequel, *Let 'Em Eat Cake*, which appeared two seasons later. These two satires suffer from humor which is too obvious and from occasional musical reminiscences of Gilbert and Sullivan, but they mark a great advance over the earlier jazz pieces. With their arrival musical comedy had become more grown-up and high-brow.

Another noteworthy feature of the twenties, beside the intimate revue and satire, was the rise of the Negro musical show. Employing the talents of performers like Josephine Baker, Florence Mills, Bill Robinson, and Ethel Waters, the colored revue specialized in blues singing and torrid dancing. The choruses too—given bizarre names like the Chocolate Drops or Plantation Steppers—played with a zest and abandon not commonly seen on the Broadway stage. Some of the typical Negro shows were *Shuffle Along* (1921), *Chocolate Dandies* (1924), *Dixie to Broadway* (1924), and *Keep Shufflin'* (1928). One of the best was *Blackbirds of 1928*, in which Bill Robinson danced and Adelaide Hall sang the catchy "Diga, Diga, Do." These revues—lively, rhythmic, rapid in pace—remained on a rather primitive and elementary entertainment level, but they prepared the way for the later and more original Negro musical.

Considered as a whole, the musical shows up to 1932 closely reflected the characteristics of the period. They were boisterous, gaudy, impudent, suggestive, brash. They had a few moaners and blues singers, but they were nevertheless predominantly gay, unlike the whining schools of depression and Second World War crooning. Living life blatantly and energetically, the Charleston steppers, the Texas Guinans, the Tin Pan Alley enthusiasts little realized that they would come to symbolize a golden and grandiose age of manic insanity. With satirical malice a musical show of 1945, *Billion Dollar Baby* by Betty Comden and Adolph Green with music by

Morton Gould, set out to recapture the flavor of this almost mythical era of bootleggers, speakeasies, night club hostesses, and marathon dancers. The musical and terpsichorean extremists of the Jazz Age had suffered the fate of all revolutionaries and become classic.

After 1932 the musical show continued its advances in craftsmanship and streamlined efficiency. Because of its frank escapism in a troubled world it generally prospered in spite of depression and war. Except for haphazard resuscitations of the *Ziegfeld Follies*, the old yearly revues perished. There was no dearth, however, of large plotless revues, of which Cole Porter's *Seven Lively Arts* (1944) was the most sumptuous, a mammoth mediocrity boasting an army of collaborators and first-magnitude stars. Olsen and Johnson revived vaudeville tricks with the addition of Luna Park bedevilment in their highly popular "Screamlined Revue," *Hellzapoppin* (1938), followed in 1941 by its sequel *Sons o' Fun*, with the recently imported Carmen Miranda from Brazil. Vaudeville under its own name was resurrected in *Priorities of 1942*, and before long buried again. The best of the variety revues was probably *Star and Garter* (1942), a brilliant show modeled after burlesque and featuring the strip-tease artistry of Gypsy Rose Lee and Ann Sothern. Expert clowning was contributed by Bobby Clark, among others, and by Professor Lamberti, who combined raffish comedy with renditions on the xylophone. One number by Irving Berlin, "The Girl on the Police Gazette," was elaborately staged in the colors and costumes of that once-famous publication and may give a faint idea of the spectacular flavor of the show.

The intimate revue, though on a grander scale than before and with a café society slant, survived in Nancy Hamilton's series—*One for the Money* (1939), *Two for the Show* (1940), and *Three to Make Ready* (1946)—all of them staged by John Murray Anderson, who laid stress on verve and informality. The second production, with Eve Arden as comedienne, gave Betty Hutton her start as a frenzied jitterbug dancer and featured the English comic Richard Haydn, fish imitator. *Three to Make Ready*, starring Ray Bolger, lived up to the tradition of the informal revue by including an excellent parody wherein *An American Tragedy* was taged with folk song and ballet in the manner of *Oklahoma!*

These shows were all entertaining, but the real advance of the post-Ziegfeld period came rather in musical comedy, which carried the trends of the twenties to their logical conclusion and made some innovations of its own. An abundance of good shows illustrated the virtues of lively "book," proper fusion of musical and literary elements, humor on not too infantile a level (though often bawdy), and smoothness of performance. Thanks to the press agent and thanks to the performers' own worth, names of the best shows are familiar to all. *As Thousands Cheer* (1933), a smart satirical show by Irving Berlin and Moss Hart, employed the headlines of a newspaper as unifying theme. Cole Porter's *Anything Goes* (1934) made good use of Ethel Merman as singing comedienne and of Victor Moore as Public Enemy Number 13. This patient, long-suffering individual was to appear later in Porter's *Leave It to Me* (1938) as a reluctan. American ambassador to Moscow and in the Irving Berlin–Morrie Ryskind *Louisiana Purchase* (1940) as a Senator with an eye on the White House, who becomes involved in New Orleans gaiety and crooked politics. Ethel Merman and Bert Lahr were co-starred in Cole Porter's *Du Barry Was a Lady* (1939), a rough and rowdy musical that trips merrily from a New York night club to the court of Louis XV. An ingenious wedding of circus and musical comedy was offered in the Rodgers-Hart *Jumbo* (1935)—book by Charles MacArthur and Ben Hecht, comedy by Jimmy Durante. Beatrice Lillie, whose clowning carried the travelogue musical *At Home Abroad* (1935) by Howard Dietz and Arthur Schwartz, was swung over the audience on a crescent moon in *The Show Is On* (1936), to everyone's delight. Ray Bolger, comic dancing

star of the Rodgers-Hart *On Your Toes* (1936), reached the
terpsichorean heights in the same collaborators' *By Jupiter*
(1942), based on Julian F. Thompson's *The Warrior's Husband,* a scarcely classic version of the struggle between the
Amazons and the Greeks. An excellent musical play, Porter's
Panama Hattie (1940), had to do with a Sadie Thompson
from Panama City, garish in dress and manner, who finds
she cannot marry the widowed hero until she has overcome
the aesthetic scruples of his very young daughter. Most of
these pieces leaned heavily upon a star, but none can be called
a one-man show like the old Ed Wynn or Al Jolson productions. Unity of impression and good ensemble work were the
aims of the directors.

The themes of the later musicals are both old and new.
Political satire, so bravely heralded in *Of Thee I Sing,* did not
come to any full realization. It appeared incidentally in
Louisiana Purchase and was pleasantly watered down in the
Kaufman-Rodgers-Hart *I'd Rather Be Right* (1937), in which
George M. Cohan, still an accomplished hoofer, gave a life-
like impersonation of Franklin D. Roosevelt. Strolling in Central Park, the President casually meets a young couple who
are unable for economic reasons to get married until he bal-
ances the federal budget. This the President obligingly tries
to do, thus launching a slender but amusing plot. A bit of
stage business at a park bench shows F. D. R. selecting a
newspaper to sit on. With evident delight he chooses the
Herald-Tribune. There are many satirical jibes, but on the
whole the treatment has more geniality than bite. A pseudohistorical fantasy by Maxwell Anderson, *Knickerbocker Holiday* (1938) with music by Kurt Weill, a production of the
Playwrights' Company, had considerable satire in its presentation of Pieter Stuyvesant (Walter Huston) as a Roose-
veltian dictator who establishes a totalitarian regime in New
Amsterdam in the 1640's. In back of the humor and fantasy
lay the author's strong conviction that government is a necessary evil, constantly to be watched and never allowed to get

out of hand, particularly when humanitarian measures like social security mask its bureaucratic intentions. Despite its serious message, however, Anderson's musical has a gay, comic-
opera manner. For the real political satire of the period one
must turn to the leftist *Pins and Needles* and *The Cradle Will
Rock*.

Except for topical references the Second World War left
only a superficial mark on musical comedy. The theme was
obviously too grim for the purposes of escapist entertainment.
Among several mild efforts, the Herbert and Dorothy Fields–
Cole Porter *Let's Face It* (1941) refurbished the ancient
Cradle Snatchers with the new setting of a soldier training
camp, offering Danny Kaye's nimble tongue a chance to rattle
off in jargon an amusing saga of a selectee's experience. *Something for the Boys* (1943) by the same authors and composer,
localized near Kelly Field in Texas, was a hodgepodge of
army maneuvers, war work, and plain farce. Ethel Merman,
the show's mainstay, was at her best in a completely non-
military song and dance, "By the Mississinewa," in which
she and Paula Lawrence impersonated Indian squaws. There
was one excellent war musical, by the same man who in 1918
as Sergeant Berlin was responsible for *Yip, Yip, Yaphank*,
namely *This Is the Army* with its magnificent songs, but of
course it was produced by the Army and did not come out
under Broadway auspices. Broadway did better with hemi-
spheric solidarity through its adoption of Latin American
music and dances.

More in line with the past were two productions by George
Abbott with a strong accent on youth. One was the Rodgers-
Hart *Too Many Girls* (1939), a lightly satirical piece about a
rich heiress in Pottawatomie College who goes about with a
bodyguard of four football players. One of the stalwarts was
played by Eddie Bracken. Perhaps moved by the scarcity of
young men of military age, Abbott turned to prep school for
the subject of the other musical, *Best Foot Forward* (1941).
Before the big prom one of the schoolboys has invited a

glamorous movie star, somewhat passée and eager for publicity. It is not difficult to foresee complications with the school
authorities and the boy's young sweetheart. The music, with
the school song "Buckle Down, Winsocki" as a fair sample,
was both gay and appropriate. The two Abbott musicals offered pleasant but not particularly novel entertainment.

The novelty and excellence of later musical comedy resulted from its experimentation in three principal and not
mutually exclusive directions: in fantasy and imagination; in
exploitation of American past and folkways; and in the use of
more intelligent plots and subjects. The first of these, with
its opportunities for artistic décor, was in particular contrast
to the pedestrianism and cheap gaudiness of most of the
earlier musicals. A new fantasy made its appearance in an
adaptation of a play by John Vaszary—*I Married an Angel*
(1938) by Richard Rodgers and Lorenz Hart. It is the story
of an angel, a real one from heaven, who comes down to earth
and marries a Budapest banker. But it takes her some time to
become adjusted to the way of the world. Her extreme
honesty almost ruins her husband's business, and she does not
find it easy to learn female wiles and coquetry, acquisition
of which eventually overcomes her unfeminine serious-
mindedness and fatal sincerity. The angel was played by a
newcomer from Germany, Vera Zorina, whose singing,
dancing, and beauty brought instant earthly fame. Sets by
Jo Mielzener and choreography by George Balanchine helped
to bring out the imaginative qualities of the play. A similar
blend of fantasy and sophistication was seen in *One Touch
of Venus* (1943) by S. J. Perelman and Ogden Nash, with
music by Kurt Weill, in which Mary Martin played a statue
of Venus that comes to life after centuries of retirement in
stone. She also appears naïvely straightforward as she falls
in love with a New York barber and takes refuge in his room.
She is quite willing to lead a mortal existence with the barber
until she surveys the scene in Ozone Heights, where they are

to reside, but then the prospect is too depressing for a goddess and she returns to marble. Life in Ozone Heights is gloriously satirized in an Agnes de Mille ballet with Sono Osata as *première danseuse,* and effective sets were devised by Howard Bay in a less realistic vein than his bathroom-fixture designs for *One Third of a Nation.* With the production of these and other musicals it became clear that sustained fantasy, integrated with story and music and combined with sophisticated realism, provided a formula that Broadway could handle with considerable skill.

As in straight comedy the musical play became conscious of the American scene, particularly in the form of excursions into the past where it could rely on period costumes and manners and—if the subject warranted—on folk music and traditions. *Show Boat,* of course, had led the way, but the most important influence of recent times came from The Guild's *Oklahoma!* (1943), a musical version of Lynn Riggs' *Green Grow the Lilacs* by Richard Rodgers and Oscar Hammerstein 2d. Here was a superior musical comedy with slight but absorbing plot, plenty of suspense when the love affair between a cowhand and an Oklahoma girl is jeopardized by a villainous hired hand, gusty humor in characterization and song, fantasy in a dream ballet, and a romantic historical setting provided by the Indian Territory around 1900 as it is about to become a state. The Rodgers tunes and Hammerstein lyrics—"Oh, What a Beautiful Morning," "People Will Say," "Pore Jud," "The Surrey with the Fringe on Top," and many others—are too familiar for comment. Quite in keeping with the play's local color and imagination were the sets of Lemuel Ayers and the choreography of Agnes de Mille. While the performers were excellent—Alfred Drake and Joan Roberts as the frontier lovers, Howard da Silva as the smokehouse villain, Joseph Buloff as a Persian peddler—it is interesting to note that there was no star. The breeziness and originality of the piece, its Western background and dances, its excellent ensemble performance, all helped to win the Pulitzer Prize for *Oklahoma!* and to provide a gold mine for the Theatre Guild.

The success of this cowboy opus encouraged other writers and composers to delve into the American past. *Bloomer Girl* (1944), with music by Harold Arlen and lyrics by E. Y. Harburg, went back to the feminist bloomer revolution during the hoopskirt days of 1861. The usual romance is present, this time between a bloomer supporter who takes part in underground railway activities on the side and (as one might suspect) a handsome Southerner. The inevitable ballet was directed by Agnes de Mille. Another period piece with similar ingredients, *Up in Central Park* (1945), with music by Sigmund Romberg and choreography by Helen Tamiris, tried to catch the romantic atmosphere of New York in the Boss Tweed era. The Romeo-Juliet love affair here involves a crusading reporter from the *Times* and the daughter of a Tammany ward heeler, but much of the show's charm lay in the reminiscent costumes and manners, one number representing a series of Currier and Ives prints posed by the players and turning into a ballet. It is sentimentally interesting to note the presence in the cast of Noah Beery Sr. as Boss Tweed and of Mabel Taliaferro in *Bloomer Girl* as the wife of a hoopskirt manufacturer. With considerable originality a period musical of 1946, Irving Berlin's *Annie Get Your Gun*, book by Herbert and Dorothy Fields, told the story of sharpshooting Annie Oakley from the Ohio hills—her employment in Buffalo Bill's Wild West Show, her rivalry in marksmanship with Frank Butler, with whom she falls in love, and the temporary estrangement between them which results from her shooting superiority. Buffalo Bill's competition and final merger with the Pawnee Bill show offer opportunity for spectacular effects, as does Annie's adoption in the Sioux tribe as daughter of Sitting Bull, a ceremony which includes a superb male ballet. The part of Annie Oakley was made to order for Ethel Merman, who played and sang it with even more than her usual aplomb, her songs ranging from the bawdy "Doin' What Comes Naturally" to the sentimental "They Say It's Wonderful."

The same trends toward fantasy and the use of native or folk material are apparent in Negro musical comedy, which made great strides since the jazz pieces of the twenties. An excellent musical version of *Porgy* with George Gershwin music, *Porgy and Bess* (1935), indicated the possibilities of serious plot and folkways in a kind of popular opera. The songs, which include "I Got Plenty of Nuttin' " and the blues number "A Woman Is a Sometime Thing," are among Gershwin's best. Two years earlier, of course, Hall Johnson's *Run, Little Chillun* with the aid of the author's famous choir had staged with music the frenzied evangelical rites among Holy Rollers and other religious groups, but this work is more concert than drama, and certainly not a musical comedy. These two productions, however, set the pattern for folk musical comedy on Negro subjects, so promisingly brought to realization by Katherine Dunham. She, with the singer Ethel Waters, appeared in 1940 in *Cabin in the Sky,* a Lynn Root fantasy, with music by Vernon Duke, in which Lucifer Jr. and the Lawd's General wage a desperate battle for the soul of "Little Joe" Jackson. He is saved finally by the faith and devotion of his wife Petunia (Ethel Waters), but Georgia Brown (Katherine Dunham) puts up quite a fight on behalf of the infernal forces. Negro folklore inspired the musical *John Henry* (1940) by Roark Bradford and Jacques Wolfe, tale of the mythical strong man whose physical prowess was not enough to cope with the wiles of men and women. Despite a good performance by Paul Robeson as John Henry, the play was too slender and static to be successful. Katherine Dunham, who had studied West Indian dances on a Guggenheim fellowship, gave a practical demonstration of her findings in *Carib Song* (1945), an idyll of the West Indies in which her frenetic and ritualistic choreography could not make up for a deficiency of action. Such partial failures, however, should not obscure the fact that Negro life and folklore, treated with imagination and fantasy, could provide fertile material for musical plays. A more conventional piece, *St. Louis Woman* (1946), about a jockey and his woman in the late nineties, had greater popular support than *John Henry* or *Carib Song*, though it lacked the folk and fantasy elements.

Negro performers distinguished themselves also in a curious but successful development of the later period—swing and boogie-woogie versions of semiclassic musical works. *The Swing Mikado* of the Federal Theatre has already been mentioned as well as its Broadway derivative, *The Hot Mikado*. In 1943 Oscar Hammerstein 2d brought Bizet's *Carmen* up to date as *Carmen Jones* by setting the story in a defense plant and other American purlieus. The music was likewise modernized, the swing orchestration being particularly successful in a torrid scene in Billy Pastor's Café. The transformation was good, though it probably seemed like committing mayhem to some music lovers.

Along with the many changes and advances in contemporary musical comedy may be seen a great improvement in the "book" itself, in the selection of subjects which would have been rejected on sight by the Ziegfelds and the Carrolls. For one thing, as in the jazz modernizations just mentioned, prospective librettists in search of original plays to work on turned to more worth-while drama, disregarding the cheap farces that had an exclusive appeal to their predecessors. In *The Boys from Syracuse* (1938), for example, Rodgers and Hart went back to Shakespeare for an irreverent adaptation of *The Comedy of Errors*. The musical version doubles the twins and the resulting mixups, with Jimmy Savo and Teddy Hart (brother of Lorenz) as the two Dromios. Good songs, such as "Sing for Your Supper" and "It Can't Be Love," and plenty of broad humor enlivened this Abbott production, which may not have seemed much like Shakespeare but which would conceivably have pleased the bard himself, who was certainly not averse to borrowing and renovating plots. As a rule the musical adapters selected more recent guinea pigs. *Sadie Thompson* (1944), with music by Vernon Duke, did a good job of reviving *Rain*, the play derived from Somerset Maugham's story of the scarlet woman and the repressed minister. An even more unexpected subject for musical treatment was Ferenc Molnar's *Liliom*, which Hammerstein and Rodgers presented as *Carousel* (1945), a surprisingly successful piece whose locale was transferred from the original Budapest to the Maine coast. The ending was expanded and somewhat sentimentalized, but the story of the carousel barker and the girl who loves him in spite of his faults offers a far more serious and touching plot than was ever provided by the old musical show. *Carousel* was graced by an Agnes de Mille ballet and such attractive songs as "June Is Bustin' Out All Over" and "If I Loved You." Success on Broadway brings imitation and it is not surprising to find that the quest for unusual, first-rate sources led the musical dramatists even to the realistic *Street Scene*.

Selection of the best modern musical would depend largely on personal taste. An excellent case can be made for *Oklahoma!* for its regional and poetical values, and the older *Show Boat* has its ardent admirers. Two other musical plays would certainly deserve consideration for any honorary title. One of them violated musical comedy conventions by giving a cynically realistic portrait of a completely unromantic hero, a "heel" and gigolo of the nightclubs who attracts a blasé older woman as patroness. She takes him on as lover, selects appropriate clothes for him, installs him in a sumptuous new nightclub, and at last dismisses him when she becomes weary of him and his flirtations. Based on *New Yorker* sketches by John O'Hara, this superior musical, *Pal Joey* (1940), had the advantage of an excellent score by Rodgers and lyrics by Hart, not to mention the inspired hoofing of Gene Kelly—the dancer in Saroyan's *Time of Your Life*—whose interpretation of an unsavory but essentially naïve character did much to make the piece acceptable. Vivienne Segal was equally able as his worldly-wise patroness, whose experience does not prevent her from becoming occasionally "Bewitched, Bothered and Bewildered." *Pal Joey* has wit and satirical force, and its introduction of hard-boiled realism to musical comedy, not in isolated sketches but in the entire script, marks a striking departure from the past.

The same kind of naturalism alternates with fantasy in Moss Hart's fine musical comedy, *Lady in the Dark* (1941), with a score by Kurt Weill and lyrics by Ira Gershwin. The realistic scenes deal with the daily life of the hard-bitten editor of a women's glamour magazine, Liza Elliott, and her worldly associates at the office or outside. But Liza is going to pieces, prey to an anxiety neurosis, hysterically unable to make decisions. She is finally driven to a psychoanalyst, who proceeds to delve into her subconscious. This treatment readily leads to the depiction with music of Liza's dream world with all its fantasies, and eventually brings to light the painful childhood experiences that have made her withdraw as a woman and avoid competition with other members of her sex. By the end of the play Liza rejects both her elderly lover and a handsome movie actor and finds her true mate in the magazine's advertising manager, a man who had particularly irritated her. The psychoanalysis, while on a rather elementary level, offers a splendid opportunity for imaginative costume, setting, song, and dance. Gertrude Lawrence as Liza gave one of the great performances of the modern theatre, but she was well supported by Danny Kaye as a flouncing photographer, Macdonald Carey as the cantankerous advertising manager, Bert Lytell as the lover, Victor Mature as a movie star, and many others. Nor should the choreography of Albertina Rasch and the sets by Harry Horner be forgotten. Some of the musical high spots were Danny Kaye's song on the names of Russian composers and Gertrude Lawrence's famous Saga of Jenny, the girl who—unlike Liza—had no trouble making up her mind. *Lady in the Dark* was an excellent show rather than a

major masterpiece, but in its own way it put into practice
Gordon Craig's ideals about the fusion of the dramatic arts.

In giving so glowing an account of the musical comedy
stage there has been no intention of overstressing the importance of its countless offerings. The authors were no Ibsens
or Shaws or Eugene O'Neills. Their themes had little social or
philosophical significance. Essentially, whether brought to
light by the Theatre Guild or by the Shuberts, the musicals
were Big Business. *Billion Dollar Baby* represented an invest-
ment of $250,000; *The Seven Lively Arts* of $300,000. But
the returns could show equally astronomical figures, if we
consider, for example, that the Guild made five and a half
million dollars during the first two years of *Oklahoma!;* by the
end of the fourth year the gross returns had risen to over
$9,300,000. The business side of musical comedy is clearly re-
flected in box-office prices. As early as 1919 the production of
Aphrodite, a diluted version of a French musical, caused quite
a stir by charging a top of $11.00 for opening night. But
opening night tickets were $22.00 for the *Ziegfeld Follies* in
1923; $55.00 for the *Scandals* in 1926; and a modest $24.50 for
the *Seven Lively Arts* in 1944, including free champagne.
These rates, of course, are exceptional, but if a musical happens to catch the fancy of the town, no Dutch boy with his
finger in the dike can prevent a flood of dollars from pouring
in. As we have seen, however, crass commercialism has not
stopped Broadway from achieving a relatively high level of
artistic achievement. And there is some irony in the fact that
the despised girl show should have been destined to bring to
Broadway most of the fantasy and imagination that the reformers of the art theatre were proclaiming so loudly a quarter of a century ago.

Chapter 8

STATE OF THE THEATRE

$\mathcal{J}$T IS THE FATE of drama to become more rapidly dated than other literary types. Many of the plays that seemed so significant in 1920 or 1925 or 1935 would appear mannered and outmoded if we were miraculously privileged to see the original performance in the present moment. Probably very little of the drama of the last quarter century will prove to have any permanent value. There have been no Molières and Shakespeares, not even Ibsens and Shaws. It would be hazardous to assert that the playwrights equaled the performance of the novelists during the same period. Nevertheless modern American drama has been anything but trivial, achieving competence and often distinction in a variety of forms. It is undeniably superior to the drama that preceded it. During the period itself it showed startling improvement both in content and in *mise en scène*. The playgoing public, too, has progressed, giving indications of being more serious minded, more sophisticated, more discerning, if we may judge from its support of better plays. Thus, while a final evaluation of contemporary drama may leave something to be desired, the picture drawn in these pages has been by no means a discouraging one; nor should the dramatists—working not for eternity but for a specific time and place in a perishable medium—be judged for what they never attempted to do.

Their contributions, as revealed in the preceding chapters, call for no apology. They brought beauty and imagination to a stodgy commercial theatre. They offered serious, unvarnished representations of American life, and they turned Broadway into a sounding board for the discussion of man's relation to society, to conventions, to the sexual urge, to himself. They debunked the pretensions of a disintegrating Victorian and Babbitt culture. Their idealism, expressed in both negative and positive form, attacked reactionary forces and championed the tenets of liberalism, sometimes of radicalism. They gradually weaned themselves from English and Continental influences, not only discovering America with its wealth of manners, customs, traditions, folkways, but also developing native dramatic forms, not the least of which were the hard-boiled comedy of manners and the musical show. To their great credit they welcomed the Negro actor and the Negro playwright. When war threatened and later arrived, they rallied to the support of democracy. All this they accomplished in the face of an unwieldy theatrical system where failure to attract immediate response after opening night brings financial nirvana and a trip to Cain's warehouse.

This system has recently been under sharp attack, but before going into particulars it may not be amiss to consider the state of American drama near the close of war and during the first season or two of peace. The cataclysms of world conflict and reconversion with their inflationary tendencies have necessarily brought an interim period in the theatre with emphasis on escapist entertainment. Yet the level of excellence on Broadway during this period was surprisingly high. The dramatic types on exhibition were mainly those of the past. As might be expected, the musical plays—*Carousel, Call Me Mister, Annie Get Your Gun*—were particularly in demand. Hard-boiled comedy survived triumphantly in Garson Kanin's *Born Yesterday,* in which the ex-chorine mistress of a millionaire junk dealer with fascist propensities learns the social facts of life from a *New Republic* writer, and in Howard Lindsay's and Russel Crouse's *State of the Union,* showing the rebellion of a Republican presidential candidate against the machine politicians and economic royalists that selected him. Both comedies, despite their light satirical treatment, had a serious intent. The sex and the domestic play respectively were well represented in the long-lived *The Voice of the Turtle* and *I Remember Mama* by the English dramatist John Van Druten, for some years now a fixture in the American theatre. Serious plays of ideas include Paul Osborn's *A Bell for Adano*, based on the John Hersey novel, which gives an absorbing account of working democracy in an occupied Italian village, and Robert Sherwood's *The Rugged Path*, in which Spencer Tracy returned to the theatre in the role of a disillusioned journalist who joins the Navy as a cook and among sailors and Philippine guerillas discovers at last the rugged America he has been searching for. Postwar problems and dislocations were treated, though unsuccessfully, in Maxwell Anderson's *Truckline Cafe* and Arthur Laurents' *Home of the Brave*. Several plays savagely attacked racial intolerance in the South—*Strange Fruit* by Lillian and Esther Smith, *Deep Are the Roots* by Arnaud d'Usseau and James Gow, and *Jeb* by Robert Ardrey—dealing with such problems as miscegenation, lynching, and the Negro veteran's return to an unsympathetic society. Social changes in Boston's Back Bay were recorded ironically in the dramatization by John P. Marquand and George S. Kaufman of Marquand's *The Late George Apley*, and another Boston portrait was drawn sympathetically in Emmet Lavery's *The Magnificent Yankee*, a biography of Chief Justice Oliver Wendell Holmes. An equally high standard was set for the new 1946–1947 season with the opening of O'Neill's *The Iceman Cometh*, discussed earlier; Lillian Hellman's *Another Part of the Forest*, a renewed attack on rapacious capitalism in which the Hubbards are represented some twenty years before the time of *The Little Foxes;* George Kelly's *The Fatal Weakness*, a domestic comedy about marriage and divorce; and Anderson's *Joan of Lorraine*, an ingenious version of the Joan of Arc story in the form of a play rehearsal with Ingrid Bergman as a contemporary actress playing La Pucelle and expressing the author's usual message of faith.

At the same time fantasy and imagination were not neg-

lected. On a rather elementary plane were Elmer Rice's
Dream Girl, which gave the author's wife, Betty Field, the
opportunity to enact the egocentric daydreams of an impres-
sionable young woman, and Mary Chase's *Harvey*, in which
the vaudeville actor Frank Fay played a harmless alcoholic
who hobnobs with a large rabbit invisible to anyone but himself. Equally theatrical but somewhat more serious was Moss
Hart's *Christopher Blake*, depicting in alternate scenes of
realism and fantasy the progress of a divorce and the dream
fantasies of the estranged parents' young son. *Lute Song*, a
poetic fantasy with music by Raymond Scott and sets by
Robert Edmond Jones, was an adaptation by Sidney Howard
and Will Irwin of *Pi-Pa-Ki*, a Chinese play about a faithful
wife. The best of the imaginative works was Tennessee Williams' *The Glass Menagerie*, a tender "memory play" about a
fragile crippled girl (Julie Haydon) who has lost all contact
with reality, finding refuge in her collection of glass animals.
Her mother—played by Laurette Taylor, her last role before
her death—lives mainly in her past as a Southern belle, and
the girl's brother escapes at first vicariously by spending every
evening in the movies and later actually by decamping. For
one brief moment the girl's secret life comes to realization
when a gentleman caller turns out to be a boy she idolized in
high school, but he departs after revealing his engagement to
another young woman. This story of pathos, calling for a narrator, nonrealistic lighting and setting, symbolic music, and
imaginative devices, marked the advent of a new poet in the
theatre, mild successor to the mantle worn so flamboyantly
by Saroyan.

These plays of 1944–1946 may not rank with the best in
modern drama, but they have solid virtues and they compare
favorably with the Broadway bill of fare during the corresponding period before and after the end of the First World
War. A representative selection from this earlier drama would
show the *Follies, Sinbad, Monte Cristo Jr., La, La, Lucille*,
and *Irene* among the musical shows. Sentimental pieces in-

cluded *Seventeen, Daddies, Smilin' Through, A Little Journey, Lightnin'*, J. Hartley Manners' *Happiness*. A measure of wit was discernible in *Clarence* and *The Squab Farm*, but there were plenty of ordinary farces, bedroom or otherwise: *Parlor, Bedroom and Bath, Up in Mabel's Room, Wedding Bells, The Gold Diggers*. Equally in popular favor were melodramas such as *Three Faces East, The Unknown Purple*, and *The Ouija Board*. For solid fare the playgoer would have to be satisfied with Charles Rann Kennedy's depressing opus, *The Army with Banners*, Knoblock's *Tiger! Tiger!*, Eugene Walter's *The Challenge*, or Zoë Akins' *Déclassée*, wherein Ethel Barrymore, exhibiting no visible marks of impact from the automobile that struck her, took half an hour to expire romantically. The realistic *Ambush* and the high comedy *Why Marry?* were off the beaten track, but for real stimulation the theatre enthusiast would have to turn to the Provincetown and Washington Square one-acters, or else to the foreign importations.

Some improvement must be conceded in a quarter of a century, yet current drama leaves much to be desired. It gives the impression of being complacent and uninspired, lacking in vigor and enthusiasm. The earlier creative impulses have worn themselves out, and the spirit has not kept up with the technical proficiency. Harold Clurman has called the early forties "the Billy Rose and Michael Todd period on Broadway," combining cheap showmanship with diluted culture, eager to satisfy every taste, deficient in force and originality. Rosamond Gilder remarks in *Theatre Arts* that "a certain middle-aged caution has descended on our theatre." Joseph Wood Krutch in a brief article about our vanishing playwrights observes the tendency to dramatize novels instead of writing plays. From these and other impressive voices the perennial query "What is wrong with the theatre?" has made itself heard with more than customary vigor and authority. What are, indeed, the specific ills and the remedies proposed for them?

The season of 1945–1946 was enlivened by several assaults
on the Broadway critics as the villains in the piece. One salvo,
delivered by Maxwell Anderson after unfavorable reviews
of *Truckline Cafe*, took the form of newspaper attacks on the
critics as a Jukes family of journalism, made up of incom-
petents and irresponsibles, "who bring to the theatre nothing
but their own hopelessness, recklessness and despair." The
public, he asserted, is far better qualified to judge plays than
are the reviewers. He was supported in his accusations by
Elia Kazan, Harold Clurman, and the Playwrights' Company,
producers of the play. A more detailed indictment of the
New York critics appeared in Irwin Shaw's preface to his
unsuccessful *The Assassin,* including such items as their
judicial and Olympian dicta; their desperate attempts at
humor and witticisms, leading to a "cult of humorous patron-
ization"; their unwillingness to learn their trade; their vague
political viewpoint, which "seems to be an amorphous liberalism"; and their bewildering critical standards, which impel
them "to salute greatness and trash with the same hysteria,
and dismiss talent and incompetence with the same spiteful-
ness." The situation is aggravated, according to Irwin Shaw,
by the fact that three men, the critics of the *Times,* the *Trib-
une* and the *News,* have power of life and death over any new
production. As one possible solution he urges that practicing
playwrights take over the task of criticism because of their
technical knowledge and their sympathetic viewpoint.

One can feel a modicum of sympathy for the critics—who
are forced to sit through many a doleful performance and
who, like baseball umpires, must call strikes and balls as they
see them—and yet admit the justness of many of these stric-
tures by the embattled dramatists. It is true that under the
Broadway system the newspaper reviewers wield an entirely
disproportionate power over the fate of their victims. It is
impossible to condone the cavalier dismissal of honest work
and the wisecracking technique that serves mainly for the
self-aggrandisement of the critic. A serious dramatic work

deserves to be treated seriously, and a fundamentally good play, though it may not completely come off, is worthy of encouragement. The crux of the matter lies in the quality of the present crop of critics, who whether or not they are Jukes are certainly no Brunetières or Bernard Shaws. Irwin Shaw's complaint about the bewildering diversity of critical standards treads on less sure aesthetic ground. No final, absolute criteria are discoverable for the judgment of drama, which depends in the final analysis on the taste and personality of the observer, so that one man's point of view is often another man's poison. That is, unless one espouses the Communist critique that calls for uniformity and judges any work of art by its ideology, which offers a far more limited standard than the "amorphous liberalism" of the Broadway reviewers. Strong convictions are not necessarily a blessing, as witness the opinionated views of William Winter, nor is the playwright-critic an infallible solution if we recall the tenure of St. John Ervine as dramatic critic for the old *World*. Solution of the difficult problem of criticism lies rather in educating the public to make up its own mind and in encouraging—if possible— the daily newspapers to select critics of literary stature and cultural background, who combine expert knowledge of drama with genuine love of the theatre. Ideally such a critic should exhibit both a sense of discrimination and catholicity of taste, at least if one believes that there is room in the same theatre for *Winterset, Three Men on a Horse,* and *Waiting for Lefty.*

Reforming the critics is only part of a campaign against the prevailing Broadway system, which Margaret Webster has called a market for best-sellers only. The extreme centralization of American drama in New York has brought about an increasingly unhealthy financial situation, which is reflected in abnormally high costs of production. Whereas in the Belasco era a play could be put on for $5,000 or less, the present average is about $50,000 for an ordinary one-set play, with musical shows, as we have seen, coming closer to

$250,000. For a relatively simple stage set alone the producer must invest in the neighborhood of $5,000. Union regulations, often arbitrary and irrational, have helped to boost costs heavenward. An acute shortage of theatres on Broadway has not only impeded the arrival of new productions but has permitted the owners to require a weekly guarantee of $3,000 to $3,500, making it impossible for a play to continue that is not an immediate hit. Any production therefore represents a sizable financial venture, which may bring fabulous returns or else complete loss, since it is impossible to predict the eventual effect of a script on critics and public. Since sixty percent or more of Broadway productions are failures, the theatre business in New York has become more than ever a gamble. One can scarcely blame many producers and their angels for playing safe to the best of their ability by selecting scripts by known dramatists on tried and true subjects with definite promise of popular appeal, but the result has been to discourage the production of serious and experimental plays. At the same time the increase in costs has forced the price of theatre tickets beyond the reach of thousands of potential theatregoers, an evil that is aggravated when a smash hit comes along. Immediately the agencies and speculators take over and seats vanish from the box office, leaving the theatre the property of the carriage trade and of visiting salesmen from out of town.

Broadway's haphazard system of free enterprise has worked special hardship on the young playwright, who faces tremendous odds in attempting to have his plays put on at all. The young actor is similarly victim of a vicious cycle; he finds it difficult to secure the necessary training in his profession, and yet he cannot get a part without experience, especially since few players today receive from the professional directors the meticulous training they enjoyed, let us say, under the tutelage of Belasco. The established actor is likely to find himself unemployed in the best of seasons, or else, if his play turns out to be a long-run hit, occupied year after year in the same mechanical routine. Little wonder that he and the playwright are often lured to Hollywood.

Under the assumption that theatrical ills may be numerous but not necessarily fatal, several remedies have already been tried out, with some success. The new playwright has been aided by various scholarships, prizes, and opportunities for experimental production. The producer John Golden has been active in organizing a plan of playwriting scholarships awarded in cooperation with the drama departments of three New York colleges. Promising scripts are to be given production at the Princess Theatre, former home of Labor Stage, which has been leased to the American National Theatre and Academy (ANTA) with privileges to Mr. Golden. In 1941 the Experimental Theatre was started by the Dramatists' Guild and Equity under the direction of the late Antoinette Perry to try out promising plays.* Also in 1941 was established the New Play Project of the National Theatre Conference with the dual purpose of helping to produce scripts by relatively unknown playwrights and of making available to community and university theatres the plays of established dramatists, either before or concurrently with their Broadway production. To supplement this project the National Theatre Conference has instituted an extensive system of fellowships. Another organization, the Dramatists' Play Service, headed by Barrett H. Clark, has been of help to young writers. Among specific prizes the Sidney Howard Memorial Award is bestowed yearly by the Playwrights' Company on any playwright who has proved his ability by having one or more plays produced on Broadway during the current season but who has not had any previous professional success. Prizes are available outside of New York, too, like the Dramatists' Alliance awards at Stanford University, including the Maxwell Anderson prize for verse drama. The new playwright may have

---

* It may be noted as an interesting development of the 1946–1947 season that the Experimental Theatre launched in February, 1947, a subscription series of five productions at the Princess Theatre under the sponsorship of ANTA.

many valid complaints, but he is not entirely without opportunity.

The young actor has been aided not only by the production of experimental scripts but by other projects as well. Here again John Golden has taken the lead by sponsoring the Equity Library Theatre, organized early in 1944 by the actor Sam Jaffe and by George Freedley, curator of the Theatre Section of the New York Public Library, to give productions of classics and revivals in the small theatres located in various sub-branches of the library. It is planned to give some of these offerings at the Princess Theatre, where John Golden's auditions for actors are also to be held semiannually. With the neophyte actor in mind ANTA has rented the same theatre for the establishment in the near future of a graduate academy, which will offer two years of professional training to about fifty apprentice players. A recent development in the New York theatre promises to benefit both the established actor and the theatregoer who resents the casual dismissal by Broadway of its dramatic heritage, for the old dream of repertory seems at last possible of successful realization. There have been, of course, many previous plans and attempts, of which the most gallant was Eva Le Gallienne's Civic Repertory Theatre on Fourteenth Street, but they invariably failed or were not financially self-supporting. Even Miss Le Gallienne's venture had to rely upon the support of a wealthy patron. During the 1945–1946 season two new groups were formed who combine talent with sound finance. The American Repertory Theatre, organized by Margaret Webster, Eva Le Gallienne, and Cheryl Crawford, scheduled for full operation in the fall of 1946, has a program for the presentation of at least six plays a season with change of bills two or three times weekly.* It began its first season with revivals of Barrie's *What Every Woman Knows*, Shakespeare's *Henry VIII*, and

---

* Because of operational costs, despite assistance from the Actors' Equity Association and ANTA, the American Repertory Theatre was forced early in 1947 to change its method of production from actual repertory to limited engagements.

Ibsen's *John Gabriel Borkman,* and among its later productions it hopes to put on at least one new play. The actors in the
company, headed by Victor Jory and Eva Le Gallienne, are
guaranteed a term of at least two years at a regular salary regardless of what roles, if any, are assigned to them in any
production. With equally notable sponsorship, including
among others the playwright Arnold Sundgaard, another
group, Theatre Incorporated, was formed as a nonprofit
organization for the presentation of repertory. It began auspi-
ciously with a revival of Shaw's *Pygmalion,* co-starring Gertrude Lawrence and Raymond Massey, and with the importation from England of the Old Vic Company for a six-week
season in New York. Theatre Incorporated opened its 1946–
1947 season with Synge's *Playboy of the Western World,*
which it planned to follow with a revival of *The Changeling*
by Middleton and Rowley. Great plays of the past, like great
music, deserve a hearing, and Broadway will be the richer
with the operation of these two companies. Both companies
fulfill one of the prerequisites for successful repertory in
America, the employment of name stars, without which the
native audience, with its feverish passion for newness, cannot
be drawn to the classics. It remains to be seen whether the
public will eventually acquire the repertory habit, for the
frequent rotation of plays seems to irritate persons accustomed
to the long-run system. Repertory itself tends to break down
under the pressure of a highly successful production as happened to Theatre Incorporated with *Pygmalion,* and to resign
itself to an extended run. It is not too much to hope, however,
that Broadway will eventually develop a first-class repertory
company, comparable to the Old Vic, the Moscow Art Theatre, or the Abbey Players, where the actors, assured of a regular income, will have the opportunity of essaying a variety
of roles and of developing an integrated ensemble technique
from working together in numerous productions.

Scholarships, experimental productions, and repertory were
designed in part to revitalize a show business suffering from

high blood pressure and hardening of the arteries. At present
Broadway is also faced with a vast plan of decentralization
calculated to lessen its dominance in American drama. Briefly
this plan calls for a truly national theatre with its roots in what
Theatre Arts calls the Tributary Theatre—the educational,
regional, community, or stock organizations that dispense
drama to the provinces. The experience of Federal Theatre
showed the existence outside of New York of a vast audience
eager for good drama, an audience that now includes thousands of returned veterans, many of whom saw actual plays
for the first time in the entertainment program for the armed
forces. The end of the war brought to vigorous awakening the
American National Theatre and Academy, a nonprofit organization which received a federal charter but no funds in the
Wagner-McLaughlin bill of 1935. The number and quality
of its directors, representing a wide range and diversity of
interests in matters theatrical, as suggested by the presence in
the same body of Alfred G. Arvold, Brooks Atkinson, Walter
Pritchard Eaton, Arthur Hopkins, Robert Edmond Jones, and
Billy Rose (to mention but a handful), offer high promise for
the future of ANTA. Its officers for 1946–1947 include an
equally impressive list: Vinton Freedley, president; Robert
E. Sherwood, vice-president; Gilbert Miller, treasurer; Rosamond Gilder, secretary; Colonel C. Lawton Campbell, chair-
man of the board; and Robert Breen, executive secretary.
ANTA'S plans for a graduate academy have already been
mentioned, but this is only one of several important projects.
In the fall of 1945 Robert Porterfield and Robert Breen
launched a specific proposal for a Public Theatre Foundation
—to resemble the great educational and philanthropic foundations—and called for a vast drive for funds, which would be
derived mainly from private sources but eventually perhaps
from federal grants. From the resources acquired ANTA
would make allocations to any dramatic group or organization
throughout the country which in the opinion of a central
board was deserving of support. An additional service might

be the financial backing of professional companies on tours to sections of the country that would not normally be visited. The Foundation blueprint for the backing of worthy projects, inspired partly by the favorable experience in recent years of the Arts Council of Great Britain and its subsidiary, CEMA (Committee for the Encouragement of Music and the Arts), was enthusiastically acclaimed by reformist groups and promptly adopted by ANTA. It is interesting to note that one of its proponents, Robert Porterfield, is founder and director of the Barter Theatre at Abingdon, Virginia, first American theatre to receive state support—a $10,000 yearly grant from the Commonwealth of Virginia.

The movement away from Broadway marks a commendable effort to develop a theatre for the American people as a whole. Both the interest and the opportunity are present, and it is hoped full advantage will be taken of them. The Tributary Theatre is already performing a valuable service; any stimulation and extension of its activities would benefit everyone concerned. The educational and community theatres are especially well equipped to handle revivals of the classics on the one hand and experimental, imaginative, and regional plays on the other. Here is a ready-made workshop for the young actor and playwright, which can become increasingly productive with time. A good nation-wide theatre may exert a salutary influence on show business and may conceivably become a springboard for a new revolutionary drive, like the little theatre movement of the past, for a second conquest of Broadway.

Encouraging a national theatre, however, does not mean that Broadway will be demoted from its eminence and become a mere appendage to the Tributary Theatre. For all its faults it enjoys certain advantages over the provincial theatre that are likely to maintain its supremacy for many years. For one thing, it possesses the money and the established professional talent that make even its ordinary productions superior to the best that the out-of-town theatre can offer. This is said

with no intent to deprecate the efforts of the many earnest
workers outside of New York who bring enthusiasm and a
splendid amateur spirit to the theatre. In the second place,
New York because of its size and diversity can provide an
audience for almost any kind of play, vulgar or precious,
poetic or realistic, leftist or rightist. It is significant that the
so-called commercial theatre in New York has been responsible for many, if not most, of the vital and significant productions from O'Neill to Saroyan, while practically all the remaining ones came from the Guild, the Group Theatre, and other
residents of the Times Square district. Then again, while it
is often cheap and unregenerated, the New York theatre has
usually avoided a tendency to solemnity and artiness, an impulse to "uplift" the drama, which is all too evident sometimes
in the community playhouses. Most important of all, Broadway has shown a broad tolerance with regard to language,
conventions, ideas, themes. It is perfectly obvious that Main
Street, except for a small minority, is far more steeped in conservatism and the Puritan tradition with its fatal propensities
for censorship, one that resides not only in overt official control, as in Boston, but also in the aesthetic taste of the community. Drama, to be great, need not necessarily run counter
to popular morality or to the prevailing political viewpoint,
but there is no question that it flourishes best in an atmosphere
of freedom. Broadway has not been without censorship or its
threat, but the particular character and significance of American drama in thirty years derives largely from the relative
freedom of the dramatist in New York to express himself
with sincerity on almost any subject. That is the real basis of
the superiority of his product over the predigested pabulum
of the movies—not to mention radio, where mere mention
of the word bed in a popular song causes the broadcasting
stations to blanch in horror and where a mild play like *Family
Portrait* is banned because of religious objections. When the
provinces overcome their tendency to emasculated orthodoxy
and social conventionalism they will be more able to compete

with Broadway drama. In tacit recognition of the general situation we find that even ANTA has established its headquarters in New York.

All this, of course, does not mean that Broadway is perfect and can afford to ignore defects and abuses. New York, which once supported eighty to ninety theatres, has now been reduced to the possession of about thirty. New playhouses are urgently needed. If and when more normal times return, the excessive costs of play production must be lowered and intelligent working agreements arrived at with the unions to correct evils and illogicalities while preserving the proper rights of labor. Following the lead of John Golden and of ANTA, the professional theatre should strive to offer better opportunities to unknown writers and young actors. Broadway has always been careless of the talent that it possesses. More than one discontented playwright, who would be happier writing for the theatre, has deserted for steady employment in Hollywood at $3,500 a week. Following a brilliant performance many an actor, like Macdonald Carey or Danny Kaye of *Lady in the Dark*, has been snatched away by Metro-Goldwyn-Mayer, Paramount, *et al.* Broadway cannot pay Hollywood salaries but it has much else to offer, as is indicated by the frequent return of its prodigals, and perhaps it could discover other inducements like the system of tenure of the repertory companies.

Unkind things may have been said here and elsewhere about the movies, but the theatre will have to take cognizance of greater competition from them, artistic as well as financial, than in the past. Hollywood has made unmistakable progress since Will Hays performed his best service to the cinema by leaving it and since the war gave it a chance to make a try at rugged realism. It has learned something, certainly, from foreign films, particularly those from England: the skillful mysteries, from Hitchcock's early thrillers to the psychological *Seventh Veil;* the semidocumentary war films like Noel Coward's *In Which We Serve;* and honest versions of the classics

like *Henry V, Major Barbara,* and *Pygmalion.* Hollywood must
have derived some further inspiration from France's ironic
realism and Russia's simple but brutal presentation of war
scenes with a propaganda slant. America's specialty has been
violent action plus romance, but good work has been done
in other directions as well. No one would cavil at the worth of
Hollywood's best efforts in recent years—*Citizen Kane, The
Long Voyage Home* (O'Neill's S.S. Glencairn plays), *The
Informer, The Man Who Came to Dinner, Casablanca, Fighting Lady, A Walk in the Sun, The Lost Weekend,* and Hitchcock's American melodramas. It has not proved so successful
artistically with the big emotional sob stories, with musicals,
with costume drama, with glamourized romance, with tech-
nicolor as a rule. But here, whether or not we like it, is the
real American national theatre. There is no question that the
stage play will survive, but it can no longer do so by marking
time or resting upon past performance.

Even radio, that case of arrested development among the
forms of entertainment, fumbling in its platitudes and advertising jingles, has made inroads in the field of drama. Best
of the serious programs devoted to the production of plays
was the Theatre Guild on the Air, started in 1945–1946 under
the sponsorship of United States Steel and the direction of
Lawrence Langner. Employing the best of actors, this weekly
broadcast gave revivals of famous plays, usually Guild productions, including *Ah, Wilderness!, Strange Interlude, Mr.
Pim Passes By, The Front Page,* and numerous others—with
the usual concessions, of course, to radio's squeamishness
about topics like illicit love and abortion. Such programs offer
a valuable supplement to the theatre as well as to the actors'
pocketbooks. They cannot be considered a real substitute for
the stage play, but they are not without artistic value and
they will serve in time to build up a larger, better audience
for American drama.

Regardless of its eventual destiny or its present doldrums,
Broadway's immediate prospect is at least bright. It has excel-

lent directors, from George Abbott to Herman Shumlin, and superb actors, from Helen Hayes to the Lunts. Its scenic artists are unequaled anywhere. New plays are promised not only by individual producers but by the Playwrights' Company and the Theatre Guild, the latter bursting at the seams with subscriptions in New York and on the road. The Group Theatre is considering a resumption of dramatic operations. The new repertory companies will resurrect the great drama of the past and the actress-manager Katharine Cornell may be expected to continue her program of revivals and new plays. Of the great writers of modern American drama only Sidney Howard is not alive. We may reasonably expect serious drama from Maxwell Anderson, high comedy from S. N. Behrman and Philip Barry, thesis plays from Robert Sherwood, satirical farce from George S. Kaufman and Moss Hart, probings into feminine psychology from Rachel Crothers, realistic genre pictures from Elmer Rice, regional social studies from Paul Green. After too long an absence Eugene O'Neill has returned to the theatre. Odets and Saroyan are unlikely to remain silent permanently. Other younger men like Irwin Shaw and Robert Ardrey and Tennessee Williams will surely continue to write. Despite their wealth of dramatic talent, all these dramatists represent the past rather than the future, and one of the primary needs of the present, as in 1918, is for the new playwright. Whether he will come from the city or the hinterlands, Broadway or the Tributary Theatre, depends upon the accident of genius, but it is scarcely conceivable that the Second World War will not produce, as did the First, a group of dramatists worthy to interpret the great issues of the day and give us a new drama for a new era.

It is important to remember that contemporary American drama was formed by three great revolutionary drives—the revolution in manners and morals that broke down the restraints and inhibitions of the nineteenth century, the artistic revolution that invested a pedestrian theatre with color, poetry, and beauty, and the leftist revolution of the thirties that brought missionary fervor and social consciousness in a crusade against war, poverty, and injustice. Some other revolution must come if Broadway is not to return to the 1912 status of escapist show business, for the theatre needs enthusiasm and ideals to endow it with the power to stir men's minds and imagination.

What form and direction will the drama of the future take? In a period of confusion, stress, and irreconcilable cleavages of ideology will it take refuge in mysticism, introspection, and bizarre speculation, as did the metaphysical poetry of the seventeenth century? Will it turn lofty and religious, emulating the dullness of the sermon? Will it recoil in horror from its erstwhile liberalism and promote the ideals of Rotarianism and Southern Democracy? Will the away-from-Broadway movement drive it into regionalism and what one of Elmer Rice's characters called epics of the cow pasture? Will it give us merely more of what we have today? The interested but cautious spectator will have to emulate the patron of the soap operas and tune in a decade from now for an answer to these perplexing questions.

INDEX

285

Ferber, Edna, G. S. Kaufman and, 146, 178, 214
Ferguson, Elsie, 22
Fernald, Chester Bailey, 11, 36
Ferrer, José, 97
Ferris, Walter, 103
Fervent Years (Churman), 155
Field, Betty, 224, 269
Field, Salisbury, 236; Margaret Mayo and, 10
Field God, The (Green), 95
Fields, Herbert, 250
—— Dorothy Fields and, 260
—— C. Porter and, 257
—— Richard Rodgers, Lorenz Hart and, 250
Fields, Joseph, 229
—— Jerome Chodorov and, 185, 223
Fields, W. C., 18, 243
Fifty Million Frenchmen, 250
Fight, The (Veiller), 20
Fighting Lady, 281
Financial situation of theatre unhealthy, 272 ff.
Firebrand, The (Mayer), 90
First Flight (Stallings and Anderson), 76
First Lady (Dayton and Kaufman), 228; designated as objectionable in part, 233
First Man, The (O'Neill), 49
First Year, The (Craven), 181
Fisher, Lola, 12
Five Star Final (Weitzenkorn), 236
Flanagan, Hallie, 164, 165, 167, 233
Flapper, 22
Flavin, Martin, 103, 155
Fledermaus, Die: Champagne, Sec, 247
Flight to the West (Rice), 136
Flint, Eva Kay, Martha Madison and, 235
Fog (O'Neill), 41, 45, 55, 68
Folk material and fantasy fused, 97
Folk musical comedy, 261
Follies, 243, 244, 245, 269
Follow Thru, 250
Fontanne, Lynn, 38, 57, 77, 132, 178, 203, 210; with Alfred Lunt, 135, 202, 282
Foolish Notion (Barry), 201

Fool There Was, A, 4
Foote, John Taintor, 177
Footlights, 27
Forbes, James, 192
Ford, Harriet, Harvey O'Higgins and, 15
Fortuny lighting system, 26
47 Workshop, graduates, 7, 9, 27, 28, 29 f., 40, 164; *see also* Baker, George Pierce
Foster, Norman, Harry Hamilton and, 238
Foster, Phoebe, 7
Fountain, The (O'Neill), 53, 57, 69, 105
"Four Little Angels of Peace," 136
Four Saints in Three Acts (Stein), 110
Four Walls (Burnet and Abbott), 235
France, Anatole, 28
France, ironic realism, 281
Franco, Francisco, 133
Franken, Rose, 182
Frankenstein, 241
Franklin, Irene, 249
Franz Josef, emperor, 79
Freedley, George, 275
Freedley, Vinton, 277
Freedom, of dramatists in New York, 279; of speech, increasing, 22, 23
Freedom (Reed), 34
Freud, Sigmund, 23; Barry's interest in, 199; discovered by movies, 241; influence, 124; moral revolution reinforced by study of, 121
Freudian psychology, 12, 57; O'Neill's dependence on, 57, 60, 68, 69
Friml, Rudolph, 246
—— Herbert Stothart and, 246
Frohman, Charles, 11; "Napoleon of the Drama," 1; preferred European to native plays, 2
—— Belasco and, joint production by, 14
Front Page, The (Hecht and MacArthur), 176, 222
Front Page, The, broadcast, 281
Funny Face, 250
Futurism, 23

Hazzard, John E., Winchell Smith and, 10
Heart of Wetona, The (Scarborough), 14
Heavenly Express (Bein), 104
Hecht, Ben, Charles MacArthur and, 222, 255
Hedman, Martha, 11
Helburn, Theresa, 29
Helena's Boys, 190
Helena's Husbands (Moeller), 33
Hell-Bent for Heaven (Hughes), Pulitzer Prize, 93
Hellman, Lillian, 126, 137, 142, 268
Hellzapoppin, 254
Heming, Violet, 234
Henry V (Shakespeare), 281
Hepburn, Katharine, 126, 200, 201
Herbert, F. Hubert, 185
Herbert, Victor, 17
—— Irving Berlin and, 17
"Here Am I," 249
Here Come the Clowns (Barry), 106, 119, 174, 201
Her Master's Voice (Kummer), 202
Hero, The (Emery), 123
Hersey, John, 268
Heyward, Dorothy, Du Bose Heyward and, 97
Heywood, Thomas, 30
Hickerson, Harold, Maxwell Anderson and, 83, 156
High comedy, 175-231 *passim*
High Tor (Anderson), 101, 102
Hillbilly play, 93
Hip-Hip-Hooray, 18
Hippodrome show, 18
Historical drama, 77 ff., 88 ff.
Hitchcock, Alfred, 242, 280, 281
Hitler, Adolf, 136
Hit the Deck, 250
Hobble, John L., 177
Hoboken theatrical venture, 241
Hoffman girls, 242
Holiday (Barry), 197
Holloway, Sterling, 251
Hollywood, assistance to Broadway, 233; attempts to humble, 217; best efforts in recent years, 281; could not capture musical show, 242; melodrama moved over to, 241;

salaries: progress, 280; *see also* Movies
Holm, John Cecil, George Abbott and, 213
Holman, Libby, 244
Holmes, Oliver Wendell, 268
Homeier, Skippy, 137
Home of the Brave (Laurents), 268
Hooker, Brian, W. H. Post and, 246
Hoover, Herbert, 154
Hopkins, Arthur, 11, 12, 28, 29, 38, 48, 73, 121, 128, 277; imaginative and poetical play taken over by, 71; revivals of Shakespeare, 74
—— G. M. Watters and, 216
Hopwood, Avery, M. R. Rinehart and, 240
Horizont, 26
Hornblow, Arthur, 11, 20
Hornblow, Arthur, Jr., 126
Horner, Harry, 264
Hotel Universe (Barry), 105
Hot Mikado, The, 262
Houseman, John, 164
—— Orson Welles and, 161
House of Connelly, The (Green), 95, 140, 142, 168
Housman, Laurence, Granville Barker and, 28
Housum, Robert, 177
Howard, Leslie, 100, 122
Howard, Sidney, 29, 38, 75, 121, 123, 125, 130, 139, 140, 164, 282; bourgeois portraits, 144 ff.
—— Will Irwin and, 269
Howard, Willie, 250
Hughes, Hatcher, Pulitzer Prize, 93
Hughes, Langston, 157
Hull, Henry, 79, 238
Hull, Josephine, 240
Hull, Shelley, 7
Human Comedy, The, 118
Hume, Sam, 27, 30
Hundredpercent Americanism, attacked by dramatists, 122
Hunter, Glenn, 32
Hurlbut, William, 11, 22, 23, 128
Huston, Walter, 52, 116, 215, 256
Hutton, Betty, 255
Hymer, John B., Samuel Shipman and, 234

One Touch of Venus (Perelman and Nash), 258
On the Art of the Theatre (Craig), 25
On Trial (Rice), 3, 14
On Your Toes (Rodgers and Hart), 256
Opening nights, top charges for tickets, 265
Operetta, 244 ff.
Orient in sensational melodramas, 237
Osata, Sono, 259
Osborn, Paul, 103, 182, 268
Osborne, Hubert, 177
Othello, presented with a Negro, 157
Ouija Board, The (Wilbur), 239, 270
Ourselves (Crothers), 23
Our Town (Wilder), 73, 99, 119; Pulitzer Prize, 108
Outward Room, The (Brand), 150
Overtones (Gerstenberg), 33

Pacifism, espoused by dramatists and novelists, 122; leftist writers held out for, 133
Pal Joey (Rodgers and Hart), 263
Palmer, Rose A., Arthur Goodrich and, 90
Panama Hattie (Porter), 256
Papa Is All (Greene), 92
"Papa Lewis, Mama Green," 162
Paradise Lost (Odets), 170; designated as objectionable in part, 233
Paramount, 280
Paris Bound (Barry), 197
Parlor, Bedroom and Bath, 270
Parnell, designated as objectionable in part, 233
Parodies, 251, 255
Pasadena Community Playhouse, 57, 112, 118
Passing Show of 1914, The, 18
Passing Shows, 18, 247
Paths of Glory (Howard), 130
Patriotism, attacked by dramatists, 121, 128 ff.; dramatists reverse their position on, 133 ff.; expressed through medium of movies, 138
Patriots, The (Kingsley), 91
Pavlova, Anna, 19, 251

Peace on Earth (Sklar and Maltz), 160
Peardon, Patricia, 185
Peg o' My Heart (Manners), 5, 142
Pennington, Ann, 18, 244
Penrod (Rose's adaptation of Tarkington), 184
"People Will Say," 259
Perelman, S. J., Ogden Nash and, 258
Perfect Fool, The, 247
Perkins, Osgood, 30, 208, 222
Perry, Alfred, 146
Perry, Antoinette, 274
Personal Appearance (Riley), 214
Peters, Paul, George Sklar and, 160
Peters, Rollo, 33
Petrified Forest, The (Sherwood), 122
Philadelphia Story, The (Barry), 196, 199 ff.
Pickford, Mary, 4, 175
Pierrot the Prodigal, 28
Pins and Needles, 136, 161, 162, 257
Pi-Pa-Ki, 269
Pirandello, Luigi, 74
Pirate, The (Behrman), 210
Platt, Livingston, 28, 30
Playboy of the Western World (Synge), 276
Playhouses, new needed, 273, 280
Play juries, 233
Plays, cost of production, 272; crusading zeal for nonrealistic, 73; excessive costs of production must be lowered, 280; experimental production, 274; percentage of failures, 273; production of serious and experimental, discouraged, 273; sentimental, 6 ff.; specific ills and remedies proposed, 270; with a punch, 15 ff.
Play without a Name, A (Strong), 193
Playwright-critic, 272
Playwrights, aids to new, 274; chief failure of American, 19; comic, 176; confused by march of history in the thirties, 132; contribution of contemporary, 266-83; desert theatre for Hollywood, 280; dif-